The Common Core,
an Uncommon Opportunity

Redesigning Classroom Instruction

Judith K. March

Karen H. Peters

CORWIN
A SAGE Company

CORWIN
A SAGE Company

FOR INFORMATION:

Corwin

A SAGE Company

2455 Teller Road

Thousand Oaks, California 91320

(800) 233-9936

www.corwin.com

SAGE Publications Ltd.

1 Oliver's Yard

55 City Road

London EC1Y 1SP

United Kingdom

SAGE Publications India Pvt. Ltd.

B 1/I 1 Mohan Cooperative Industrial Area

Mathura Road, New Delhi 110 044

India

SAGE Publications Asia-Pacific Pte. Ltd.

3 Church Street

#10-04 Samsung Hub

Singapore 049483

Acquisitions Editor: Arnis Burvikovs

Associate Editor: Desirée A. Bartlett

Editorial Assistant: Ariel Price

Production Editor: Amy Joy Schroller

Copy Editor: Amy Rosenstein

Typesetter: C&M Digitals (P) Ltd.

Proofreader: Dennis Webb

Indexer: Sheila Bodell

Cover Designer: Anupama Krishnan

Copyright © 2014 by Corwin

Printed in the United States of America

A catalog record of this book is available from the Library of Congress.

ISBN 978-1-4522-7182-8

This book is printed on acid-free paper.

SFI Certified Sourcing
www.sfiprogram.org
SFI-00453

13 14 15 16 17 10 9 8 7 6 5 4 3 2 1

The Common Core, an Uncommon Opportunity

This book is dedicated to the thousands of people with whom we have had the pleasure to work over the last three decades. We salute all of the people who gave us opportunity to promote our thinking and to work in different settings—individual school districts, Educational Service Centers, and our University colleagues. To have worked in all types of districts in seven different states and Canada has been amazing!

Specifically, we extend this dedication to the teachers and administrators in our client schools. Each district has provided its own distinct contribution to our work and has given us a unique array of insights to share with others. Our work reflects the impact of different groups from urban, suburban, and rural districts, and all of you have had a unique influence on the work that we do. The various partnerships with districts and teacher teams set the stage for the next school we would serve. Each of you made us smarter for having worked with you. Thank you for that, and know that some piece of each of you is represented in this book. As you read the examples and explanations, you will find yourself saying— "Hey! They did that when they worked with us!" Yea, for you, and yes we did!

To our families who have made the sacrifices of allowing us to be gone and do "our thing," we thank you so very much. Without our huge support teams behind us, we could never have put any of these ideas into practice. You made that possible, and we appreciate your continued support.

—Judy and Karen

Contents

Preface

By the time this book is published, the Common Core and newly approved content standards in Social Studies and Science will have become the new normal in most school districts across the nation. As approved providers for the Ohio Department of Education, we are currently working with several districts attempting to transition to the new standards. And despite the flurry of attention being paid to the new standards in every education journal and at virtually every conference, the truth is that most districts are *not ready!*

Like buying a flat-screen TV without new operating software, the mere adoption of new content standards without proportionate improvements in classroom instruction is relatively useless. Because the new standards are so different in scope and depth from the prior standards, districts who attempt to implement them without redesigning their instructional delivery systems accordingly are experiencing failure and frustration. In contrast to the current standards—many of which are isolated skills, knowledge, and ideas that could be taught and measured in relative isolation—the new standards are an interconnection of skills and require a deep-level understanding of complex relationships among several concepts and ideas. Those who crafted the new standards proudly hail them as essential to college and career readiness for life in the 21st century.

The Common Core in Math and English Language Arts are the kick-off to what may become a national curriculum and assessment system in all four major subjects. And with so much negative press about America's education system, the last thing school districts need is to fumble on their first possession. We wrote this book to help schools and school systems successfully adopt and implement the new content standards.

We designed this book as a process guide for districts who are sincere about adopting the new standards and realize they are embarking on what is essentially the systematic redesign of classroom instruction. Because it contains suggestions for how to accomplish this goal—accompanied by actual examples, as well as quotes from practitioners who have been directly involved—the book offers an authenticity and relevance that are absent from more theoretical publications.

With so many similar books out there, why should readers buy THIS one?

1. It addresses all four core content areas, K–12, rather than only one subject or only one grade range (e.g., elementary, middle school, or high school).

2. It shows districts how to translate the new standards into a holistic, comprehensive instructional delivery system—not just a piece of one or a single component; it includes both the content and the cognitive demand of the new standards.

3. It helps teachers develop an entire suite of course tools for each grade level and subject, including curriculum maps and unit plans; daily lessons are easily derived from these unit plans and are flexible to permit differentiation as needed. In addition, the book addresses assessment of the standards through various strategies that help teachers adjust their teaching to be sure that they are truly meeting the rigor of the standards.

4. It accommodates the reality that a transformed curriculum—enriched by the new content standards and the 21st century skills—cannot be taught with traditional classroom strategies. It incorporates the best-practice techniques to deliver and assess classroom instruction, taking it to the level required by the new standards.

5. It is based on several years of experience in districts of various sizes and demographics (rather than only one district or only one demographic group).

Our book is equally appropriate for administrators and teachers. For administrators, the book offers both wide-angle and close-up advice about districtwide readiness; adjustments in the infrastructure; and the role of principals, coaches, and grade-level teams to launch and then sustain the new instructional program. For teachers, the book provides evidence-based, best-practice approaches to the delivery and assessment of classroom instruction and includes proven examples of specific techniques.

To allay the understandable skepticism of many readers, the messages from practitioners throughout the book are a testament to the processes described and the positive impact of these processes on staff and students. As educators, we must be willing to continue to grow and learn as the expectations change for our students. The following quote, from one of the people with whom we have worked, says it best.

. . . And from those who REALLY know. . . .

One of the things I love most about the teaching profession is the commitment educators make to being life-long learners. But I wonder how many teachers have really followed through with this commitment. I wonder how many teachers have simply been recycling skills, lesson plans, and worksheets, and become stagnant learners. While we often talk about how the Common Core and State Standards will challenge our students, and provide them with more in depth and rigorous learning experiences, I am most excited and hopeful about how these new standards will encourage . . . or in some cases, force . . . our nation's educators to grow as professionals, instructional leaders, and as learners.

(Continued)

(Continued)

The cliché is that a patient would not go to a doctor who refused to keep current with new medical practices and research. Our students deserve no less. They deserve to be taught by teachers who are passionate about student learning, and their own personal and professional learning. The Common Core will not have a positive impact on students' learning unless our teachers are compelled to seek new instructional resources and strategies, build collaborative relationships with their colleagues, and renew their commitment to continually grow as learners.

*As I help teachers to understand the Common Core standards and the implications they will have on their teaching, I am optimistic about the positive impact these standards will have not only on our students' achievement and growth, but on the professional learning of our teachers.—**Jennifer M. Walker, 2009 Ohio Teacher of the Year, instructional consultant, Mahoning County (Ohio) Educational Service Center***

With the commitment to being life-long learners, we hope that you enjoy the book as the tool to help you accomplish that goal.

—*Judith K. March and Karen H. Peters*

Acknowledgments

Corwin wishes to acknowledge the following peer reviewers for their editorial insight and guidance.

Deanna Brunlinger, Science
   Department Chair
Elkhorn Area High School
Elkhorn, WI

Robert A. Frick, Retired
   Superintendent
Lampeter-Strasburg School
   District
Pennsylvania, PA

Jane Hunn, Sixth-Grade Science
   Teacher
Tippecanoe Valley Middle School
Akron, IN

Susan N. Imamura, Retired
   Principal
Manoa Elementary School
Honolulu, HI

Katherine M. D. Lobo,
   ESL Teacher
Chenery Middle School
Belmont, MA

Lynn Macan, Superintendent
Cobleskill-Richmondville Central
   School District
Cobleskill, NY

Lauren Mittermann, Social Studies
   Teacher
Gibraltar Middle School
Fish Creek, WI

Jeanine Nakakura, STEM Resource
   Teacher
State of Hawaii Department of
   Education
Honolulu, HI

Dana Sanner, Middle School Science
   Teacher
Sanibel School
Sanibel, FL

Belinda J. Raines, Administrator
Northwestern High School
Detroit, MI

Bonnie Tryon, SAANYS
   Representative
NY State Education Department's
   NCLB Committee of Practitioners
Albany, NY

Betty Brandenburg Yundt,
   Curriculum Coordinator
Walker Intermediate School
Fort Knox, KY

About the Authors

Judith K. March and Karen H. Peters are senior consultants for EdFOCUS Initiative, a nonprofit consulting group that provides customized services to schools and school districts. Dr. Peters and Dr. March have worked in school reform for more than two decades in Canada, California, Florida, Indiana, Minnesota, New Jersey, and Ohio.

Dr. March taught high school English, speech, and drama and served as a high school assistant principal. She has also been a curriculum supervisor, curriculum director, and assistant superintendent for an Educational Service Center. In addition, she was the director of Developmental Education and an associate professor at Ashland University; Dr. March has also served on the graduate faculty at Kent State University. Dr. March continues to serve as an adjunct member of the graduate faculty of Ashland University. Her special areas of focus are (a) standards-based curriculum redesign; (b) the Best-Practices research for classroom instruction; (c) assessment and accountability, including the construction of diagnostic and benchmark tests; (d) long-term and short-range planning; (e) capacity building for continual improvement, featuring Collaborative Observation; and (f) data-based decision making.

Also an experienced educator, **Dr. Peters** has taught at the elementary and middle school levels in Ohio and Florida, focusing on math and science. In addition, she has served as an elementary principal, curriculum supervisor, and director of curriculum as well as a member of the graduate faculty of Kent State University. Dr. Peters is currently an adjunct member of the graduate faculty of Ashland University. Her special areas of focus are (a) standards-based curriculum redesign; (b) the Best-Practices research for classroom instruction; (c) assessment and accountability, including the development of diagnostic and mastery tests; (d) the training and development of principals; (e) capacity building for continual improvement, featuring Collaborative Observation; and (f) data-based decision making.

While at Kent State, Drs. March and Peters operated an outreach center for school reform and developed the Instructional Design process to integrate standards-based reform with the Best-Practices research to deliver and assess classroom instruction.

Both **Drs. March and Peters** are approved providers for the Ohio Improvement Process, and as such are authorized by the Ohio Department of Education to provide consultation to schools and school districts to improve their standing. Drs. March and Peters have worked in school reform for more than two decades, providing services to school districts in Canada, California, Florida, Indiana, Minnesota, New Jersey, and Ohio. Their work has included urban, suburban, and rural districts. In addition to their current status as Ohio Improvement Process providers, both Dr. March and Dr. Peters have served as providers for federally funded Comprehensive School Reform projects. Further, March and Peters have been contracted by the Battelle-for-Kids Division of the Battelle Institute to work in with various research initiatives with Value-Added. In addition, March and Peters have served as consultants in formative assessment to the CTB/McGraw-Hill Corporation.

The secret to their consulting work has always been that they work directly with teachers and administrators in the redesign of classroom instruction and assessment. They are "hands-on" consultants who admit that their job is to build capacity among the school staff members with whom they work to sustain the reforms put in place. By developing their own leadership capacity, the districts can continuously examine and adjust their curriculum, instruction, and assessment programs in the light of student and staff performance.

Dr. March earned her bachelor's and master's degrees in arts from Bowling Green State University (Ohio) and her doctorate in curriculum and instruction from the University of Toledo (Ohio). **Dr. Peters** earned her bachelor's degree at the University of South Florida, her master's degree from Youngstown State University (Ohio), and her doctorate in educational administration with a minor in curriculum and instruction from Kent State University (Ohio).

No Longer 1
Business
as Usual

"It is not so very important for a person to learn facts. For that he does not really need school. He can learn them from books. The value of an education is . . . not the learning of many facts but the training of the mind to think things that cannot be learned from textbooks."

—Albert Einstein

For American education, the past few decades have promised one reform after another. But until 2010, these recommendations have been long on philosophy and short on actually changing what happens between teachers and students. With the advent of the Common Core State Standards in Math and English Language Arts (ELA), the new state Science and Social Studies standards, and the 21st century skills, an unprecedented transformation in American classrooms is underway.

The new standards, combined with the 21st century skills, will force a complete redesign of the PK–12 curriculum and instructional programs in 46 of the 50 states. Students are expected to see interrelationships, to think at deeper levels, to construct meaning for themselves, and to process information independently. This is a radical shift from the current focus on textbook-based and teacher-centered instruction, on providing students as much information as possible, and a reliance on repetition and memorization. In addition, because the new standards are internationally benchmarked, American students who master the new curriculum will be equipped to achieve respectable scores on such world-class tests as TIMSS, PISA, ACT, and SAT. This too, will represent a positive turnabout, since the United States is currently 32nd among nations of the world in student achievement (Hanushek & Peterson, 2011). As *Good to Great* icon Jim Collins (2001) said of blue-ribbon businesses that brought themselves back from failure, quality organizations (and we feel education is certainly one of these!) must honestly confront the brutal facts about their performance and be willing to transform themselves.

To accomplish and sustain this new curriculum and its instructional requirements, the entire district—teachers, principals, central office, and the Board of Education—must assume a portion of accountability.

- Teachers will need a new skill set, including (a) how to develop effective course tools to deliver and assess the new curriculum—including strategies for *differentiation;* (b) how to replace traditional teaching methods with "best-practice" techniques that are equal to the *cognitive demands* of the new standards; and (c) how to provide intervention as needed—both remediation and enrichment. Course tools include a curriculum map or pacing guide, unit plans that specify what is to be taught and how, as well as unit tests and authentic assessments to measure student mastery of the standards.

- Principals must facilitate the classroom implementation of the new curriculum and continuously monitor its instructional delivery. They will need to (a) identify teacher behaviors that yield more and less effective student responses and (b) prescribe corrective action plans as needed—including specific suggestion for best practices that are aligned with the new standards. With the appropriate training and involvement, principals will share with their teachers the responsibility for implementing the new curriculum. Within each school, the faculty and administrative team will forge a strategic partnership to help students master these more rigorous standards. The importance of the principal's responsibility for the new curriculum cannot be overstated. In fact, the principal's job description should set forth specific duties in the areas of curriculum, classroom instruction, and student assessment. Moreover, each principal's annual performance review should reflect his and her level of success in these important new duties.

- School leaders and Boards of Education must provide structured opportunities for staff training, allocate the time and resources needed, and enact policies and procedures that will provide ongoing support. They must have the courage and commitment to hold themselves and the entire school staff accountable for each of their respective roles and responsibilities to move the quality of the curriculum and classroom instruction to that next level of rigor essential to student success in the 21st century.

MAJOR DIFFERENCES BETWEEN THE FORMER STANDARDS AND THE NEW CORE

. . . From those who REALLY know . . . .

All students need strong fiction and nonfiction skills to achieve general knowledge required for career and college. In fact, the Common Core suggests that by the time students graduate, 70% of what they read—and understand—should be quality nonfiction. The new emphasis on robust nonfiction skills across the content areas of ELA, mathematics, science, and social studies is a critical lynch pin for students to successfully interpret the information they will encounter every day. In real life, there will be no teacher and no textbook to guide their thinking. So while we still have them, we must equip them to be independent and savvy consumers of what they read, see, and hear.—Sue Long, PhD, retired assistant superintendent of Curriculum and Instruction, Akron Public Schools

With the former standards, most curriculum skills and concepts could be taught and assessed one standard at a time. Many were designed to allow for mastery from memorization and algorithmic, formulistic thinking directed by the teacher and texts. In contrast, the new standards combine skills and concepts into holistic, integrated webs of ideas. Mastery of the new standards requires students to think at deeper levels about integrated concepts and to make *independent* connections among concepts and ideas. See the following examples:

English Language Arts, Grade 6	
Former State Standards	**Common Core**
R.6.2. Identify the features of setting, and explain their importance in literary text.	**RL 6.5.** Analyze how a particular sentence, chapter, scene, or stanza fits into the overall structure of a text and contributes to the development of the theme, setting, or plot.
R.6.3. Identify the main and minor events of the plot, and explain how each incident gives rise to the next.	
R.6.5. Identify recurring themes, patterns, and symbols found in literature from different eras and cultures.	

Math, Grade 2	
Former State Standards	**Common Core**
NS.2.6 Model, represent, and explain subtraction as comparison, take-away and part-to-whole; e.g., solve missing addend problems by counting up or subtracting, such as "I had six baseball cards, my sister gave me more, and I now have ten. How many did she give me?" can be represented as $6 + ? = 10$ or $10 - 6 = ?$	**2. OA.1** Use addition and **subtraction** with 100 to solve one- and two-step word problems involving situations of adding to, taking from, putting together, taking apart, and comparing, with unknowns in all positions, (e.g., by using drawings and equations with a symbol for the unknown number to represent the problem.

Social Studies, Grade 9	
Former State Standards	**New State Standards**
H.9.14 Explain causes/consequences of fall of Soviet Union and end of Cold War.	**WH.23** The break-up of the Soviet Union ended the Cold War and created challenges for its former allies, the former Soviet republics, Europe, the United States and the nonaligned world.

Science, Grade 5	
Former State Standards	**New State Standards (Note: The new standards for Grade 5 reflect what was previously in Grade 8 standards.)**
ES.5.1 Describe how night and day are caused by Earth's rotation.	**ESS. 5.3** Most of the cycles and patterns of motion between the Earth and sun are predictable: a. Earth's revolution around the sun takes approximately 365 days. b. Earth completes one rotation on its axis in a 24-hour period, producing day and night. This rotation makes the sun, stars, and moon appear to change position in the sky. c. Earth's axis is tilted at an angle of 23.5°. This tilt, along with Earth's revolution around the sun, affects the amount of direct sunlight that the Earth receives in a single day and throughout the year. d. Average daily temperature is related to the amount of direct sunlight received. Changes in average temperature throughout the year are identified as seasons.

As these examples show, making the conversion from the former to the new standards is not a simple matter of inserting the new content into the existing documents. Several steps are required, and the effort must be a strategic one. In and of themselves, the standards are not the curriculum, and they must be (a) examined and discussed by grade level or course work teams to determine the specific skills and concepts contained in each. From there, the teams decide (b) how student mastery will be measured, (c) what classroom delivery strategies will be appropriate, (d) which print and nonprint materials will be needed, (e) how technology fits in, and (f) whether there are readiness or lead-up skills and concepts to be included. Combined, these elements become the curriculum—an umbrella label often used by districts to subsume the course content, classroom instruction, materials and technology, and student assessment.

These steps must be completed by grade level and course writing teams whose members include not only the general education teachers but also teachers of special needs, gifted, and English as a second language students who work at each grade level and in each course. Moreover, to ensure administrative involvement with and accountability for the new curriculum, members of the central office staff, principals, and academic coaches should each be appointed to at least one writing team in each subject. This will provide the opportunity for that important partnership among teachers, support staff, and administrators to share the accountability for transforming the curriculum.

As they complete these steps, the work teams will produce teaching documents or course tools (curriculum maps, unit plans, and unit assessments) that will be used to implement the new curriculum in school classrooms. Once a work team has "unpacked" the standards for its grade-level and/or course, the team decides how best to cluster the standards into meaningful units of instruction. With previous standards, a Math unit might contain only Number Sense, or a Language Arts unit might be confined to Writing Conventions. But the Common Core in Math and ELA directs districts to use an *integrated approach* to provide a more authentic and broad-based context for student learning. So a Math unit might now contain Measurement and Data, Geometry, and Operations and Algebraic Thinking; and a Language Arts unit might include Reading for Information, Writing, Speaking, and Language.

The writing team then determines how to sequence these units across the school year for the most effective developmental flow. This is captured in a year-long curriculum map, which guides the pacing, sequence, cross-strand integration, and strategic repetition of the new standards. It is also during this step that the work teams should examine the standards required of students in the previous and subsequent grade levels. This will guarantee articulation across grade levels to ensure that the degree of sophistication builds each year to culminate in college and career readiness.

From the curriculum maps, the teacher work teams then devise unit plans to actually guide the delivery and assessment of the standards in each classroom. Currently, most elementary instruction is guided by the teacher's manual, and secondary teachers rely on the textbook's table of contents. But the precise interpretation of these manuals and textbooks is left to each teacher, jeopardizing the consistency of instruction and eliminating any quality control within a grade level or subject. Given the huge content and cognitive difference in the new standards, the major shift required in teaching methods, and the uncomfortable (but undeniable) fact that the present system of "academic freedom" has failed to yield the desired results, a more definitive and structured approach is called for.

In contrast to the current approach to classroom delivery, the unit plans proposed in this book:

- are anchored by the cluster of standards,
- specify valid teaching strategies and student responses that actively engage students in processing their learning and constructing new meaning,
- include traditional assessments to monitor selective mastery; and
- include authentic or performance assessments to determine independent mastery.

However, they are not scripted units that attempt to make teachers clones of each other with prescribed dates and page numbers. Each unit follows a consistent format that sets forth teaching-learning activities derived from the research on best practices and constructivist learning. Teacher work teams who develop the units include several options from which their colleagues may choose to allow for personal style. Each unit plan also designates print and nonprint materials to be used, technology needed, and techniques for differentiation. Also included are paper-pencil assessments and authentic assessments with scoring rubrics, based on the unit standards. In their study of high-achieving schools from across the country, Harvey Daniels and Marilyn Bizar (2005) discovered that one common feature was the use of thematic, integrated units that included constructive and authentic learning activities. We have carefully researched each of these components (March & Peters, 2007) and used them with numerous school districts.

Combined, these curriculum maps and unit plans should be approved by the Board of Education as the district's new curriculum, and they thus become the course tools by which the new curriculum is implemented in every classroom. The inclusion and alignment of all these necessary components are what Larry Ainsworth (2010) calls a "rigorous curriculum" (pp. 4, 24). Following this, teacher-developed but standard-based curriculum becomes the expectation for every teacher to teach, every principal to monitor, and every central office administrator to facilitate.

IMPLICATIONS FOR CLASSROOM INSTRUCTION AND ASSESSMENT

While the writing teams work to transform the curriculum, they will also discover that most of the traditional classroom teaching and learning strategies are no longer appropriate or adequate. With the Common Core, the new Science and Social Studies standards, and the 21st century skills as the basis of WHAT students learn, the instructional methods for HOW they learn will need to change accordingly. Teachers will need to actually teach students how to think—and how to think differently and more deeply than was previously required. Art Costa and Bena Kallick (2010) refer to a shift from transmitting meaning to constructing meaning, saying it's not the content that students store but the memory of constructing it (p. 224). As shown in the sample standards (Table 1.1), teachers will need to create opportunities for students to see how skills are combined to solve a problem or how multiple ideas are integrated to create a new concept. Students will experience a new level of learning that is more about relationships, comparisons, cause and effect, and what-ifs than the memorization of information. Virtually none of the new standards is a matter of rote recall of facts or a mechanical application of naked algorithms and rules. Instead of mimicking what they see in class or textbooks to show mastery, students must construct new meaning on their own. Table 1.1 illustrates this shift in detail. Grant Wiggins and Jay McTighe (2008) see this process of making meaning and then transferring it to life as the core mission of school reform. Larry Ainsworth (2010) calls this "raising the level of teaching" (p. 5).

Table 1.1   A Comparison of Previous Classroom Strategies With Those Needed for the New Standards

With Previous Standards . . .	With the New Common Core and 21st Century Standards . . .
Teachers have focused most of their planning on their behaviors and what they would provide to students.	Teachers will need to focus on what students will do to show mastery and from that decide what teaching strategies will be most likely to yield those results.
Teachers have typically provided the single best way to perform a task or solve a problem. Alternative methods have not been a priority.	Teachers will need to show students multiple ways to approach tasks and to solve problems, and it will be essential that students can explain which approach they used and how it worked for them.
Students have been passive learners; they have been given information and directed how to apply it. With sufficient, controlled repetition and directed practice, students could appear to have mastery, when it may be only mimicry of what they've seen.	Students will need to become active learners; they will need to be shown how to: ✓ discover and interpret information independently, and ✓ apply skills and concepts independently and in unfamiliar contexts to solve problems and complete tasks. Because they are required to construct their own meaning—and in varied contexts—it is less likely that students can mimic mastery.
Practice has been limited to "controlled" examples that were identical with or parallel to those used in class (i.e., text passages, experiments, math problems, and various social studies events and scenarios). Contexts have been limited to the familiar, and students have not been led to stretch. Correct answers were largely predetermined.	Practice will need to begin with controlled examples but quickly move to unfamiliar examples that require students to construct meaning for themselves in unfamiliar contexts. This more authentic problem solving will prepare students to deal with problems they encounter in real life—many of which cannot be anticipated by the classroom teacher. Several correct answers will be possible, providing they are aligned with the criteria set forth in the standards—both in terms of content and cognitive demand. Students will be expected to explain and justify their answers.
Students have taken in information by observing teacher demonstrations, listening to teacher lectures, reading assigned texts, or viewing various media.	Students will take in information from various sources and from a diverse and greatly expanded array of electronic sources and media. In addition, students must show they can (a) gather the appropriate information and (b) distinguish relevant from irrelevant information and authentic from invalid evidence.
Students have processed information by taking notes, doing seat-work, and filling in blanks—all using language and numbers mimicked or paraphrased from the text or teacher.	Students will still take notes but not fill in controlled blanks; they will interpret details of what they see and hear through such constructive techniques as paraphrasing; summarizing; formulating questions or problems; sketching or diagramming; or completing

(Continued)

Table 1.1 (Continued)

With Previous Standards . . .	With the New Common Core and 21st Century Standards . . .
	"if-then" statements. Most of the new standards require students to cite evidence for their observations, inferences, and conclusions.
Mastery has been determined by filling in blanks or selecting from among multiple choices—using language mimicked or paraphrased from the text or teacher.	Mastery will be determined on several levels. To prepare students for high-stakes tests, some multiple-choice and short-answer items are essential. But reflecting the cognitive demand of the new standards, students must also perform authentic or performance tasks that certify they can apply what they have learned to solve real-world problems; analyze concepts and ideas to identify determinant relationships; synthesize information to create original products; and critically but objectively evaluate ideas, products, and information using valid criteria.

To be fair, this current generation of classroom teachers has not been trained to provide such instruction, and simply telling them they must begin to do so is not only unfair, it's naïve. But the development of the new curriculum with its accompanying course tools to deliver provides the perfect opportunity to embed the needed training into the context of teachers' daily work and regular team meetings. The writing teams can be trained as they work with the new standards to transform the curriculum and as they develop the course tools for classroom implementation.

In some districts, all teachers at each grade level and every teacher assigned to specific courses will be involved in one or more work teams and thus will participate in this first level of training. For larger districts, the work teams will be representative. But as these additional teachers join their work team colleagues in using the course tools, they too will develop the new teaching behaviors and skills. Whatever the size of the district, as the course tools are piloted, all teachers will be involved. They will participate in the continuous monitoring of student performance and bring the results to the regularly scheduled team meetings. In addition, they will offer edits and suggestions to the writing teams to improve the quality and usefulness of the course tools for the following school year. In our experience, no external "professional development"—no matter how famous the presenter—can ever replace this embedded, contextual growth training. They shift from what Bruce Joyce and Beverly Showers (2002) called passive users of someone else's material to active developers of their own tools.

This book will highlight the necessary adjustments in classroom instruction and the new teaching practices and skills using examples from all four core subjects. It is especially important that principals and academic coaches fully understand these changes as well and can help teachers transition to the new practices. Involving administrators on the writing teams will ensure that they too become fluent in these best practices. As Larry Ainsworth (2010) puts it, transforming education "makes us jugglers, attempting to keep 100 balls in the air simultaneously . . . including the many new practices we expect our teachers and administrators to be learning rapidly and implementing immediately in their daily work" (p. 17).

A Word About Special Needs

In the prefatory remarks, the Common Core acknowledges that the standards themselves do not provide for students with special needs, students who are gifted, or students who are English language learners. Each district is tasked with providing for such needs locally in the form of differentiated instruction.

For special needs or ESL students, they too are expected to work toward on-level standards and have access to on-level reading material, math problems, social studies scenarios, and science activities. Any differentiation or accommodation is to involve adjustments in teaching-learning techniques (including materials) and should not be a reduction to below-level standards or diminished performance expectations. This approach differs considerably from current practices in many districts, which are to provide these students with below-level instruction and reduced learning expectations to ensure student success.

In terms of response to intervention, Tier I and Tier II students remain in the classroom as part of the learning community, but they are provided in-class support services by auxiliary or special needs staff. Again, they are provided differentiated instruction but are expected to master on-level standards. Tier III students are the 1–5% of all students who have the most severe academic, behavior, or emotional problems. They are typically assigned to self-contained classes to receive individualized interventions with very frequent progress monitoring.

In the case of gifted students, they should be offered more challenging materials or assignments and may be required to read above-level material. Whether these students remain in the classroom as part of the learning community or are taken out for special services is up to the district. But the Common Core makes it clear that districts are expected to make provisions both for remediation and enrichment.

To these ends, each of the unit plans will include strategies and materials for differentiation—both for remediation and enrichment. The dual blunders of "one-size-fits-all" and "tracking for less and more successful students" are—thankfully—finally being corrected.

. . . And from those who REALLY know. . . .

*As a self-contained teacher of children with special needs, I know that my students must function in the same 21st century society as their general education classmates. The speech therapist and I developed units similar to the units in general education but containing standards at multiple grade levels. We are intentional about setting high expectations for learning, applying learned skills, and maximizing the potential of all students. I can't imagine doing it any other way!—**Denny Devine, special needs teacher, Maryland School, Bexley City Schools**

A corollary to the issue of student tracking is teacher tracking. On a blog posting, Linda Darling-Hammond (2011) is still worried that the most expert teachers teach the most advantaged and capable students and that the lower track students are still assigned the least experienced and least capable teachers. Worse, she fears, lower track students are still given less demanding material and not expected to perform at grade level—even with supplemental assistance.

The Impact of the 21st Century Skills

If students are to be successful citizens of the 21st century, mastery of the new content standards is only part of their preparation. The other part is mastery of the 21st century skills—workplace and communication competencies that enable students to successfully apply their academic knowledge and skills to function as productive adults. Because they must begin at the primary level and progress developmentally through high school, the 21st century skills should be fully integrated into the course tools at each grade level. The connection between the new content standards and the 21st century patterns of thinking is solid and reciprocal, and the continuous flux of world events underscores the urgency to incorporate the 21st century skills into the redesign of classroom instruction.

Throughout this book, reference will be made to integrating the 21st century skills into the Common Core skills as well as the new content standards in Science and Social Studies. The following categories have been used as reference points:

(a) General References in the New Standards to the 21st Century Skills

(b) Global Awareness

(c) The Literacies (financial and economic, civic, health and environmental)

(d) Thinking and Reasoning for Effective Decision Making

(e) Communication and Collaboration

(f) Information Technology and Media Literacy

(g) Initiative, Flexibility, and Collaborative Skills

These have been drawn from the Partnership for 21st Century Skills at www .p21.org and published in print (Trilling & Fadel, 2009; Rotherham & Willingham, 2009).

Some of the specific connections between the standards and the 21st century skills details are described later. Note that the sources will be cited only once but are included in the References section.

(a) General References in the New Standards to the 21st Century Skills

English Language Arts. The developers of the ELA standards see part of their mission as helping schools prepare students to be "a literate person in the 21st century" (Common Core State Standards Initiative, 2012a).

Math. While the documents setting forth the Common Core Math standards do not contain specific wording relative to the 21st century skills, the depth of the standards, their stress on modeling, and requirement for real-world application are synchronous with the requirements of the 21st century skills. The Science and Mathematics Education Policy Advisory Council (SMEPAC), headed by Thomas Friedman, author of *The World Is Flat*, has made specific suggestions to teachers of Math and Science content standards to the 21st century skills. They underscore the importance of mastering the Common Core Math and the 2010 Science standards as requisite to college and career readiness.

Social Studies. In Ohio (which is indicative of other states), the new Social Studies standards are designed to "allow teachers to elicit a greater depth of understanding on the part of students" [and] "to meet the needs of students in the 21st century." This 21st century connection has been based on the *Framework for 21st Century Learning* from the Partnership for 21st Century Skills. Included are skills in historical thinking, spatial thinking, civic literacy and participation, financial and economic literacy, and decision making and global awareness (Ohio Department of Education, 2012). Links to other 21st century skills such as problem solving, communication, media literacy, and leadership are also included in the content standards.

Science. In the "Introduction" to the Ohio Revised Science Education Standards and Model Curriculum" (Ohio Department of Education, 2011), the developers insist that 21st century skills are integral to the science standards and the curriculum revision documents. They are an essential part of the model curriculum through the integration of scientific inquiry, science skills and processes, and technological and engineering design. As enumerated in Ohio Amended Substitute H.B. 1, these skills include creativity and innovation; critical thinking, problem-solving, and communication; information, media, and technological literacy; personal management, productivity, accountability, leadership, and responsibility; and interdisciplinary, project-based, real-world learning opportunities.

(b) Global Awareness

Global awareness is defined as understanding and respect for the growing diversity of religions, cultures, and world views. Among the chief proponents of expanding both the curriculum and instructional practices to embrace global thinking is Hayes Jacobs (2010).

English Language Arts. Students who are college and career ready "actively seek the wide, deep, and thoughtful engagement with high-quality literary and informational texts that builds knowledge, enlarges experience, and broadens worldviews" (Common Core State Standards Initiative, 2012a, Introduction). The ELA standards are internationally benchmarked to prepare American students to compete successfully in a "globally competitive society" (Common Core State Standards Initiative, 2012a, Introduction). In addition, college- and career-ready students realize that the 21st century workplaces are settings that include people from widely divergent cultures with diverse experiences and perspectives who must learn and work together. Students actively seek to understand other perspectives and cultures through reading and listening, and they are able to communicate effectively with people of varied backgrounds. They evaluate other points of view critically and constructively. Through reading great classic and contemporary works of literature representative of a variety of periods, cultures, and worldviews, students can vicariously inhabit worlds and have experiences much different from their own (Common Core State Standards Initiative, 2012a). In the Reading for Literacy strand, students in a majority of grade levels are required to read authors from different cultures or authors from outside the United States (Common Core State Standards Initiative, 2012a).

Math. SMEPAC, headed by Thomas Friedman, author of *The World Is Flat*, has emphasized the importance of providing instructional activities that will prepare every student to succeed in the global economy and a worldwide society.

Social Studies. In strategic grade levels, the Social Studies standards require students to (1) "analyze and interpret significant events, patterns, and themes in the history of the state, the United States, and the world"; (2) "use knowledge of geographic patterns, locations, and processes to show the interrelationship between the physical environment and human activity," particularly the "practices, products, and perspectives of cultural and ethnic groups within local, regional, and global settings"; and (3) use economic reasoning skills and knowledge of major economic concepts, issues, and systems to make informed choices . . . as citizens of an interdependent world" (Ohio Department of Education, 2012, Overview).

Science. The centerpiece of the Ohio Science standards is the "Science Eye of Integration," displayed at each grade level, K–8, in the Ohio Revised Science Education Standards and Model Curriculum. One of the giant sections surrounding the "eye" is Global Connections. In the Grade 3 "eye," for example, is specified (1) investigations of soil erosion problems in other countries (e.g., China, Central America, and South America) and (2) studies of the desertification process because of soil erosion in Southern Mexico. Each grade level includes one or more activities to promote global understanding.

(c) The Literacies

As defined in the 21st century skills documents, the literacies will help students realize the reciprocal impact of human behavior on the economic, civic, health, and environmental conditions in which they will live:

- Financial and Economic Literacy
- Civic Literacy
- Health Literacy
- Environmental Literacy

English Language Arts. There are no specific ELA standards that speak to Financial or Economic Literacy, nor to Civic, Health, or Environmental Literacy.

But throughout the ELA standards—including the Literacy standards for Math, Science, and Social Studies—is the expectation that students will become literate in every content area. That is, they will be able to distinguish objective from biased information and legitimate from questionable sources of evidence.

Math. Throughout the K–8 Common Core Math, the standards require students to solve and construct problems involving money, measurement, and data in real-world applications and situations. This provides an important mathematical foundation for Financial, Economic, and Civic Literacy. In Grades 9–12, all of the Literacies are integrated into the contextual problem solving where math skills are to be applied.

Social Studies. At K–8, the Government strand includes the topic of Civic Participation and related skills. These include the principles of government and the students' role as citizens. The Geography strand includes the understanding of humans' interdependency on the physical environment. The Economics strand specifies Economic Decision-Making and related skills and Financial Literacy, including wants, needs, resources, production, and consumption (Ohio Department of Education, 2012, K–5). In Grades 9–12, the recommended courses include "Government" (containing the topic of civics) and "Economics and Financial Literacy" (Ohio Department of Education, 2012, High School Syllabi).

Science. The centerpiece of the Ohio Science standards is the "Science Eye of Integration," displayed at each grade level, K–8, in the Ohio Revised Science Education Standards and Model Curriculum. One of the giant sections surrounding the "eye" is Environmental Literacy.

(d) Thinking and Reasoning for Effective Decision Making

- Creative and Innovative Thinking
- Working Creatively With Others
- Effective Reasoning
- Systems of Thinking (e.g., whole to part)
- Effective Judgments and Decision Making
- Solving Unfamiliar Problems
- Asking Appropriate Questions to Clarify Alternate Points of View

All Subjects. As they construct their course tools (the curriculum maps and unit plans), the writing teams will receive embedded professional development in the best practices and constructivist teaching-learning techniques shown in Table 1.1. Among the 21st century skills, several are particularly associated with the new classroom delivery and assessment techniques. They include the following:

(1) *Creative and innovative thinking* (i.e., student responses to each teaching strategy will require them to process the information on their own and to construct meaning for themselves. As part of the authentic or performance

assessments for each unit, students will be required to create or construct an original product, activity, solution, or set of problems that show independent mastery of designated standards).

(2) *Effective reasoning* (i.e., among the teaching-learning and assessment activities in the unit plans will be those requiring students to evaluate a set of problems, a document, or a product to determine if there are errors. They then analyze those errors to discover the reasoning used, the type of errors made, what should have been done instead, and what can be done now to make corrections).

(3) *Systems of thinking* (i.e., teachers will be shown how to help students analyze the structure of text or arguments to discover the organizational pattern or "system" used by the author to communicate his or her message. These patterns include chronological sequence, cause-effect, problem-solution, compare-contrast, and so on. From this analysis, students learn to construct accurate graphic organizers that display the author's thinking, to write valid summaries, and to take effective notes).

(4) *Solving unfamiliar problems* (i.e., the foundation of constructivist learning is that students construct their own meaning for a concept, skill, or idea by applying it to an unfamiliar situation. In math, they would solve a new problem; in science, they would encounter a quandary they'd not seen before. In social studies, they would examine a document for the first time, and in language arts, they would respond to unknown text. Twenty-first century citizens must be able to apply what they have learned to solve all sorts of unfamiliar problems—many of which have not yet even been identified).

(5) *Asking appropriate questions* (i.e., one of the most popular best practices is levels of questioning, and each unit plan will contain leveled questions to model for students how to formulate and then answer them. Level I questions are literal, asking students to identify stated detail; Level II are inferential, asking students to read between the lines or see implications; and Level III are hypothetical or extensions beyond the material, asking students to apply the material to another situation or make higher-order connections).

English Language Arts. At Grades K–5, students are expected to read a broad range of high-quality, increasingly challenging literary and informational texts, and history and science content texts to give them the background they need to be better readers in every subject (Common Core State Standards Initiative, 2012a, K–5). The specific standards at each grade level require them to understand the author's reasoning and patterns of thinking. Students are expected to see connections and interconnections from multiple perspectives and to document their analyses with text detail.

In the Reading strand, students are to identify the reasons an author gives to support his or her points.

In Writing, students are to analyze text and write arguments using valid reasoning and sufficient evidence, conduct research projects based on focused questions, gather relevant information, and assess the credibility and accuracy of each source.

In Speaking/Listening, students are to evaluate a speaker's point of view, reasoning, and use of evidence and rhetoric and present information, findings, and supporting evidence to reflect valid reasoning.

In Language, students use context to make reasoned predictions of the meaning of unfamiliar and multi-meaning words, figurative language, and connotations.

In Grades 6–12, students are to "grapple with works of exceptional craft and thought whose range extends across genres, cultures, and centuries. Such works offer profound insights into the human condition and serve as models for students' own thinking and writing" (Common Core State Standards Initiative, 2012a). Students must read high-quality contemporary works, including seminal U.S. documents, the classics of American literature, and the timeless dramas of Shakespeare. "Through wide and deep reading of literature and literary nonfiction of steadily increasing sophistication, students gain a reservoir of literary and cultural knowledge, references, and images; the ability to evaluate intricate arguments; and the capacity to surmount the challenges posed by complex texts" (Common Core State Standards Initiative, 2012a, 6–12).

In Reading, students must determine the meanings of unknown technical, connotative, figurative words; analyze text structures and their impact on the whole piece; delineate and evaluate the arguments and specific claims in a text—including the validity of the reasoning involved as well as the relevance and sufficiency of the evidence.

In Writing, students are expected to write arguments to support their analysis of text, using valid reasoning and sufficient evidence; conduct research projects based on focused questions; gather relevant information; and assess the credibility and accuracy of each source.

In Speaking/Listening, the standards ask students to hold a range of conversations and collaborations with diverse partners, building on others' ideas and expressing their own ideas clearly and persuasively. Students are to evaluate a speaker's point of view, reasoning, and use of evidence and rhetoric; they are to present information, findings, and supporting evidence to reflect viable reasoning.

In Language, like Reading, students are to determine the meaning of unfamiliar and multi-meaning words, figurative language, and connotations—all from context.

Math. The Common Core Math Standards specify a set of eight Math Practices, K–12 (Common Core State Standards Initiative, 2012b). These are to be integrated into the unit plans throughout the school year in each grade level and course. They are to (a) make sense of problems and persevere in solving them; (b) reason abstractly and quantitatively; (c) construct viable arguments and critique the reasoning of others; (d) model with mathematics; (e) use appropriate tools strategically; (f) attend to precision; (g) look for and make use of structure; and (h) look for and express regularity in repeated reasoning.

Social Studies. Throughout K–12, the standards require students to examine primary and secondary sources to consider the multiple perspectives from which historic and contemporary decisions have been made.

At K–8, each grade level from Grade 1 forward includes Geography standards dealing with collaboration and group problem solving. From Grade 2 forward, these standards include interactions among cultures to promote sharing and mutual gain. From Grade 3 forward, the Government strand includes standards about compromise and the common good, and the Economics strand features critical decision making among choices. From Grade 7 forward, the Government strand includes standards that require students to understand individual and group perspectives as essential to analyzing historic and contemporary issues. From Grade 8 forward, the Government strand involves students in decision making that has present and future consequences (Ohio Department of Education, 2012, K–5).

In Grades 9–12, the recommendations for service learning involve students in creative and innovative problem solving, systems thinking, solving unfamiliar problems, and asking appropriate questions to clarify points of view. The "Contemporary World Issues" course includes the dynamics of competing beliefs and goals, methods of engagement, and conflict versus cooperation versus collaboration in solving global problems (Ohio Department of Education, 2012, High School Syllabi).

Science. Key to the Science standards is the "Scientific Inquiry/Learning Cycle" (Ohio Department of Education, 2011, Introduction). This cycle includes "Use evidence and scientific knowledge to develop explanations" and stresses the importance of (1) knowing, using, and interpreting scientific explanations of the natural world; (2) generating and evaluating scientific evidence and explanations, distinguishing science from pseudoscience; (3) and understanding the nature and development of scientific knowledge.

(e) Communication and Collaboration

- Oral, Written, and Non-Verbal Communication for Various Purposes
- Effective Listening
- Working Effectively With Others to Reach Common Goals

English Language Arts. The ELA standards have an entire strand on Speaking and Listening, K–12. Students are required to actively participate in a variety of rich, structured conversations as part of a whole class, in small groups, and with a partner—built around important content in various domains. Each student must contribute appropriately to the conversations, make comparisons and contrasts, and analyze and synthesize ideas in accordance with standards of evidence for a particular discipline. In addition, students are required to listen to others and respond to what they say (Common Core State Standards Initiative, 2012a, K–5).

Math. The eight Math Practices specified in the Common Core Math Standards (listed in category [d] earlier) are relevant to the three Communication and

Collaboration skills. In addition, students are expected to talk about the mathematical reasoning they used and the processes they applied and evaluate the quality of their and others' work.

Social Studies and Science. For the Communication portion of this category, the K–5 Social Studies and Science standards have embedded various Literacy activities, including group discussion, listening, verbal and nonverbal forms of communication, and evaluating media (Ohio Department of Education, 2011, K–5; Ohio Department of Education, 2012, K–5).

In Grades 6–12, the Social Studies and Science curricula are expected to include specific Reading and Writing Literacy skills. These are set forth in the ELA Common Core standards, Grades 6–12 (Common Core State Standards Initiative, 2012a).

The Reading Literacy skills include the analysis and evaluation of printed, oral, or media text to:

- identify explicit detail and supportable inferences;
- determine central ideas or themes, summarizing key details and ideas;
- interpret language, including figurative, technical, and connotative meanings;
- discern point of view or purposes of the text; and
- determine the validity of reasoning and legitimacy of the thesis idea.

The Writing Literacy skills include writing arguments to support claims in an analysis of topics, text, speeches, or media. In addition, students are to write informative or explanatory texts to examine and convey complex ideas, drawing on viable evidence and research. Finally, students in Grades 6–12 are expected to write routinely over extended time frames in both Social Studies and Science classes.

Science. In addition to the Literacy Skills listed previously, the "Scientific Inquiry/Learning Cycle" (Ohio Department of Education, 2011, Introduction) includes participating productively in scientific practices and scientific discourse and "communicating the results [of scientific investigations] with graphs, charts, and tables."

(f) Information Technology and Media Literacy

- Access, Manage, and Evaluate Information
- Analyze Media for Purpose and Bias
- Create Effective Media to Communicate a Message
- Use of Digital Technology to Access, Manage, and Create Information

English Language Arts. The Writing standards, K–12, require the use of technology, including the Internet, to produce and publish writing and to interact and collaborate with others. Students are to "make strategic use of digital media and visual displays of data to express information and enhance understanding of presentations" (Common Core State Standards Initiative, 2012a, K–5, 6–12).

New technologies have broadened and expanded the role that speaking and listening play in acquiring and sharing knowledge and have tightened their link to other forms of communication. Digital texts confront students with the potential for continually updated content and dynamically changing combinations of words, graphics, images, hyperlinks, and embedded video and audio (Common Core State Standards Initiative, 2012a, 6–12).

The Internet has accelerated the speed at which connections between speaking, listening, reading, and writing can be made, requiring that students be ready to use these modalities nearly simultaneously. Technology itself is changing quickly, creating a new urgency for students to be adaptable in response to change (Common Core State Standards Initiative, 2012a, K–5, K–6).

Math. In the Mathematics Common Core Standards Initiative (2012b, Appendix A), the following is specified: "Strategic use of technology is expected in all work. This may include employing technological tools to assist students in forming and testing conjectures, creating graphs and data displays, and determining and assessing lines of fit for data. Geometric constructions may also be performed using geometric software as well as classical tools and technology may aid three-dimensional visualization. Testing with and without technological tools is recommended."

Social Studies. Most of the references to Informational Technology and Media Literacy are in the Geography strand as part of Geospatial Technologies.

In Grades K–2, the following representational skills are included: pictures, symbols, and signs that communicate and create associations and photographs, artifacts, and letters to document events across time (Ohio Department of Education, 2012, K–5).

In Grades 3–5, students are required to (1) interpret timelines or multitier timelines and regional maps to display interrelationships among events and diffusion of ideas and people, (2) understand systems of communication and transportation, (3) describe how technological innovations from the early 1800s benefitted the United States, and (4) interpret data organized into tables and charts to expedite communication (Ohio Department of Education, 2012, K–5).

For Grades 6–8, the standards expect students to realize that visual displays, maps, and tables show information from the perspective of the "developer" and thus may contain bias to shape agendas and influence attitudes. Students are to trace information flow and determine the objectivity of information. Moreover, students are required to understand how media and information condition human behavior, impact trade routes, and affect the movement of humans in the United States and all parts of the world. In addition, students need to realize how goods and services foster the spread of technology to new sections of the world (Ohio Department of Education, 2012, K–5).

At the high school level (Grades 9–12), the standards include most of what is listed in K–8, plus requires media literacy in each course (Ohio Department of Education, 2012, High School Syllabi).

Science. The K–12 Science standards include a focus on technological design and engineering or "a problem-based way of applying creativity, science, engineering, and mathematics to meet a human needs or wants" in the 21st century. Moreover, the standards presume that "technology modifies the natural world through innovative processes, systems, structures, and devices to extend human abilities." Coupled with technology, the knowledge and methods derived from science "profoundly influence the quality of life" (Ohio Department of Education, 2011).

(g) Initiative, Flexibility, and Collaborative Skills

- Adaptability to Change and Diversity
- Effective Use of Positive and Corrective Feedback
- Effective Goal Setting and Resource Management
- Commitment to Self-Direction and Advanced Skill Levels
- Work Effectively With Others and Leverage Diversity to Achieve Innovation
- Demonstrate Integrity, Professional Etiquette, and Responsibility for the Greater Good

All Subjects. This cluster of 21st century skills is more about each student's personal development as a learner and citizen-to-be than about specific content standards. While the writing teams develop their course tools, they will also be learning how to use the best practices and constructivist teaching-learning techniques shown in Table 1.1, many of which include the 21st century skills in this category. By design, the course tools will include the following: "Initiative, Flexibility, and Collaborative Skills" to help every student prepare him and herself to function successfully in the 21st Century. Costa and Kallick (2012) have published a Web page interpreting these and a few additional habits such as persistence, managing impulsivity, metacognition, finding humor, and posing problems.

(1) *Adaptability to Change and Diversity:* Ironically, most 21st century students will have been subjected to far more change and diversity than most of their teachers. With advances in technology, the proliferation of social networking, and the ever-expanding globalization in every aspect of their lives, students experience change daily.

Schools must help students develop work habits and self-discipline sufficient to take control of their lives—despite continuous and unanticipated change. Teachers will establish clear and efficient classroom routines and specific procedures to complete learning activities and out-of-class assignments. The point isn't to punish students or to stifle their creativity; it is to help them learn to follow directions, manage time and resources well, and complete assigned tasks successfully.

At the core of this self-discipline and the power to stay focused is the ability to adapt to change quickly and efficiently. Confident, self-directed students are not shaken up when facing surprises and not rendered helpless when the rules suddenly change. To teach students this sort of flexibility, classroom activities must occasionally "throw them a curve" by introducing new details. Further, students need to depart from their customary, typically homogeneous circumstances and learn to function equally well with diversity in cultures, values, and interpretations.

(2) ***Effective Use of Positive and Corrective Feedback:*** In each unit plan, teachers will be prompted to provide affirmative feedback to students for correct answers, including *why* the response was correct to provide students an "anchor" they can use again. When students provide an incomplete or incorrect answer, teachers will provide corrective but encouraging feedback. Again, it is important that the feedback be substantive; rather than a simplistic, unhelpful "no," the teacher will indicate why the response was not correct and prompt the student toward the correct one. The entire point is to help students know the *why* of their responses and that an incorrect answer is not so much a mistake as an opportunity to rethink and reconsider the information to arrive at the correct answer.

Equally important is modeling for students. If this type of feedback is the norm in each classroom from kindergarten on, by the intermediate grades, students are expected to respond to each other in similar fashion. This two-step process of "teacher models-students apply" will help students internalize these behaviors for use in their own lives.

Positive and corrective feedback is included in most of the best-practices lists currently circulated among school reformers (Marzano, 2003a, 2011).

(3) ***Effective Goal-Setting and Resource Management:*** Goal-setting is certainly not a new practice for most teachers. But the typical practice has been to set class goals and for an entire quarter or semester. In our experience, these goals are more rhetorical than substantive. But when teachers help students set individual goals related to an individual unit plan—connected to the requirements of that unit—the goals are taken more seriously. The key is to allow students to give themselves credit for making progress toward their goals and counting that credit toward the letter grade. Of course, the criteria for this credit are established at the outset of the unit, and students must document their progress. But experience has shown that students become more invested in this type of goal-setting and take it more seriously.

Consistent with the 21st century skills requirement, each student's goals must include "resource management." This may involve the improved stewardship of time, supplies, materials, technology, and any other resources necessary to master the standards of the unit. As with other 21st century skills, as students become accustomed to and successful at "goal-setting and resource management" in *school,* they will transfer those skills to their work and college Marzano, 2003a, 2011).

(4) ***Commitment to Self-Direction and Advanced Skill Levels:*** This particular 21st century skill set undergirds most of the others. It is also closely related to all of the new content standards in that mastery and retention of these more rigorous expectations will require students to attain advanced skill levels. And because only a portion of what students will need to know can be learned in 13 years of schooling, they will need serious self-direction to continue to learn beyond their public school years. With the previous standards,

teachers attempted to guide students through the entire curriculum. By contrast, the new standards drive a curriculum in which teachers prepare students to think and reason and critically analyze, and then the students will be expected to discover the rest by themselves. Every unit plan will include activities to reinforce independent learning, self-direction, and higher-order thinking. These are also core tenets of *Understanding by Design* by Jay McTighe, Eliot Seif, and Grant Wiggins (2004).

(5) ***Work Effectively With Others and Leverage Diversity to Achieve Innovation:*** A common thread running through most of the 21st century skills is the expectation that students work collaboratively with others and take their full share of responsibility for completing the task. In many districts, cooperative learning has long been a frequent practice, but in others, isolation or even competition is more the trend. Each unit plan will include some activities that students complete in collaboration with others. In districts with a highly diverse cultural population, students are accustomed to diversity, and this portion of the 21st century skill will not be new to them. But in more homogeneous districts—be they urban or rural—students may need to consider alternate points of view and diverse perspectives from sources other than their peers. But with the enormous variety of information available instantly from across the globe, the new curriculum and its classroom experiences will show students how to leverage diversity to accomplish innovative solutions to any number of problems.

(6) ***Demonstrate Integrity, Professional Etiquette, and Responsibility for the Greater Good:*** This set of 21st century skills is indeed a very personal one—and difficult to teach as well as to measure. These skills are—or are not—part of an individual's value system and actually most noticeable by their absence.

Integrity isn't so much a skill as an attribute that distinguishes someone who can be trusted from one who cannot. But schools can help students see the importance of integrity by making sure they see the positive consequences when it is *present* and the negative consequences when it is *missing.* The outward manifestations of integrity include the willingness to admit mistakes or errors, to respect another person's work and property, and to be scrupulous about the truth. School staffs need to (a) make it easier for students to admit mistakes; (b) create situations where students and their property are treated with respect, and in turn, they extend respect to others; (c) reinforce students for being truthful and honest; and (d) consistently model.

Professional etiquette is the observance of accepted rules in attitude and decorum when dealing with others. In boxing, it's like following the *Marquis of Queensbury* rules, or in playing cards, one does it according to *Hoyle.* In school—both in and out of the classroom—it means that students are polite, mannerly, and observe restraint. They respect alternate opinions, even ones that differ widely from their own, and they work at giving others the benefit of the doubt. School administrators need to model it with teachers, teachers with each other, and teachers with students. Again, students must see the benefits of behaving this way as well as the disadvantages of not doing so.

Responsibility for the greater good is one's personal conviction that he or she has a duty to others and to society as a whole—not just to him or herself. The intent is not to foster socialism or any other political belief but to develop a legitimate and healthy commitment to the welfare of others, to be "our brother's keeper," and to make decisions that will benefit the common good. School personnel need not only to consistently model this behavior but also to create opportunities for students to demonstrate concern for others and for society as a whole.

. . . And from those who REALLY know. . . .

*Our school serves students with disabilities, so, as we worked with the new standards, we deliberately incorporated 21st century skills into the unit plans and our daily routines and procedures for each class. There was a time when we left it to each teacher to include these skills, but it's become clear to me that if we are not deliberate and strategic about helping students develop these skills, they'll never be ready to perform them on their own. We don't want our students suffering from "learned helplessness" by having them leave our school with the impression that just because they face challenges, everything will be DONE FOR them. We want them to use these skills to successfully navigate through their education, careers and everyday lives.—**Lydia Brown-Payton, school director, Mollie Kessler School**

International Benchmarking for Global Competition

When the National Governor's Association and the Council of Chief State School Officers commissioned the development of the Common Core standards in Math and ELA, they intended to raise the level of academic rigor in America's schools to that of competing nations. Not only were they hopeful for better results on the National Assessment of Educational Progress, this international benchmarking would permit students of the United States to earn respectable scores on the PISA, PIRLS, TIMSS tests, and other worldwide assessments.

The urgency of this need for rigor and accountability in American education came to the world's attention with Exxon-Mobil's sponsorship of the 2012 Masters Tournament in Augusta. Viewers and sponsors from all over the world were reminded on television that the United States ranked 25th among the competing nations.

Even more important than test scores and bragging rights is the anticipation that American ingenuity, technical expertise, economic savvy, and academic competence will once again be sufficient to compete globally. It has been difficult for America's corporate leaders, politicians, and most of its citizens to imagine the United States lagging behind smaller, less endowed nations in anything. True to America's indomitable spirit, no one wants to give up on finding a solution, and so the "solution wars" continue. The Common Core and new state content standards are the next best hope to return the nation's schools—and the quality of education they provide—to their former world prominence.

IMPLICATIONS FOR LEADERSHIP

The current generation of district superintendents and building principals were mostly trained during the last decade when the previous standards were still in place. Without training to do otherwise, they will attempt to use their current understanding of curriculum and classroom instruction to implement the new standards.

Principals need to know how to facilitate and monitor the classroom implementation of the new curriculum. They will be expected to identify teacher behaviors that yield more and less effective student responses and how to prescribe corrective action plans as needed—including specific suggestions for best practices that are aligned with the new standards. With the appropriate training and involvement, principals can regain the respect of their teachers and become viable partners in the implementation of the new curriculum. Each principal's annual performance review should reflect his and her level of success in these important new duties.

The implications for leadership are focused at three levels: First is the Board of Education, followed by central office, and then building administrators. Michael Fullan (2002a, 2002b) stresses the need for solid leadership at all levels in the district as the primary strategy for sustainable school reform. If curriculum and instruction are to be a part of central office and building administrators' job expectations, the Board of Education must include the specifics of what is expected in the administrative job description, and then hold the administrators accountable for completing the tasks outlined in that document. It is not enough to put the expectations in a job description and expect people to perform a series of tasks not previously expected. In collaboration with the National Association of Secondary School Principals, Doug Reeves (2004b, 2005) insists that the principal's job description must include the role of continuously monitoring classroom instruction. The board must provide principals with the professional development and ongoing support needed to perform their roles in the implementation of the new standards. Michael Fullan, Al Bertani, and Joanne Quinn (2004) contend that boards must mandate the structure and align finances and human resources necessary for principals to closely monitor instruction. Further, M. Hayes Mizell (2004) calls for boards to avoid wasting dollars on professional development for any activity that *will not be applied* in the classroom.

Once the Board of Education has established the policies for performance, then central office and building administrators must work to determine how this can happen. If there are curriculum experts in the district—content supervisors, coordinators, or content coaches—they should be a part of the plan to provide support for the building principals. The central office team should regularly discuss content standards, how to interpret them, and where they are placed in the curriculum map. Moreover, the central office staff should pay close attention to the delivery of instruction and how quality assessments are being used to determine student learning. Otherwise, they remain disconnected from what is actually taking place in the district classrooms. We suggest that central office staff be assigned to buildings and content areas, maintaining visibility and providing support to teachers as well as the building administrators.

Finally, it is the building administrators—principals and assistant principals—who shoulder the primary responsibility for seeing that the curriculum is implemented in all subjects in every classroom of their buildings. Wow! It even sounds daunting to say it! But it can be done. Terrance Quinn

(2002), former principal, emphasizes the need for principals to reorder their priorities to be visible throughout the school and spend the majority of time in classrooms. James Bernauer (2002) insists that obtaining feedback about student performance and teaching practices is the "glue" that holds the process of continuous improvement together. Without timely information to assess progress, teachers and administrators are unable to evaluate the effectiveness of instructional methods and therefore, not able to make mid-course corrections. Michael Fullan (2002a, 2002b) urges principals to exercise leadership and guide staff members through the work.

. . . And from those who REALLY know. . . .

*Since the beginning, we've worked hard to make sure that our curriculum maps capture a developmental flow across the grade levels. Our teachers have done most of their best practices professional development (PD) in cross-grade level teams to hear from each other and to understand the "before and after" of their work. That's also helped replace less effective practices like "telling" and "worksheets" with drawing students out and having them construct their own meaning. I attend the PD sessions as an active participant, and the teams appreciate that I see instruction as a priority. My conferences with teachers are professional conversations about which teaching behaviors yield the most effective student results.—**Jon Hood, principal, Maryland Elementary School, Bexley City Schools**

Building administrators rightly insist that they cannot be expert in all content areas, and while that is true, there are strategies that can be employed to assist them in learning about those content areas where they may lack sufficient background knowledge. It is critical that each administrator be a member of at least one curriculum writing team in the district as the curriculum is being developed. Michael Mills (2001) sees it as the building administrator's duty to work with teachers in devising the curriculum and using data to know if they are making the difference needed. This does not mean show up at curriculum or standards meetings and do other work while the teachers write the curriculum. It is about being part of the discussions and listening to the issues raised by teachers who will have to implement the standards in their classrooms. By being legitimately involved in these discussions, and being part of the solutions for how "we" will approach these issues in this district, everyone gets on the same page. Without helping to decide what will each new standard look like when students demonstrate it, how the new standards differ from the current curriculum, how the standards flow developmentally across grade levels, a building administrator cannot appreciate what teachers face in the delivery of the new curriculum.

Without this knowledge, how can an administrator possibly know if a teacher is doing what is required for a group of students? Hayes Mizell (2003) insists that when teachers and principals collaborate to understand the content standards and to determine the best means for organizing their schools to help students meet them, amazing things happen for students. Michael Fullan

(2002a) describes the principal's leadership as the "core feature of sustainability" in the transformation of schools. Further, Victoria Bernhardt (2002), executive director of Education for the Future Initiative, speaks to the notion of leading by modeling instructional excellence.

It is not about being expert in all content areas, but about being willing to *learn with the teachers* what is needed to get students to master these new expectations set for in the standards. And once the curriculum is established, the major burden for overseeing the implementation in the classrooms of the district falls squarely on the shoulders of the building administrators. So what skill set is needed to accomplish this awesome task? For this to happen, Virginia Hurley (high school assistant principal), Ruth Greenblatt (educational consultant), and Fordham University professor Bruce Cooper (2003) teamed up to stress the need for administrators to replace traditional approaches (i.e., top-down behaviors with interrogation-like tones) with "professional conversations" that are focused on effective practice. These conversations include open-ended, probing questions that feature use of paraphrasing, summations, and clarification to gain common understanding of what is needed to be successful with students.

. . . And from those who REALLY know. . . .

*When we began working with the Core Standards, we found a need to build capacity in our principals to become active participants in the process of designing curriculum maps and units of instruction. Each principal determined areas where she or he would work with teachers—some choosing areas of greatest strength in content knowledge and others choosing areas where she or he wanted to become stronger in the content knowledge. Knowing the curriculum and the discussions that went into the development of the units allowed principals to work as a team with their teachers for the delivery of instruction to students as well as monitor what was happening in classrooms.—**Cherie Mourlam, assistant superintendent, Washington Local Schools***

For building administrators to monitor the new curriculum, they need to spend time in classrooms. They should script the teachers' behaviors and their impact on students. In addition, they should notice what is happening relative to the standards, paying particular attention to each teacher's fidelity to the curriculum maps and unit plans. In particular, the building administrator must be trained to be familiar with the following:

(a) Understanding the content and cognitive demand of the standards.

(b) Knowing what is in the curriculum maps and what teachers are to be focused on for a given point in time. This might mean keeping a wall chart or clipboard chart in the office to know what should be being taught and where teachers should be in their units during walk-throughs).

(c) Understanding instructional practices that are in the unit plans and what is in the research about these practices and alternatives; the unit plan becomes the lesson plans for teachers.

(d) Understanding differentiation—knowing how to discuss response to intervention and examine practices with teachers to accomplish this without "tracking" students.

(e) Being able to ask questions about instruction and engage in a conversation with teachers about specific practices that are used and how these impact students.

(f) Reviewing unit assessments for validity to be sure they are well constructed and the questions assess the designated standards; offering feedback on how to improve the quality of the assessment.

(g) Reviewing the results of unit or common formative assessments and knowing the data in terms of the instructional implications.

(h) Offering specific prescriptions to teachers to upgrade their instruction and/or to address specific student weaknesses.

(i) Attending regular departmental or grade level meetings to listen to and be part of the discussions on the course tools—unit plans and maps.

Complete detail about the logistics and protocols for these tasks will be included in Chapter 7.

Developing Course Tools to Build the Instructional Program

2

"Choose always the way that seems the best, however rough it may be. Custom will soon render it easy and agreeable."

—Pythagoras

For 46 of the 50 states, the Common Core standards in Math and English Language Arts is no longer a matter of "whether" or "if"—it is a matter of "how." And for many states, Science and Social Studies content standards have also been adopted to completely transform the curriculum. And despite the good intentions of the standards, the professional literature has continued to reflect concern about *how they will be implemented*—the old "dragging a ham bone through a pot of water doesn't make soup." Simply claiming to have adopted the new standards does not transform the curriculum.

A few of the most recent observations of this effect are as follows:

- In a blog describing the formula used by several countries to increase student achievement, Marc S. Tucker (president and chief executive officer of the National Center on Education and the Economy) cites the standards as only the first step to improve student performance (Tucker, 2012, para. 3). He reports that these countries then "worked backwards to define a curriculum framework for each grade level" (Tucker, 2012, para. 4). Also included were carefully crafted syllabi and high-quality examinations based directly on the curriculum standards. Tucker (2012) also observes that teachers be trained to deliver this curriculum.

- Stephanie Hirsh, veteran professional development specialist for the National Staff Development Council, worries about the push for upgrading student expectations. While upgraded content standards offer an agenda for what students should know and how they should learn it, "We have not yet committed to offering teachers the deep learning they will need to transform the way they work" (Hirsh, 2012, p. 22). She charges that too many curriculum transition plans read like communication talking points "rather than serious roadmaps" (Hirsh, 2012, p. 22) to guide teachers in actually teaching the standards.

- In a statement released by the Marzano Center for Teacher Leadership and Evaluation, John Edwards strongly suggests that the new standards be implemented in every classroom using a model of teaching that both teachers and administrators follow. The model must contain a common language to discuss about what good teaching looks like and how to make adjustments when students fail to master the specified content. Edwards and the rest of the Marzano team are confident that in all those states where student performance will constitute 50% of the teacher's performance evaluation, a new interest has been kindled in such "models" to improve classroom instruction (Edwards, 2012).

- Deborah A. Taub is director of research at Keystone Assessment, a Kentucky-based firm specializing in devising alternate assessments for children with cognitive disabilities. She is concerned that special needs students not be overlooked in the standards-frenzy. In a recent Special Education Advisor (Taub, 2012), she makes four suggestions to general and regular education teachers to give every student access to the new standards.

   o Build sample lessons and curriculum for teachers to use.
   o Use interim assessments that are compiled to create the end of year assessment.
   o Devise learning progression frameworks to inform teaching activities.
   o Use dynamic learning maps to continuously monitor student learning.

These and scores of similar admonitions endorse the underlying premise of this book. That is that while the new standards are vital to the restoration of American education, they are just print on paper without a districtwide delivery system. This system is empowered by course tools to implement and monitor the standards in every classroom. Chapter 2 is devoted to how such a delivery system can be built.

MAKE THE COMMITMENT AND THEN GET A GAME PLAN

In spite of pressure on the nation's schools to adopt the new content standards as quickly as possible, most districts are using a staggered approach. Many are beginning with the first students impacted by the 2014–15 testing; these are the "bookends" of PK–3, with the new high-stakes tests, and 9–12, with the end-of-course assessments. This strategic phase-in approach of two to three years will allow districts to work within their resources and staff capacity. Taking on too much too quickly would jeopardize the entire process and actually delay its accomplishment.

The new standards and the 21st century skills are such a radical departure from the previous standards that to implement *any of them* will transform the entire educational program—but in a good way. The transformation will have a positive impact on staff and student performance, and the new habits of leadership and classroom practice will be well worth the effort. This section will speak to the importance of making adequate preparations.

Once a Board of Education makes the commitment to take on the transformation process, step one is to articulate the vision as a districtwide priority, allocate the necessary time and resources, and then establish a strategic plan to accomplish the task. The most successful plans make crystal clear what is to be done, how it will be accomplished, and in what time frames, holding every teacher and administrator accountable for the success of the new curriculum.

> *Lesson Learned!* An important lesson from experience has been to include the building schedules in the overall planning. One district made the investment in time and resources to adopt the new standards in all four core content areas and appointed teachers to devise a best practices curriculum. They had even planned for double periods in math and English language arts to allow for ongoing intervention and differentiation. But they did not devise the building schedule ahead of time and had to settle for 45- to 48-minute periods, thus severely weakening their entire project. A second misjudgment was waiting to order needed supplies until just before the year began. The delay in receiving science and math equipment, social studies maps, and some reading selections has seriously interfered with their implementation of a well-designed delivery system.

The overall game plan to develop the delivery system and its course tools should include the following steps:

(a) Appoint teachers to grade-level (or course) work teams; each work team (or at least grade band; e.g., PK–2) should also include a principal, an academic coach or similar support staff, and a central office staff member. In most districts, the "representative-critical friends" model is appropriate. As the work teams complete drafts of the course tools, they are circulated among the other teachers at that grade level (or who teach the course) for reaction and input. Facilitated by the principal and content area coaches, this feedback loop not only ensures that each teacher has a voice, but also it involves the principal and other support staff as visible partners in the process.

(b) Schedule work sessions in grade bands to maximize developmental flow and continuity. The divisions should be appropriate to the district's organization, but one sample is PK–2; 3–5; 6–8; and 9–12. Experience has shown that monthly work sessions allow for circulation of the drafts and provide work team members opportunity to reflect on their efforts in preparation for the next session. Several models will be provided.

(c) Devise "rubrics" for each course tool and ask those furnishing technical assistance to provide feedback to the work teams on their drafts. This will enhance the structural integrity of each tool and maintain quality control of the content and cognitive demand required of the new standards. Because the teachers, principals, and support staff are involved in this feedback process, the rubrics will strengthen the district's internal capacity to continuously review and upgrade the course tools.

(d) Include progress reports by work team members on the course tool development in the agenda of at least one grade-level or department meeting per quarter. Some districts have grade-level and/or building leadership teams who monitor the results of curriculum design projects. As the course tools are piloted or field-tested, those testing should share any results as an indication of how the material "worked" with students. This will also provide opportunity for participants to make revisions. These meetings are actually dry runs of what will become standard operating procedure at all grade level and department meetings during full implementation. Having the principals and academic coaches as active participants in these progress reports solidifies them as partners in the process and strengthens their credibility among the teaching staff.

(e) Provide parallel training (with relevant field assignments) to the principals and other support staff concurrent to the course tool development. The more familiar they are with the standards and the course tools, the better prepared they will be to support their implementation. The principals (the collective term; includes coaches, supervisors, etc.) will distinguish effective from ineffective teaching practices and their respective impact on students. Through strategic questioning, these principals help teachers honestly examine their delivery and how students responded. By working with teachers to devise collaborative action plans, principals affirm what is going well and specify corrective measures for improvement. For strong teachers, these action plans are about continued growth and reaching new levels of competence. For strugglers, the action plan is a blueprint for remedial action and sets forth precise expectations for improvement. While the principals do not deliver the newly enacted curriculum, they are accountable for making certain that it is taught with fidelity in every classroom.

> *. . . And from those who REALLY know. . . .*
>
> *When I took this job, the district had been through dozens of plans and programs. It jumped into one reform after another—one for the reading curriculum, the next one for science teachers, then one for middle school principals. But there was never one program that pulled everything together—a K–12 curriculum project that involved all the teachers and every principal. What I knew we needed was a comprehensive project that would create a K–12 standards-based curriculum. The board had to commit to a long-term plan that included release time, staff retraining, and a total revamping of our assessment system. And then once we had a plan, we had to KEEP it . . . and maintain it with regular checks and adjustments. For sure, we could never again go back to business as usual.—**Connie Hathorn, PhD, superintendent, Youngstown City Schools***

UNPACKING, BUNDLING, AND SEQUENCING THE STANDARDS

The all-important first stage of curriculum transformation is to examine the standards themselves. Although there are any number of off-the-shelf products that claim to be the "standards explained" or the "standards unwrapped," there is no substitute for teacher work teams physically reading and discussing the standards, nailing down the precise content and cognitive demand of each. Team members need to agree on what students will do to demonstrate mastery of each standard and how the standard will look as it is being taught. It is in this seemingly simple act of defining, clarifying, and interpreting that a work team establishes its own culture of transformation and creates a special bond to carry them forward. Once examined and understood, the standards are then bundled or clustered into thematic or topical "units" that provide an authentic context for the skills and concepts included in those standards. This, too, is where the 21st century skills are embedded.

> *. . . And from those who REALLY know. . . .*
>
> *When the district started talking about the changes coming with the Core Math standards, we contracted with an outside expert (who works internationally) to lead our Grades 6–12 math department, including special education teachers (24 members) in what the standards would mean for our teaching. We spent time in the summer of 2012 to begin the process, and people were a little unsure the first day. But by the end of the first three days, the acceptance was amazing! Teachers began researching rich tasks immediately, sharing ideas with other department members, and showing a willingness to "dig in." We are now working on rich tasks for the Common Core integrated into an authentic context.— **Dana Edmonds, Math Department Chair, Whitmer High School, Washington Local Schools***

It is the authenticity that separates these new units from their predecessor. Unlike many traditional units, these are not sterile clumps of facts, rules, or skills. Instead of a unit on Fractions, the new unit will be something like "Using

Fractions at Disney World." Instead of a unit called "The Short Story," the new unit will be "Rising to Our Challenges" and include a mix of the short story, poetry, and nonfiction. Unlike the old units that may include only one strand (e.g., just Number Facts or Reading), the new Units will integrate strands, such as Number Facts and Measurement or Reading, Writing, and Speaking. The Science and Social Studies units will include the integration of literacy skills dealing with vocabulary, author bias, and writing content-based research reports.

Once the units are roughed out, the work teams then place them into the most appropriate teaching-learning sequence for classroom implementation. In schools where the core content areas are teamed, this sequence will be a cooperative venture between, for example, social studies and English language arts. That way, the argumentative research paper (a standards requirement in BOTH subjects) can be coordinated.

This unpacking-bundling-sequencing process yields the cornerstone of the entire curriculum. How each team interprets the content and the cognitive demand of the new standards (in sync with the 21st century skills) and their implications for classroom instruction will set the tone for the rest of the work. In effect, this step accomplishes the "what" of the new curriculum.

To save them time and improve their efficiency, every work team needs to understand some basic assumptions behind the "new" standards and the 21st century skills.

The Common Core. Most districts begin with the Common Core in Math or English Language Arts (ELA). Both subjects are built around the premise that each school year is its own vital step in the developmental progression toward college- and career-readiness. Moreover, these two bedrock subjects are the foundation for all learning and the metric by which school districts are judged. However, each of the two is organized around its own set of categories and sub-categories, and it is essential that work teams become familiar with these overall structures and the precise wording of each standard. As shown in the Chapter 1 example (from Table 1.1), the Common Core in Math and ELA deliberately and purposefully bind together individual skills and concepts to replace fragmented, splinter skills with holistic and deep-level understandings of "how things work." To help students accomplish this integrated learning, teachers must show them how to think about the subject in a new way. Obviously, the work teams must first understand this concept themselves. It is no longer rules and drills; it is now application to solve problems and construct meaning for oneself.

One new twist brought by the Common Core standards to ELA is the requirement that students experience a steady diet of literary nonfiction. In fact, by graduation, the standards insist that 70% of the materials students read in ELA be literary nonfiction.

For special needs, gifted, and English as a second language students, the Common Core directs that districts make suitable adaptations and modifications. No "adjusted" standards are provided. But it is strongly recommended that special needs students do not work with standards below their grade placement. It is understood that materials and teaching methods may be adjusted, but the Common Core hopes that students are encouraged to master on-level standards in Math and ELA.

. . . And from those who REALLY know. . . .

I have been teaching for 19 years, and I have always considered myself a challenging teacher. However, the new standards are much more rigorous and demanding, both for the students and the teachers. They have made me realize how much deeper I need to get the students to think. The new standards really require the students to construct meaning for themselves more than ever before, which means that we have to adjust the way we teach as well. If we expect students to construct meaning, we have to model for them how to do that.

*My colleagues and I are excited to see that the bar for students has been raised; we know that they are capable of so much more. At the same time, we're a little scared about how we are going to get it all done well. We are also struggling with incorporating our standards with our science and social studies colleagues in a way that makes sense and helps the students learn and grow across all of our disciplines.—**Julie Dudones, eighth-grade integrated language arts teacher, Roberts Middle School, Cuyahoga Falls City Schools***

Revised Standards in Science and Social Studies. New Science and Social Studies standards were adopted by each state, rather than as national curricula. The process of unpacking-bundling-sequencing for Science and Social Studies is similar to that of the Common Core, but with a major difference in *internal* structure. Math and ELA standards are more *process* than *content*, and as such, they are recursive; many will need to be repeated in various contexts for mastery to occur. Science and Social Studies standards are more *content* than *process*, and thus many are not as likely to be repeated in multiple grade levels or even in several units across the school year.

A special twist on the Social Studies and Science standards is that the Common Core standards for ELA include Literacy standards specifically designated for Social Studies, Science, and Technical Subjects. The intent is to move students away from textbooks (secondary sources) into primary sources such as eyewitness accounts, field notes from live research, diaries and journals from actual participants in the scientific or historic event. The Literacy standards include both Reading and Writing and are to be embedded in K–6. But for 6–12, they are specified as to the skills that students must demonstrate in analyzing nonfiction text, conducting research, and writing papers for different purposes.

. . . And from those who REALLY know. . . .

*The new standards really reduce the role of memorization in learning. Instead, students are required to think about the HOW and WHY of things and construct their own explanation. It's like we can no longer tell them what they need to know; we have to involve them in learning experiences where they discover for themselves what's going on. For example, I'll never forget the a-ha moment when my kids realized there were no individual rights in the U.S. Constitution and that led to the Bill of Rights. Or when they traced the ideas from the Enlightenment thinkers to American democracy. Oh it's not easy! In fact, it's probably just as tough on the teachers as it is the students.—**Eboni Williams, social studies teacher, Chaney High School, Youngstown City Schools***

Part of the unpacking-bundling-sequencing process in the 6–12 work teams for math, science, and social studies will be the placement of these Literacy standards. The sample course tools at the end of this chapter include these Literacy standards in Science, Social Studies, and Math.

The 21st Century Skills. These workplace-success skills were promulgated in 2002 by a collaborative partnership of prominent global businesses (e.g., Verizon, Microsoft, Apple, DELL, and Cisco), the International Society for Technology in Education, and the U.S. Department of Education. The intent of that group was and remains that the nation's schools insert into their curriculum specific skills that will be needed by students to be successful in the workplace. The hope is that these 21st century skills (listed in Chapter 1, Table 1.1) will influence public education in America through policies and practices as well as comprehensive pedagogical, curricular, and assessment frameworks.

Unlike the Common Core standards in Math and ELA and the state-based standards in Science and Social Studies, the 21st century skills are not assigned to individual grade levels. Hence, the work teams collectively decide how to distribute the standards across grade levels and what specific activities will be associated with each. Experience has shown that many of the 21st century skills are identical to or strongly resemble the various content standards, expediting their integration into the new curriculum.

For example, students will be expected to use the following:

1. **Global Thinking** when units include activities that involve the Middle East, Europe, Asia, Africa, South America, the Pacific Rim, Canada, and Mexico. One instance of this is that students consider the impact of decisions made in one country on other countries—not only in that region but elsewhere around the globe.

2. **The Literacies**—Financial and Economic, Civic, Health, and Environmental—by solving authentic problems in each area as a part of Math, Social Studies, Science, and Health units. For instance, students will demonstrate their grasp of Environmental Literacy by proposing an equitable solution to the Keystone pipeline dilemma or to resolve the fracking dispute in Youngstown, Ohio.

3. **Thinking and Reasoning for Effective Decision Making** when they are challenged to make group and individual choices throughout the curriculum, including finding solutions to real and hypothetical problems. For example, what are multiple ways that several more people might have been saved from the Titanic disaster—and what are the relative merits of each over the other.

4. **Communication and Collaboration** when they make written and spoken presentations—individually as well as in teams. These apply with re-enactments, readers' theater, debates, and skits.

5. **Information Technology and Media** when planning, devising, delivering, evaluating the impact of, and upgrading various technology applications as well as media presentations. These occur as PowerPoints, blogs, webinars, and so on.

6. **Initiative and Flexibility** to accomplish tasks when faced with obstacles to their routine and barriers to their normal way of proceeding. In addition, when direction is not provided, can students proceed on their own and accomplish the task according to, or at least reasonably close to, expectations?

DEVISING CURRICULUM MAPS (OR PACING GUIDES)

Once the writing teams have decided how to cluster the content standards and the 21st century skills into units of instruction and place them in the correct developmental sequence, this work is committed to print as a *curriculum map*. Also known as a pacing guide or a yearlong overview, a curriculum map is prepared for each grade level in each of the subject areas addressed. The purpose of the curriculum map is to provide an aerial view of the school year to document the implementation of the content standards.

Collectively, the PK–12 curriculum maps for each grade level should be adopted by the Board of Education as the official curriculum of the district for that subject. As such, each curriculum map is the foundational course tool for each grade level and subject. It is the "document of record" for central office staff, principals, coaches, teachers, and parents. The ultimate intent is for the district to transform the curriculum in all four of the major subjects, but time and resources limitations will require most districts to adopt a staggered approach to this across a two- to three-year period.

Experience has shown that although each district prefers to design its own maps—and may design a different format for primary grades, intermediate, junior high, and high school—the following components are those most frequently selected:

- ✓ Time Frames (quarters or grading periods)
- ✓ Unit Titles
- ✓ The Standards Assigned to Each Unit
- ✓ Literacy Standards (for Science, Math, and Social Studies—set forth in the Common Core English Language Arts standards)
- ✓ Labs or Inquiry Projects (for Science)
- ✓ Cross-Curricular Connections
- ✓ High-Stakes Tests or Benchmark Assessments
- ✓ The 21st Century Skills

> *. . . And from those who REALLY know. . . .*
>
> *Another veteran English teacher and I developed the first draft of the Grade 11 and 12 curriculum maps for English language arts. Although it was certainly a challenge, it has helped organize all of us who teach the 7–12 sequence–especially deciding what major literary selections we'll use at each grade level. Our writing teams continue to meet every few weeks, and I really appreciate that we can adjust the Map, given extenuating circumstances and the inevitable delays that happen in school. As we edit this first draft, we are looking forward to NEXT year, when we'll know more about what order and pacing have worked the best.* **–Angela Dooley, English teacher, Chaney High School, National Writing Project teacher consultant, and High Schools That Work site coordinator, Youngstown City Schools**

Very simple curriculum maps may look like the following shown in Table 2.1. Others become very complex. Individual pages from three sample curriculum maps—showing different formats—will follow.

In districts where the work teams include representatives rather than all teachers who teach a course, the first draft of the curriculum map should be circulated among the other faculty who will teach it. This "critical friend" technique gives the other teachers a voice in the development of the map and provides helpful feedback to the writing teams. By incorporating the suggestions of the larger group, the final map is a work of greater consensus and thus more

Table 2.1 Grade 9 American and World History

UNIT 2: ENLIGHTENMENT	QUARTER 1	TIME FRAME: 4 WEEKS
CLUSTER OF STANDARDS	**LITERACY STANDARDS**	**HISTORICAL THINKING/ 21st CENTURY**
WH.5 The Scientific Revolution impacted religious, political, and cultural institutions by challenging how people viewed the world. WH.6 Enlightenment thinkers applied reason to discover natural laws guiding human nature in social, political, and economic systems and institutions. WH.7 Enlightenment ideas challenged practices related to religious authority, absolute rule, and mercantilism.	RH.4 Determine the meaning of words and phrases as they are used in a text, including vocabulary describing political, social, or economic aspects of history/social studies. RH.6 Compare the point of view of two or more authors for how they treat the same or similar topics, including which details they include and emphasize in their respective accounts. WHST.4 Produce clear and coherent writing in which the development, organization, and style are appropriate to task, purpose, and audience.	Historical Thinking 1. Historical events provide opportunities to examine alternative courses of action. 4. Historians analyze cause, effect, sequence, and correlation in historical events, including multiple causation and long and short-term causal relations. 21st Century Skills Global Awareness; Thinking and Reasoning for Decision-Making Initiative, Flexibility, and Collaboration

accepted by the entire staff. As the official document approved by the Board of Education, the curriculum map will dictate the official order and pace of the curriculum for each grade level and course. However, in the spirit of continuous improvement, the map is reviewed annually in the context of student performance and adjusted as needed. This phase is discussed in Chapter 4. Moving forward, the curriculum map continues to be the compass that guides to the remainder of the curriculum transformation process. Tables 2.2, 2.3, and 2.4 show other formats that teachers or districts have developed.

Table 2.2 Sample Grade 8 Language Arts Curriculum Map for First Quarter

Unit 2 "Strange and Mysterious" [4½ weeks September–October]

SYNOPSIS: The students will reflect on the life and death of Edgar Alan Poe and read his short story "The Tell-Tale Heart." They will use Poe's work and other sample texts to consider various literary elements such as author's style, irony, mood, tone, and figurative language. In addition, they will analyze other narrative techniques such as dialogue, pacing, description, and reflection; transition words and phrases; and sensory language. At the end of the unit, students will write an epitaph or obituary for Poe, create an original story that follows narrative conventions and is "strange and mysterious," compare the various versions of Poe's death, and evaluate the progress they have made on their personal and academic goals for the unit.

Resource Materials	Differentiation Ideas
• "Tell-Tale Heart" by Edgar Allan Poe (Elements of Lit. pp. 536–545) • "Out-Out" by Robert Frost (Elements of Lit. pp. 707–710) • Writing Effective Sentences continued (e.g., Elements of Lit. pp. 943–970, Elements of Lang. pp. 274–319) • Adjectives (e.g., selections from Elements of Lang. pp. 358–362) • Verbs (e.g., selections from Elements of Lang. pp. 371–379)	• "Masque of the Red Death," "Black Cat," or another short story narrative by Edgar Allan Poe • "The Monkey's Paw" (Elements of Lit. pp. 84–100) • Urban legends • Ss work in 2s; pair-share for reading aloud • T will work 1:1 to get Ss started; circle back • Smaller chunks of reading at one time • Journals may be bullet points rather than complete sentences

Standards

READING LITERATURE

RL 8.6. Analyze how differences in the points of view of the characters and the audience or reader (e.g., created through the use of dramatic irony) create such effects as suspense or humor.

RL 8.7. Analyze the extent to which a filmed or live production of a story or drama stays faithful to or departs from the text or script, evaluating the choices made by the director or actors.

RL 8.9. Analyze how a modern work of fiction draws on themes, patterns of events, or character types from myths, traditional stories, or religious works such as the Bible, including describing how the material is rendered new.

(Continued)

Table 2.2 (Continued)

Standards

READING INFORMATIONAL TEXT

RI 8.3. Analyze how a text makes connections among and distinctions between individuals, ideas, or events (e.g., through comparisons, analogies, or categories).

RI 8.9. Analyze a case in which two or more texts provide conflicting information on the same topic and identify where the texts disagree on matters of fact or interpretation.

WRITING

W 8.3. Write narratives to develop real or imagined experiences or events using effective technique, relevant descriptive details, and well-structured event sequences.

    a. Engage and orient the reader by establishing a context and point of view and introducing a narrator and/or characters; organize an event sequence that unfolds naturally and logically.

    b. Use narrative techniques, such as dialogue, pacing, description, and reflection, to develop experiences, events, and/or characters.

    c. Use a variety of transition words, phrases, and clauses to convey sequence, signal shifts from one time frame or setting to another, and show the relationships among experiences and events.

    d. Use precise words, phrases, relevant descriptive details, and sensory language to capture the action and convey experiences and events.

    e. Provide a conclusion that follows from and reflects on the narrated experiences or events.

W 8.4. Produce clear and coherent writing in which the development, organization, and style are appropriate to task, purpose, and audience. (Grade-specific expectations for writing types are defined in standards W 8.1–W 8.3.)

Table 2.3 Curriculum Map—Grade 7 Mathematics

Unit: #1   **Name: ADDING AND SUBTRACTING RATIONAL NUMBERS**   **Time: Quarter 1:4 weeks**

TECHNOLOGY	PRODUCTS	RESOURCES
NO Calculators National Libra ry of Virtual Manipulatives website to get color chip addition and subtraction activity—nlvm.usu.edu	Analyze problems worked for correctness and explain any errors and correct.	Glencoe Pre-Algebra Teacher Manual: sections 2.2 and 2.3 on adding integers Scott Foresman Course 3: Chapter 2, sections 1, 2, 3

STANDARDS

7.NS.1   Apply and extend previous understandings of addition and subtraction to add and subtract rational numbers; represent addition and subtraction on a horizontal or vertical number line diagram.

a. Describe situations in which opposite quantities combine to make 0 (e.g., a hydrogen atom has 0 charge because its two constituents are oppositely charged).

b. Understand $p + q$ as the number located a distance $| q |$ from p, in the positive or negative direction depending on whether q is positive or negative. Show that a number and its opposite have a sum of 0 (are additive inverses). Interpret sums of rational numbers by describing real-world contexts.

c. Understand subtraction of rational numbers as adding the additive inverse, $p - q = p + (-q)$. Show that the distance between two rational numbers on the number line is the absolute value of their difference, and apply this principle in real-world contexts.

d. Apply properties of operations as strategies to add and subtract rational numbers.

7.NS.3   Solve real-world and mathematical problems involving the four operations—addition and subtraction only in this unit—with rational numbers. (Note: Computations with rational numbers extend the rules for manipulating fractions to complex fractions.)

Note: Addition and subtraction are in this unit and multiplication and division are in unit 2. In this unit, we focus on whole numbers, fractions, and decimals (e.g., −4, +4, +1/4, −1/4, +.25, −.25, etc.). Calculators should not be used since students are learning how to perform these operations.

LITERACY	MATH PRACTICES	VOCABULARY
• Learn to read mathematical text (including textbooks, articles, problems, problem explanations). • Communicate using correct mathematical terminology. • Listen to and critique peer explanations of reasoning. • Justify orally and in writing mathematical reasoning.	1. Make sense of problems and persevere in solving them. 2. Reason abstractly and quantitatively. 3. Construct viable arguments and critique the reasoning of others. 4. Model with mathematics. 5. Use appropriate tools strategically. 6. Attend to precision. 7. Look for and make use of structure. 8. Look for and express regularity in repeated reasoning.	Absolute Value Absolute Value Notation Additive Inverse Positive and Negative Numbers Rational Numbers Irrational Numbers Real Numbers Counting Numbers Natural Numbers Whole Numbers

SYNOPSIS: In this unit, students will gain a greater understanding of how to add and subtract positive and negative rational numbers. Students learn that rational numbers include fractions, mixed numbers, and decimals. Students will solve real-life problems where addition and subtraction of rational numbers are used.

Table 2.4 Curriculum Map: Grade 8 Science

Unit Title: UNIT #2 Tectonic Plate Motion	Time Frame: Quarter 1 Weeks 4–5	
Cluster of Standards	**Literacy Standards**	**Labs/Investigations**	**Resources**

Cluster of Standards	Literacy Standards	Labs/Investigations	Resources
ESS.8.2 Earth's crust consists of major and minor tectonic plates that move relative to each other. **ESS.8.2.a** Historical data and observations such as fossil distribution, paleomagnetism, continental drift, and seafloor spreading contributed to the theory of plate tectonics. **ESS.8.2.b** The rigid tectonic plates move with the molten rock and magma beneath them in the upper mantle. **ESS.8.2.c** Convection currents in the crust and upper mantle cause the movement of the plates. The energy that forms convection currents comes from deep within the Earth. **ESS.8.2.d** There are three main types of plate boundaries: divergent, convergent, and transform. Each type of boundary results in specific motion and causes events (such as earthquakes or volcanic activity) or features (such as mountains or trenches) that are indicative of the type of boundary.	Conduct short research projects to answer a question (including a self-generated question), drawing on several sources and generating additional related, focused questions that allow for multiple avenues of exploration. **WHST .6** Follow precisely a multistep procedure when carrying out experiments, taking measurements, or performing technical tasks. **RST .3** Determine the meaning of symbols, key terms, and other domain-specific words and phrases as they are used in a specific scientific or technical context relevant to *Grades 6–8 texts and topics.* **RST .4**	Pangaea activity (Steve)—Earth's plates fit together Speed of Waves Kinds of Waves Refraction of Waves Predicting Plate Reversals Continental Drift Theory—Wegener Demo—Seafloor Spreading Map study of location of earthquakes and volcanoes using U.S. Geological Survey real-time data. Global positioning system data documenting plate movements—where will North America be in 600 million years? Plate Boundaries	Newspaper sheets 9 × 13 glass baking dish or flat container Stopwatch Flashlight Slinky Black line master 2.2 (p. 317 *Our Dynamic Planet*)

> *. . . And from those who REALLY know. . . .*
>
> *The curriculum map has helped me manage my classroom time so much better than before. Although the maps aren't carved in stone, they give us an idea of how much time to spend on each unit, what sequence we're following, and which Literacy Skills are placed where. Taken together, the maps at each grade level give us an aerial view of the whole Social Studies curriculum. But I'm also on the writing team for the unit plans, and I really appreciate the ability to make adjustments in the maps as we go along.—**James Kosek, social studies teacher, Woodrow Wilson Middle School; Youngstown City Schools***

UNIT PLANNING

The curriculum map determines the "what" of the new curriculum and provides the overall direction. However, the curriculum map does not address how the teaching-learning or the assessment will be addressed. The next step is the "how," or the actual delivery and assessment of the standards in the classroom. The second course tool—the unit plan—is a research-based template to organize teaching-learning activities that lead students toward mastery of the standards. Using the "units" identified on their curriculum map, each grade-level work team typically develops between 8 to 12 unit plans for the year, or two to three units per quarter. This division works well with either short-cycle (midquarter) or quarterly benchmark assessments.

Sudden Impact. If the work teams haven't already, they will discover the full impact of the new standards and how dramatically classroom instruction will need to change during the development of the unit plans. It dawns on each team that truly, this is no longer "business as usual." While more capable teachers will feel validated—albeit a bit challenged, struggling teachers will become anxious and resistant, and weak teachers will be thoroughly intimidated and may even become uncooperative. But herein lies the importance of direct and supportive involvement of the central office staff, the principals, coaches, and other support staff. Every teacher—who sincerely wishes to—can be successful in learning these new techniques and habits of mind. For those not wishing to, the district may wish to offer other career choices that would be more appealing. Refusing to help their students master the new content standards and the 21st century skills is simply not an option—for any teacher or administrator. Indeed, as veteran teachers have been working with the new standards and the teaching that is necessary to accomplish these, many report that they feel as though they are in their first year of teaching with all of the new things they must consider.

. . . And from those who REALLY know. . . .

*Working through unpacking standards and chunking them into a curriculum map laid the framework for the yearlong process of developing grade-level unit plans. The map and the units became the guiding framework for what was to be taught, when it was to be taught, and how it should be taught and assessed. The analysis of what type of instruction was required to address the new Core prompted the richest discussion for our group. Our team, representing teachers across the district, developed contextualized activities for our students to gain a deep-level understanding of what the standards require of them to be successful and prepared for high school course work—and that is how to **think** about math, **not** just perform algorithms! Getting students to want to think has been our greatest challenge! But we see growth, and they CAN do it!—**Jan Ross, math coach, and Stacey Mulder, teacher, Youngstown City Schools**

The Research Base. The unit plan format is based on more than two decades of teaching and learning research, beginning with pioneers like Piaget (1952), Taba (1962, 1966), Tyler (1950), and McCarthy (1990) and proceeding through the current work of Daniels and Bizar (2005), Danielson (2008), Darling-Hammond (2000, 2011), Marzano (2002, 2003a, 2003b, 2011), Schmoker (2004, 2011), Strong, Silver, et al. (2001), Tomlinson (2005, 2012), and Yaple (2012).

The unit plan format is based on how learning occurs. The basic structure of the unit plan is provided as two intersecting lines as shown in Figure 2.1.

Figure 2.1   Unit Plan Format

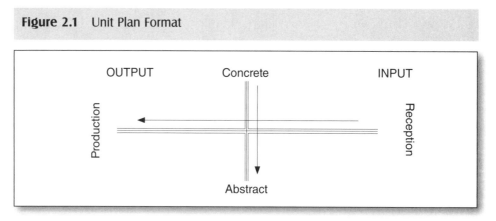

On the **vertical axis**, the mastery process begins with **Concrete** experiences and progresses to **Abstract** thinking, where the learner can talk or write about the Concrete without having to directly experience it. As very young learners, we all had concrete experiences with a variety of concepts before being asked to think abstractly (e.g., manipulating blocks to count and compute when first learning about numbers, and moving to being able to visualize or think abstractly about a number without actually having to manipulate objects).

On the **horizontal axis**, classroom instruction provides for the **Reception** of information (INPUT) and progresses toward student **Production** (OUTPUT) that illustrates the learning. The Reception allows for students to take in information and work with it, concretely and abstractly. The Production allows for students to show what they have learned in different ways—on a paper-pencil test (abstract) as well as an authentic application of the learning (concrete). While the abstract level is important to do well on high-stakes tests, it is the Concrete or constructive level of production that shows independent mastery of the concepts and skills in the standards.

The structure of the unit plan drives the decisions that teachers must make with regard to the instructional input needed to learn the standards for the unit, and the assessment that will allow students to show mastery of the standards for the unit. The elements that make up the unit plan are explained here, and following this explanation is a graphic that summarizes the process.

Unit Plan Criteria

Standards

For the teacher's benefit, the actual standards for the unit plan are included as the guiding endpoint for what students need to do to show mastery. Experience in many districts has shown that when the standards are not directly stated or only code numbers appear for each standard, there is a tendency for individual teachers to read into the standard what they like to teach or skip over certain parts or all of some standards, falling short of the required level of cognitive demand. The standards are also connected to what is in the various sections of the unit by using a code number for each standard. This is evident throughout the teaching-learning activities and assessments parts of the unit. In districts using common grade-level or course tests and/or benchmark assessments, these codes are integral to the reporting schema and to discover patterns in the analysis of student performance data.

As mentioned previously, the introductory material to the Common Core and the 21st century skills allude to "integration" and "inter-strand connections" dozens of times. The expectation is that none of the strands or categories is meant to be taught in isolation. For example, "Number Concepts" in Math makes no sense without the context of, for example, applications in the Measurement strand. The 21st century skill of "economic literacy" and "solving unfamiliar problems" would provide real-world context. Conversely, because they are more content-driven than process-driven, many of the individual strands in Science and Social Studies standards are more stand-alone. However, they too would be accompanied by such 21st century skills as "civic literacy" (Social Studies) and "environmental literacy" (Science).

In addition, the Common Core standards in English Language Arts include Literacy standards to be included in the curriculum for Social Studies, Science, and technical subjects, including Math. These Literacy standards must be strategically included in the cluster of standards powering each unit plan.

Unit Synopsis

This is a brief aerial view of the unit plan that consists of a sentence or two of what the students will receive during the unit (INPUT) and what they will produce by the end (OUTPUT). It answers the basic question, "If a student misses this unit, what will be lost?" It is also a handy reference for teachers and administrators to the "big picture" of the unit without getting "into the weeds." If strung together end-to-end, the synopses comprise an effective course overview. Table 2.5 shows the standards and unit synopsis.

Table 2.5

Component and Definition	Format	Notes/Examples

Content Standards
 	
• taken from curriculum map
• include multiple strands
• may include other subjects (integration)
• represent a common theme or topic
• imply or state teaching and testing strategies
• typically involve a product
• reference one or more 21st century skills
	STANDARDS
	SYNOPSIS
	MOTIVATION
	TEACHING–LEARNING
	TRADITIONAL ASSESSMENT
	AUTHENTIC ASSESSMENT
		Integrated
		   popular in self-contained classrooms
		Single Subject
		   more prevalent
		Cross-Overs
		   activities are shared (e.g., the English teacher allows the science essay to satisfy an English requirement—or vice versa)

Motivation

The Motivation activities are intended to pique students' curiosity and to grab their attention by providing a Concrete experience with one or more of the unit concepts or skills. The Motivation segment of the unit plan also includes, as shown in Table 2.6, Motivation outlines:

- determining what students know (and do not know) about the unit standards;
- establishing the rationale for taking time to do the unit; that is, with so much to cover and so little time, why use time to do THIS topic? How will it relate to the student's own life?);
- setting academic and personal goals for the unit; and
- previewing expectations for students as per the authentic assessments.

Table 2.6

Component and Definition	Format	Notes/Examples
Motivation (Concrete-Reception) • actively involve students in a direct experience • determine what students know and don't know • establish connections to prior and subsequent learning • pique students' interest • set expectations for completing the *Unit* • help students set personal learning goals	STANDARDS SYNOPSIS MOTIVATION TEACHING–LEARNING TRADITIONAL ASSESSMENT AUTHENTIC ASSESSMENT	• pretest • brainstorm • KWL chart • video • manipulation of objects or ideas • intriguing question or puzzlement • concept web • song • artifacts • oral reading • conduct a poll • what-if scenario • demonstration • role-play or simulation • expert speaker • error analysis • extended analogies or extended metaphors

Teaching-Learning Activities

This section of the unit plan, as outlined in Table 2.7, is devoted to organizing and ordering the presentation of information pertinent to the unit skills and concepts and to the processing of that information by students. Each teaching-learning activity designates what the teacher will do and what the student will do to process information. The cognitive demands of the new standards and the 21st century skills make passive student responses inappropriate. The filling in of blanks from rote recall or supplying other predetermined answers from memory will not involve students in constructing meaning for themselves. The following table shows a sampling of teacher behaviors and possible student responses through which students construct meaning. Through **Differentiation**, several alternative strategies are typically included to account for different learning needs and to supply "plan B" for students who need enrichment or remediation. The key here is that these activities and events are planned in advance so that individual student needs are met.

As indicated in the most valid research, the primary focus of the unit plan format is on active student engagement, the use of real-world contexts, and having students construct meaning for themselves. This approach to the planning, delivery, and assessment of classroom instruction is directly parallel to the requirements of the new standards and the 21st century skills set forth in Chapter 1, Table 1.1. Table 2.8 outlines how the teaching will need to be different.

Table 2.7

Component and Definition	Format	Notes/Examples
Teaching-Learning Activities (Abstract-Reception) • teacher behaviors and student responses that match the content standards • students have an active, constructive role • include variety in grouping patterns and learning modalities • indicate how all content standards will be taught (including options for differentiation: remediation, enrichment) • require multiple levels of thinking • involve continuous assessment, feedback	STANDARDS SYNOPSIS MOTIVATION TEACHING—LEARNING TRADITIONAL ASSESSMENT AUTHENTIC ASSESSMENT	**Learning Constructs—e.g.,** • organizational patterns • summarizing • note-taking • graphic or visual organizers • context and structural clues for vocabulary • various levels of questioning • similarities and differences **Delivery Strategies—e.g.,** • lecture • demonstration • guided discussion • inquiry • Socratic seminar • literature circles • action research • advance organizer

. . . And from those who REALLY know. . . .

Rolling out the standards and discussing what they mean for students allowed our high school math team to keep focus on designing lessons for real contextual applications instead of constant traditional mathematics skills. Computational fluency and procedural skills are important, and I found that there were some lessons that cannot be taught through applications until fluency is completed by students. The units allow for a perfect integration to achieve both.

*The chunking of the standards into the curriculum map and the design of the units were the interrelated links, which allowed teachers to make connections for our students to see the sequence of the learning outcomes. Students are now able to see how one topic and standard are related to another. Students are exposed to math skills, abstract thinking, and problem-solving with real-world applications for what they learn. A perfect trifecta!—**Kenneth Andrews, math teacher, Stockbridge High School, Stockbridge, Georgia***

Drawing from the Table 2.8 showing the requirements of the Common Core and the 21st century skills, the components of the unit plan provide a structure that—if implemented with fidelity—ensures that the quality of instruction and assessment is appropriate to the new expectations. Each district may select additional components, but the following are the basic requirements supported in the research. It is worthwhile to note that when we say "not business as usual," it is what happens in the way students receive information and construct meaning that focuses on active student engagement where teachers actually talk with students about their thinking and have students discuss with each other what they do to make meaning of new ideas and concepts. In the technology era, we so often see teachers more concerned about projecting something, showing a YouTube video, or moving through problems that there is virtually no time given to discussing with students how they think, analyzing the thinking in terms of what students need to learn, and correcting mis-learning. Indeed, there seems to be more done to not talk with students than to engage them in dialogue about their learning. Working pages and pages of problems, or filling in reading guides, and so on are also strategies that prevent dialogue between and among students with students and students with a teacher, and these practices actually slow the learning process and reinforce that learning is nothing more than copying or filling in blanks. We are teaching students who will work with ideas and technology that have not yet been invented, so performing tasks such as worksheet drills are not preparing them for the future they will encounter.

Traditional Assessment

As shown in Table 2.9, one level of student mastery is determined by a paper-pencil test. This more traditional method infers mastery of the standards by asking students multiple-choice and constructed-response questions. Typically, more content is taught than can be assessed in a 50-minute test, so teachers must prioritize the most important concepts and develop or select appropriate items. Since high-stakes tests do not include matching, true-false,

Table 2.8 Teacher Behaviors and Student Responses—A Comparison of the Current Standards With the Common Core Standards and 21st Century Skills

With Previous Standards . . .	With the New Common Core and 21st Century Standards . . .
Teachers have focused most of their planning on their behaviors and what they would provide to students.	Teachers will need to focus on what students will do to show mastery and from that decide what teaching strategies will be most likely to yield those results.
Teachers have typically provided the single best way to perform a task or solve a problem.	Teachers will need to show students multiple ways to approach tasks and to solve problems, and it will be essential that students can explain which approach they used and how it worked for them.
Students have been passive learners; they have been given information and directed how to apply it. With sufficient, controlled repetition and directed practice, students could appear to have mastery, when it may be only mimicry of what they've seen.	Students will need to become active learners; they will need to be shown how to accomplish the following: ✓ Obtain and Interpret Information Independently. ✓ Apply Skills and Concepts Independently and In Unfamiliar Contexts to Solve Problems and Complete Tasks. Because they are required to construct their own meaning—and in varied contexts—it is more difficult for students to mimic mastery.
Practice has used "controlled" examples that were identical to those used in class (i.e., text passages, experiments, math problems, and various social studies events and scenarios). Contexts have been limited to the familiar, and students have not been led to stretch. Correct answers were largely predetermined.	Practice will need to begin with controlled examples but quickly move to unfamiliar examples that require students to construct meaning for themselves in unfamiliar contexts. Several correct answers will be possible, providing they are aligned with the criteria set forth in the standards—both in terms of content and cognitive demand. Students will be expected to explain and justify their answers.
Students have taken in information by observing teacher demonstrations, listening to teacher lectures, reading assigned texts, or viewing various media.	Students will take in information in much the same way as before, but with a greatly expanded and diverse array of electronic sources and various media; in addition, students must show they can distinguish relevant from irrelevant information and authentic from invalid evidence.
Students have processed information by taking notes, doing seat-work, and filling in blanks—all using language and numerals mimicked or paraphrased from the text or teacher.	Students will still take notes but not fill in controlled blanks; they will interpret details of what they see and hear via such constructive techniques as paraphrasing; summarizing; formulating questions or problems; sketching or diagramming; or completing "if-then" statements.
Mastery has been determined by filling in blanks or selecting from among multiple choices—using language mimicked or paraphrased from the text or teacher.	Mastery will be determined on several levels. To prepare students for high-stakes tests, some multiple-choice and short-answer items are essential. But reflecting the cognitive demand of the new standards, students must also perform authentic or performance tasks that certify they can apply what they have learned to solve real-world problems; analyze concepts and ideas to identify determinant relationships; synthesize information to create original products; and critically but objectively evaluate ideas, products, and information using valid criteria.

Table 2.9

Component and Definition	Format	Notes/Examples

Traditional Assessment (Abstract-Production)
 	
• traditional tests to determine mastery (paper-pencil or teacher observation); i.e.,
  o multiple-choice and 2- and 4-point constructed response
  o validly constructed to match the content and cognitive demand of the content standards
  o aligned with teaching-learning activities
• are diagnostic to identify needed intervention
• selective; infer mastery
	STANDARDS
	
	SYNOPSIS
	
	MOTIVATION
	
	TEACHING—LEARNING
	
	TRADITIONAL ASSESSMENT
	
	AUTHENTIC ASSESSMENT
		Tests/quizzes that parallel high-stakes tests:
		• multiple-choice items (with choices that are diagnostic upon analysis)
		• short answer items that involve:
		  ✓ problem-finding, solving
		  ✓ making inferences
		  ✓ evaluating, making judgments
		  ✓ explaining
		
		observation checklists, journal entries, maps, data compilation, etc.

or fill-in items, districts are discouraged from including these types of items on their unit tests. For quality control and maximum objectivity, traditional tests are convergent and have a narrow range of correct answers.

The high-stakes tests in each state, national tests such as NAEP and ACT or SAT, and the international tests like PISA and TIMSS all use the multiple-choice and constructed-response format. Although there is considerable criticism about how unfair and biased these tests can be, they are the reality. And since students are required to take these tests, it is incumbent upon school districts to make sure they have plenty of practice and are not taken by surprise. It is recommended that each unit include at least one such test, composed of multiple-choice and extended response items—but which are appropriately constructed and criterion-referenced to the standards they purport to measure.

Authentic or Performance Assessment

A second type of assessment (shown in Table 2.10) requires each student to demonstrate independent mastery by performing a holistic or stand-alone task that displays one or more of the unit standards. Students might develop an original product, solve unfamiliar problems, perform action research, analyze a finished work for errors, or devise and conduct original experiments. In contrast to traditional assessments—for which there are limited correct answers—authentic or performance assessments permit a wide array of correct responses to maximize students' creativity and critical thinking. In the spirit of the 21st century skills, some of these authentic assessments may be group activities that involve strategic collaboration. However, it is essential that teachers determine each student's mastery of the designated standards as well as his and her performance as part of the group.

The complete unit plan criteria summary appears in Table 2.11.

Table 2.10

Component and Definition	Format	Notes/Examples
Authentic Assessment (Concrete-Production) • are holistic, life-related tasks extending beyond the classroom • draw together the unit learning experiences • encourage divergent thinking; allow students options for completing the tasks • help students measure their own goals • scored with a rubric based on the content standards	STANDARDS SYNOPSIS MOTIVATION TEACHING–LEARNING TRADITIONAL ASSESSMENT AUTHENTIC ASSESSMENT	• writing an original piece of literature or a composition • devising a treaty or a contract between two parties • collecting, displaying, and analyzing data • designing and conducting an original experiment • analyzing error patterns in a series of "solved" problems • developing original problems to solve • preparing a script for a TV talk show or newscast • formulating arguments, etc.

. . . And from those who REALLY know. . . .

*As Department Chair, working in a large high school with 16 people teaching each course, the unpacking of the standards and developing unit plans provided opportunity for a disparate group to bring thoughts together and arrive at consensus on how best to teach the new standards. We also developed common assessments for each unit to ensure that we were in sync. Everyone in the department who teaches a course had opportunity to input into what was incorporated in a unit plan and the discussion that happened as we developed these units was unique to any curriculum work we had ever done. Additionally, time was built into department meetings to reflect on how a unit was progressing and discuss what adjustments were needed to make the unit stronger. The process with the new Science standards was the first time our Science department worked as "one team;" and we are all stronger teachers as a result of the work.—**Jodi Fryman-Reed, Science Department Chair, Whitmer High School, Washington Local Schools**

Table 2.11 Unit Plan Criteria

Component and Definition	Format	Notes/Examples
Title: The title and length of the unit plan are taken directly from the curriculum map.		
Synopsis: The synopsis provides an overview of what students will LEARN in the unit and HOW MASTERY is demonstrated.		
Content Standards • taken from curriculum map • include multiple strands • may include other subjects (integration) • represent a common theme or topic • imply or state teaching and testing strategies • typically involve a product • reference one or more 21st century skills	STANDARDS SYNOPSIS MOTIVATION TEACHING-LEARNING TRADITIONAL ASSESSMENT AUTHENTIC ASSESSMENT	**Integrated** popular in self-contained classrooms **Single Subject** more prevalent **Cross-Overs** activities are shared (e.g., the English teacher allows the science essay to satisfy an English requirement—or vice versa)
Motivation (Concrete-Reception) • actively involve students in a direct experience • determine what students know and don't know • establish connections to prior and subsequent learning • pique students' interest • set expectations for completing the *Unit* • help students set personal learning goals	STANDARDS SYNOPSIS MOTIVATION TEACHING-LEARNING TRADITIONAL ASSESSMENT AUTHENTIC ASSESSMENT	• pre-test • brainstorm • KWL chart • video • manipulation of objects or ideas • intriguing question or puzzlement • concept web • song • artifacts • oral reading • conduct a poll • what-if scenario • demonstration • role-play or simulation • expert speaker • error analysis • extended analogies or extended metaphors
Teaching-Learning Activities (Abstract-Reception) • teacher behaviors and student responses that match the *Content Standards* • students have an active, constructive role • include variety in grouping patterns and learning modalities	STANDARDS SYNOPSIS MOTIVATION TEACHING-LEARNING TRADITIONAL ASSESSMENT	**Learning Constructs—e.g.,** • organizational patterns summarizing • note-taking • graphic or visual organizers • context and structural clues for vocabulary • various levels of questioning • similarities and differences

	AUTHENTIC ASSESSMENT	**Delivery Strategies—e.g.,**
• indicate how all *Content Standards* will be taught (including options for differentiation: remediation, enrichment) • require multiple levels of thinking • involve continuous assessment, feedback		• lecture • demonstration • guided discussion • inquiry • Socratic seminar • literature circles • action research • advance organizer

Traditional Assessment (Abstract-Production)	STANDARDS	Tests/quizzes that parallel high-stakes tests:

• traditional tests to determine mastery (paper-pencil or teacher observation); i.e.,
   o multiple-choice and 2- and 4-point constructed response
   o validly constructed to match the content and cognitive demand of the *Content Standards*
   o aligned with teaching-learning activities
• are diagnostic to identify needed intervention
• selective; infer mastery
	SYNOPSIS
	
	MOTIVATION
	
	TEACHING-LEARNING
	
	TRADITIONAL ASSESSMENT
	
	AUTHENTIC ASSESSMENT
		• multiple-choice items (with choices that are diagnostic upon analysis)
		• short answer items that involve:
		  ✓ problem-finding, solving
		  ✓ making inferences
		  ✓ evaluating, making judgments
		  ✓ explaining
		observation checklists, journal entries, maps, data compilation, etc.

Authentic Assessment (Concrete-Production)	STANDARDS	• writing an original piece of literature or a composition
• are holistic, life-related tasks extending beyond the classroom • draw together the unit learning experiences • encourage divergent thinking; allow students options for completing the tasks • help students measure their own goals • scored with a rubric based on the *Content Standards*	SYNOPSIS MOTIVATION TEACHING—LEARNING TRADITIONAL ASSESSMENT AUTHENTIC ASSESSMENT	• devising a treaty or a contract between two parties • collecting, displaying, and analyzing data • designing and conducting an original experiment • analyzing error patterns in a series of "solved" problems • developing original problems to solve • preparing a script for a TV talk show or newscast • formulating arguments, etc.

SAMPLE UNIT PLAN

_____School District

GRADE 2: MATH: UNIT # 1: ALL ABOUT ME   **Quarter 1: 4 weeks**

Synopsis: In this unit, students work with facts about themselves to enter into making measurements and calculations of information on classmates. They work with addition and subtraction with 100 and write equations for problem scenarios. Students work with number facts and make computations with two-digit numbers. During the unit, students measure using standard and nonstandard tools and generate measurement data that they use to create different types of graphs. Students use all of the strategies learned in the unit to create an "All About Me" sand baby, with the relevant information about themselves; they share the "baby" with their parents. In addition, students create addition and subtraction problems from the data about classmates (e.g., Jan is 2 inches taller than Tom, but 1 inch shorter than Sam).

STANDARDS

2.OA.1	Use addition and subtraction with 100 to solve one- and two-step word problems involving situations of adding to, taking from, putting together, taking apart, and comparing, with unknowns in all positions, (e.g., by using drawings and equations with a symbol for the unknown number to represent the problem).
2.OA.2	Fluently add and subtract within 20 using mental strategies (explanations may be supported by drawings or objects). By the end of Grade 2, know from memory all sums of two one-digit numbers.
2.NBT.6	Add up to four two-digit numbers using strategies based on place value and properties of operations.
2.MD.1	Measure the length of an object by selecting and using appropriate tools such as rulers, yardsticks, meter sticks, and measuring tapes.
2.MD.4	Measure to determine how much longer one object is than another expressing the length difference in terms of a standard length unit.
2.MD.5	Use addition and subtraction within 100 to solve word problems involving lengths that are given in the same units (e.g., by using drawings, such as drawings of rulers) and equations with a symbol for the unknown number to represent the problem.
2.MD.7	Tell and write time from analog and digital clocks to the nearest 5 minutes, using a.m. and p.m.
2.MD.9	Generate measurement data by measuring lengths of several objects to the nearest whole unit, or by making repeated measurements of the same object. Show the measurements by making a line plot, where the horizontal scale is marked off in whole-number units.
2.MD.10	Draw a picture graph and a bar graph (with single-unit scale) to represent a data set with up to four categories. Solve simple put-together, take-apart, and compare problems using information presented in a bar graph.

MATH PRACTICES:

1. Make sense of problems and persevere in solving them.
2. Reason abstractly and quantitatively.
3. Construct viable arguments and critique the reasoning of others.
4. Model with mathematics.
5. Use appropriate tools strategically.
6. Attend to precision.
7. Look for and make use of structure.
8. Look for and express regularity in repeated reasoning.

MOTIVATION	TEACHER NOTES
1. Unit inventory test from text series. 2. Brainstorm ways that we are alike and different. Focus on the height of students, foot length, length of arms, etc. 3. "What's in My Bag?" Teacher prepares a bag with personal items and pulls one item out at a time to give information about her/himself. A bag might contain a tennis racket, pictures of family, a baby picture, and a favorite snack. Information is shared about the number of brothers and sisters, birth date, birth length, and weight measurements, time of birth, etc., particularly in comparison to current weight, height, and other measurements. 4. Preview Authentic Assessment: The students will make babies with their birth measurements; they will collect and display data based on class weights, heights, other measurements, and personal information. (The teacher should preview the Mathline video with Sand Babies activities before the unit.) 5. Work with students to establish individual goals related to unit content and study skills.	NOTE: Boxed text represents "best-practice" strategies

TEACHING-LEARNING	TEACHER NOTES

1. Send letter to parents requesting birth information: weight/length/date/time of day (see list of requested data in #2).
 	
2. Teacher works with students to show comparisons between birth measurements and "now" using language of "greater than, less than, and equal to" create a class comparison matrix from the data collected about each student: (MP-4; MP-7)
 	
  - birth time (specify a.m./p.m.) (2.MD.7)
  - birth weight
  - birth length (2.MD.1) (2.MD.4) (2.MD.5)
  - older brother(s)
  - younger brother(s) (2.OA.2)
  - older sister(s) (2.OA.2)
  - younger sister(s) (2.OA.2)
 	
3. Teacher models how to show the measurements by making a line plot, picture graph, or bar graph, depending on which data set is being used (where the horizontal scale is marked off in whole-number units); teacher shows students how to measure to the nearest whole unit; students practice with other pieces of data to show they can do this. Students make comparative statements about the data they have (e.g., 8 students were less than 25 inches long, but 11 were more than 25 inches long at birth). (2.MD.9) (2.MD.10) (MP-4; MP-5)
 	
4. Daily: Compare a daily fact wheel for addition and subtraction drill. (2.OA.2) (MP-6)
 	
5. Teacher reviews strategies for addition and subtraction of basic facts and the place value system; students work with the teacher to create a graphic organizer to represent the strategies. (2.OA.1) (2.NBT.6) (MP-4; MP-8)
 	
  - doubles
  - doubles + 1, −1, +2, −2
  - odd and even numbers
  - counting on and back	

(Continued)

(Continued)

TEACHING-LEARNING	TEACHER NOTES
6. Teacher uses base 10 blocks and/or hundred charts to model problems involving 2-digit addition. Students work on word problems that are related to the data on their "personal facts list" and use various strategies for computing. (2.OA.1) (2.NBT.6) (MP-1; MP-4; MP-7)	
7. Teacher has students practice place value concepts with base 10 blocks; include regrouping up and regrouping down. Have students explain that 10 can be a bundle of 10 ones called a "ten"; and explain counting by 10s. (2.NBT.6) (MP-3; MP-8)	
8. Have children use standard and nonstandard units to measure their length (height), and compare and measure their current length (height) with their birth length. They can also compare their height to a classmate's height. [Optional material: colored yard, paper strips, straws, and string.] Use (>, <). Read *How Big Is a Foot?* by Rolf Myller. Have groups of children construct a bed for the queen. Compare finished products, and identify and discuss the importance of accuracy in measurement. Develop metaphors or analogies to describe the measurements and show relationships among them. Work in small groups (per teacher selection) to measure individual heights in inches. Students compare their current height to the height of their classmates. Each group makes a bar graph charting birth length and current height. (2.MD.1) (2.MD.4) (2.MD.5) (2.MD.9) (2.MD.10) (MP-4; MP-6)	
Once students have generated measurements, the teacher models how to create addition and subtraction problems with an unknown from their data (e.g., Jen is 1 inch taller than Justin, and Justin is 2 inches shorter than Mollie, who is 48 inches tall. Show a problem to determine how tall Justin is and how tall Jen is using the letter of the students name to represent the unknown). (2.MD.5) (MP-2; MP-7)	
9. Teacher uses clock to have students show time of birth; record information in class comparison matrix. Teacher follows with questions such as: Who was born the closest to 12 noon? 12 midnight? Who was born in the morning, afternoon, evening? Associate a.m. and p.m. with time of birth. (2.MD.7) (MP-5)	
10. Teacher shows students how to use links to create a clock. (1 link = 1 minute). Students make clocks and mark 5-minute intervals and quarter-hour intervals, add hands, and hours (1–12). Build and rebuild every day. (2.MD.7) (MP-4; MP-7)	
11. Teacher models how to create, estimate, and solve problems comparing student heights using addition and subtraction of two-digit numbers with regrouping. (2.OA.1) (2.OA.2) (2.NBT.6) (MP-2; MP-6)	
12. Teacher poses questions such as how much taller is Jake than Kevin? Students examine differences between their birth statistics and current statistics to analyze quantitative changes and make computations. (2.MD.10) (MP-2; MP-3)	
13. From data collected, make two interpretive statements; also, identify two things the data do *not* tell us. (MP-1: Make sense of problems; MP-2: Reason abstractly and quantitatively) (2.MD.10) (MP-1; MP-3)	
14. Use a September calendar month to determine the number of days before the birthday of a particular student; show this in terms of addition (days ahead) and subtraction (days behind). (2.OA.2) (2.NBT.6) (MP-1; MP-2)	
15. Students trace their hands, the teacher's hand, and or other objects and estimate the number of nonstandard items it would take to measure the length. Then verify the estimate by measuring. After modeling this, students select an object to trace, estimate number of units long, and verify estimate. (2.MD.1) (2.MD.4) (MP-6; MP-7)	

TEACHING-LEARNING	TEACHER NOTES
16. Estimate (then verify) if objects are greater than or less than the size of a given object. (2.MD.1) (2.MD.4) (MP-2)	
17. Students create a bar graph showing the number of students: (a) born in a given month; (b) born in the a.m. and p.m.; (c) the number of brothers and sisters who are younger than the number of brothers and sisters who are older. Students will make story problems for other students to solve and practice their math computation skills. (2.NBT.6) (2.MD.4) (2.MD.5) (2.MD.7) (2.MD.9) (2.MD.10) (MP-1; MP-2)	
18. Students create a picture graph of their favorite: (a) food; (b) TV show; (c) thing to do; (d) subject in school. (2.MD.10) (MP-4; MP-7)	
19. Teacher reads *The Bigness Contest.* Students write sentences using comparative language about characters as they are introduced. Teacher then shows students how to develop metaphors and analogies to make these comparisons more interesting. (2.OA.1) (2.OA.2) (2.NBT.6) (MP-4; MP-7)	

TRADITIONAL ASSESSMENT	TEACHER NOTES
1. Daily ✓s with review questions. (2.OA.1) (2.OA.2) (2.NBT.6) (2.MD.1) (2.MD.4) (2.MD.5) (2.MD.7) (2.MD.9) (2.MD.10)	
2. Checklist: Measure segments and objects to nearest inch, foot, yard, centimeter, and meter; tell time to nearest minute. (2.MD.1) (2.MD.4) (2.MD.7)	
3. Student computations with both addition and subtraction problems that relate to real-world situations where they show variety in strategies used (doubles/1 less-1 more, etc.). (2.OA.1) (2.OA.2) (2.NBT.6) (2.MD.5)	
4. Compare the graphs of student data from different groups and make a comparative statement about the data. (2.MD.10)	

AUTHENTIC ASSESSMENT	TEACHER NOTES
1. Evaluate progress on goals.	
2. Each student will do the following: Create a "Sand Baby" that measures the same as his/her personal birth measurements; (a) fill a bag with sand, and weigh it, then make the bag the length of his/her birth length; (b) use markers to draw facial features on the bag; (c) compare current body measurements to birth measurements; and (d) calculate the difference. Students will present the "Sand Baby" to parents. Each student will display his/her birth height with the other students in the class as a bar graph. Students will also show current weight and height with birth weight and height, as a "Then and Now" graphic organizer that compares baby measurements to current measurements.	
a. Make personal "Then and Now" book with height and measurements in inches and centimeters and weight. Add time of birth to figure out age with years *and* hours. (2.MD.1) (2.MD.4) (2.MD.5) (2.MD.7) (2.MD.9) (2.MD.10)	
b. Make a class graph of data collected at school. (2.MD.9) (2.MD.10)	
c. Evaluate two students' interpretations of the data from the survey, and explain why you think the student used the data correctly. (2.MD.9) (2.MD.10)	
d. Generate two addition and two subtraction problems with two-digit numbers from the survey and class data sets and/or comparison matrix. (2.OA.1) (2.OA.2) (2.NBT.6)	

ENGLISH LANGUAGE ARTS—Grade 9

Grade 9 Unit #3 "STRANGE AND MYSTERIOUS" (4.5 weeks)

SYNOPSIS: Students will read and discuss several fiction and nonfiction selections about "legendary" icons of United States and world folklore (e.g., the Loch Ness monster, crop circles, King Tut's tomb, Bagger Vance, *The Legend of Sleepy Hollow,* etc.). From these selections, they will predict and verify the meaning of unfamiliar words (using context clues, word parts, syntax); analyze figurative language and connotative meanings; analyze the validity of an author's argument; and interpret universal themes. Students will write responses to literature, hold Socratic seminars to discuss the literature, write correspondence describing their observations, and compose a letter to the Board of Education relative to the viability of the unit and whether it should be kept or removed from the curriculum.

STANDARDS

RL 9.1.   Cite strong and thorough textual evidence to support analysis of what the text says explicitly as well as inferences drawn from the text.

RL 9.2.   Determine a theme or central idea of a text and analyze in detail its development over the course of the text, including how it emerges and is shaped and refined by specific details; provide an objective summary of the text.

RL 9.4.   Determine the meaning of words and phrases as they are used in the text, including figurative and connotative meanings; analyze the cumulative impact of specific word choices on meaning and tone (e.g., how the language evokes a sense of time and place; how it sets a formal or informal tone).

RI 9.3.   Analyze how the author unfolds an analysis or series of ideas or events, including the order in which the points are made, how they are introduced and developed, and the connections that are drawn between them.

RI 9.4.   Determine the meaning of words and phrases as they are used in a text, including figurative, connotative, and technical meanings; analyze the cumulative impact of specific word choices on meaning and tone (e.g., how the language of a court opinion differs from that of a newspaper).

RI 9.8.   Delineate and evaluate the argument and specific claims in a text, assessing whether the reasoning is valid and the evidence is relevant and sufficient; identify false statements and fallacious reasoning.

W 9.4.   Produce clear and coherent writing in which the development, organization, and style are appropriate to task, purpose, and audience.

W 9.9.   Draw evidence from literary or informational texts to support analysis, reflection, and research.

SL 9.4.   Present information, findings, and supporting evidence clearly, concisely, and logically such that listeners can follow the line of reasoning and the organization, development, substance, and style are appropriate to purpose, audience, and task.

L 9.2.   Demonstrate command of the conventions of Standard English capitalization, punctuation, and spelling when writing.

   a. Use a semicolon (and perhaps a conjunctive adverb) to link two or more closely related independent clauses.

   b. Use a colon to introduce a list or quotation.

   c. Spell correctly.

L 9.4.   Determine or clarify the meaning of unknown and multiple-meaning words and phrases based on Grades 9–10 reading and content, choosing flexibly from a range of strategies.

   a. Use context (e.g., the overall meaning of a sentence, paragraph, or text; a word's position or function in a sentence) as a clue to the meaning of a word or phrase.

   b. Identify and correctly use patterns of word changes that indicate different meanings or parts of speech (e.g., analyze, analysis, analytical; advocate, advocacy).

Materials [Core list, adjust to reflect student findings. As often as possible, use reprints so students can mark them up.]

Fiction	Nonfiction	Poetry	Drama
"Legends" from the literature anthology and the Internet; e.g., *The Legend of Sleepy Hollow,* Washington Irving	Explanations, research findings relative to specific legends; National Geographic; PBS; the History Channel; the Internet	"At Stonehenge," Katherine Lee Bates "Sneaky Curse—King Tut's Tomb," Ernest Clary	Radio script of *War of the Worlds* (Orson Welles) Movie: *The Philadelphia Experiment*

Key Terms [Synthesis of standards and teaching-learning activities]

General	Literary Skills	Writing Skills	Speaking/ Listening Skills	Language Skills
analyze explicit detail inferences summarize formal tone informal tone fact vs. opinion evaluate fallacy reflection research	explicit text details inferences supported by theme central idea summary figurative language connotative meaning denotative meaning technical meaning how language evokes a sense of time, place evaluate argument re: valid reasoning relevant evidence sufficient evidence legend	clarity coherence development organization style task audience purpose	presentation skills appropriate language delivery style use of evidence clarity coherence conciseness substance respond to listener questions demonstrate appropriate listening skills	conventions capitalization grammar punctuation semi-colon colon spelling multimeaning words context word changes regarding syntax (analyze, analysis, analytical)

MOTIVATION	TEACHER NOTES
1. Teacher leads a discussion on the concept of mysterious "legends" and folklore about the unexplained, offering a few examples and "pinpointing" them on a U.S. and world map— <table><tr><td>Loch Ness Big Foot (Sasquatch) The Flying Dutchman King Tut's Tomb The Philadelphia Experiment The Bermuda Triangle</td><td>How the pyramids were built The Mothman Prophecies The Disappearing Roanoke Colony Vampires in Transylvania The Legend of Sleepy Hollow The Gettysburg Ghosts</td><td>Bagger Vance The Jersey Devil Stonehenge UFOs (Area 51) Crop Circles Easter Island</td></tr></table>	

(Continued)

(Continued)

MOTIVATION	TEACHER NOTES
Which do students already know? Teacher asks students to think about what characteristics these "legends" have in common; *record responses on chart paper* for later use [the conventions of mystery, "legend" or folktale; be sure Ss realize there is usually a set of "facts" somewhere in MOST of the legends]. 2. T asks Ss what it is about humans that makes them "want" to believe in legends, weird stories, and unexplained mysteries. Why don't we just "stick to the facts"? 3. [If objectives are to be posted] T explains that during the unit, they will: (a) read several *fiction and nonfiction* accounts of famous "legends"; (b) add *key vocabulary* to their lexicon, using the tools of context, word parts, and syntax; (c) examine figurative, connotative, and technical language used by authors; (d) identify *central ideas* and universal *themes* and how "legends" convey these; (e) analyze authors' *styles* and how they unfold events or ideas and make connections; (f) *evaluate an author's arguments* for validity and adequate support; (g) draw evidence from text selections to support reflections and responses; (h) produce *clear and coherent written responses* to some of the literature they will read; and (i) make an *oral presentation* to classmates about one or more legends. 4. T assists Ss in goal-setting (at least one personal and one academic goal); Ss record in their journals notebooks, including how their goals will be measured. T reminds Ss to keep track of their progress on each goal. 5. T previews expectations—what Ss will be expected to do upon completion of the unit.	

TEACHING-LEARNING ACTIVITIES	TEACHER NOTES
1. Teacher reminds students about continuing their continuing lexicons and to add terms and phrases from this unit's readings as well. Either projects lexicon entry on SmartBoard or wall chart: (RL 9.4; RI 9.4; L 9.4)	

Selection:	Author:
Word or phrase: Page _____	
Predicted meaning from context:	
Actual (technical) meaning from dictionary □ same as predicted—BRAVO!! or adjusted:	
Multiple meanings?	Used figuratively? Explain
Roots/Affixes?	Connotative meaning? Explain
Alternate forms of the word/phrase based on syntax:	
Original sentence showing comprehension of the word/phrase:	

2. Teacher previews Selection #1—nonfiction piece about one of the legends (e.g., The Philadelphia Experiment) with provocative questions (e.g., how did the Star Trek transporter work?—making someone disappear and then reappear somewhere else? What would you say if I told you there is actual proof that in 1943, the U.S. Navy made a ship disappear from the Philadelphia shipyard and reappear in Norfolk, Virginia?). The class reads the piece* using a variety of techniques, and students complete lexicon and note-taking as they read. (RI 9.4)

3. Teacher shows snippets of the movie *The Philadelphia Experiment,* and students compare the nonfiction text with the movie version.

4. Each student writes a journal entry addressing his or her skepticism about or belief in the Philadelphia Experiment, including details from the nonfiction piece. (W 9.4; W 9.9)

5. Teacher previews Selection #2—nonfiction piece about New England at the time of Washington Irving and his *The Legend of Sleepy Hollow.* Class reads selection together, teacher pausing to decide how the author unfolds the piece, how he develops his points, and how he makes connections among them. Students take notes. (RI 9.3)

6. Teacher previews Selection #3, *The Legend of Sleepy Hollow.* Due to its length and 19th century language, teacher should divide it strategically and plan to read much of it orally to the class or coach them through some choral reading. Teacher helps students decide on lexicon words/phrases and key details. Students diagram sequence of events and note how Irving connects each to the other. (RL 9.3; RL 9.4; and L 9.4)

7. Students work in teams of two or three to devise various levels of questions about Selections #2 and #3, prepared to exchange them and answer another group's questions. (RL 9; RI 9.8; and L 9.2)

8. Teacher assigns students to work in twos or threes to locate (in print or online) an American-based legend or strange tale (i.e., the Roanoke Colony, the Mothman Prophecies, Big Foot, the Jersey Devil, Orson Welles's *War of the Worlds,* the Bermuda Triangle, the Ghosts of Gettysburg, and Area 51). The teams:

TEACHER NOTES

*Various Reading Strategies include:

(a) teacher read-aloud; students work on note-taking and lexicon

   (1) alone

   (2) in pairs or triads

(b) student volunteers read aloud; students work on note-taking and lexicon

   (1) alone

   (2) in pairs or triads

(c) students work in 2s or 3s to read to each other, and collaborate on note-taking and lexicon

(d) students read silently, but work on note-taking and lexicon with a partner (con't.)

(e) different groups read different sections and then jigsaw

(Continued)

(Continued)

TEACHING-LEARNING ACTIVITIES	TEACHER NOTES

(a) prepare a synopsis of literal detail and valid inferences (RL 9.1; RI 9.3; RI 9.8);
 	
    (b) draw from online or print sources information about whether the "legend" is true or strictly a legend—with SOME truth in it—and what VALID, unbiased researchers are saying; and
 	
    (c) present findings to classmates, including entertaining their questions (SL 9.4).
 	
Other students listen, take notes, and prepare questions.
 	
9. Teacher explains that we will now shift from American mysteries to Global ones. Selection #4 is a nonfiction account of the discovery of King Tut's tomb. Teacher previews the selection by asking provocative questions about the curse of the tomb and showing online scenes of the artifacts in the King Tut exhibit.
 	
10. Teacher and students read the selection,* and the students take notes and complete the lexicon work. Teacher assigns students to read "The Sneaky Curse—King Tut's Tomb" by Ernest Clary. (RI 9.4 and RL 9.8)
 	
11. Students write a letter home as a "foreign correspondent" to describe the discovery of the tomb; they should include details from the selection and the poem and refer to the "curse." (W 9.4; W 9.9; L 9.2; L 9.4)
 	
12. Teacher previews Selection #5—a nonfiction piece about Stonehenge, including pictures. Using the various reading strategies (see Task 2), the class collectively reads the piece and completes the note-taking and lexicon work.
 	
13. Students read the poem "At Stonehenge" by Katherine Lee Bates, comparing the poet's work to the nonfiction piece.
 	
14. Teacher divides class into two groups; each engages in a Socratic seminar about Stonehenge and its strange enchantment for 21st century readers (alternate strategy: fishbowl—one group does the seminar as the other observes and provides feedback). (RI 9.3; RI 9.4; and RI 9.8)
 	
15. IF TIME: Teacher previews Selection #6—a fictional account of the vampires of Transylvania. Students take notes and complete the lexicon work. Class discusses the possibility of "vampires" actually existing—why or why not. (RL 9.1; RL 9.2; RL 9.4; and L 9.4)
 	
16. Each student writes a short story about the vampire "tradition," placing himself or herself in a scenario where he or she encounters a supposed vampire and must try to escape. (W 9.4; W 9.9; L 9.4)	

TRADITIONAL ASSESSMENT	TEACHER NOTES
1. Unit test, including multiple-choice items; 2- and 4-pt. responses. 2. Completed journals, notes taken, and writing tasks. 3. Completed lexicon tasks.	

AUTHENTIC ASSESSMENT	TEACHER NOTES

Each student will:
 	
1. Evaluate progress on unit goals.
 	
2. Analyze a passage from a NEW (not read during the unit) FICTION passage dealing with the strange and mysterious; each student will [on a response form, provided]:
 	
   a. cite strong and thorough textual evidence to support analysis of what the text says explicitly as well as inferences drawn from the text (RL 9.1);
 	
   b. determine a theme or central idea of a text and analyze in detail its development over the course of the text, including how it emerges and is shaped and refined by specific details (RL.9.2);
 	
   c. write an objective summary of the pieces (RL 9.2);
 	
   d. determine the meaning of words and phrases as they are used in the text, including figurative and connotative meanings; analyze the cumulative impact of specific word choices on meaning and tone (e.g., how the language evokes a sense of time and place; how it sets a formal or informal tone) (RL 9.4); and
 	
   e. use context to determine the meaning of marked words and phrases in the text, including figurative and connotative meanings (RL 9.4; RI 9.4; L 9.5).	

Integrating Best Practices to Help Students Construct Meaning

3

"One definition of insanity is to keep doing things the same way and expecting different results."

—Albert Einstein

In these next two chapters, we will examine research-based "best practices" to deliver classroom instruction that is equal to the demands of the standards and the 21st century skills. Work teams will need a "menu" of best-practice options from which to choose to insert into their unit plans. Some of the practices should be considered for every unit, and others are more effective if used to address particular standards in specific units. We decided there are just too many to cram into one chapter, so we divided them into two.

The mistake made by so many best-practices consultants is to trot out a list of practices, explain the merits of each (and in some cases, offer a few examples), and leave town. They presume that listeners will be *so convinced,* they will rush right out to apply the practices in every classroom. In selecting which practices to use with which unit plans, it is essential that work teams are made aware of the various practices and what the research has shown about their positive impact on student achievement. Experience has proven that only when users deliberately plan how to incorporate the best practices into their unit plans—and are subsequently accountable for using them—do the practices ever really work. Best practices cannot be left as optional or elective; they must become a job expectation for both teachers and administrators. Over time, as student performance improves, there is really no temptation to revert to the old way. What is key here is the "over time." Lackluster student achievement did not set in across one year, and it will not recover in one year. It may take two to three years to begin seeing improvements.

. . . And from those who REALLY know. . . .

As teacher leader in a K–6 elementary school, I have worked with my colleagues on unit plan development and the incorporation of best practices into our teaching at every grade level and in every content area. In having teachers work through best-practices professional development that is hands-on and then make these practices part of our units to address our course standards, we have dramatically changed our teaching to be more focused on student engagement and higher levels of thinking. We have worked with both the unit development and the best practices at the same time for a holistic approach. As teachers develop units, our grade-level teams review and discuss the instructional flow, and provide feedback with additional ideas to strengthen the overall unit.— **Melanie Newman, teacher leader, Maryland Elementary School, Bexley City Schools**

The research supporting the integration of best practices into classroom delivery has filled volumes in publication. It is impossible to reference it all. But a few of the most widely referenced sources are summarized here as validation for the ideas set forth in this chapter and the next.

The name most commonly associated with best practices is Robert Marzano, and his team (Marzano, Frontier, & Livingston, 2011) has established "effect sizes," or how strongly a practice impacts student performance. These practices have been worked into a comprehensive teacher evaluation system of four domains. The best practices enumerated in this chapter are consistent with those in two of Marzano's domains—*Content* and *Student Engagement*. Our intent is that these practices become fully integrated into every unit plan and that they guide not only teachers' delivery and assessment practices but also principals' supervision of classroom instruction.

John Hattie (2012) has compiled research on teaching techniques proven to have the most visible impact on students. He has identified a mind-frame that characterizes the most successful instruction: Effective teachers collaborate to thoughtfully plan which techniques to use and then honestly reflect on the impact—or not—of those strategies on student learning.

In his compilation of "Learning to Do What Matters Most" in leading change, Michael Fullan (2012) refers to organized lessons (a.k.a. units) as "critical learning instructional pathways" to be consistently followed. This follows Fullan's earlier work (2011b) on the most important drivers of whole-system reform. One such driver is that teams of teachers create a powerful centrality of a learning-instruction-assessment nexus. In addition, he insists that the district "go all out" to power these new teaching innovations with the requisite resources and technology.

Previously, Harvard researcher Benjamin Levin (2008) had examined instructional reforms in 5,000 schools. He discovered that the heart of successful school improvement is the continuous improvement of daily teaching and learning practices. And rather than being random and voluntary, they are deliberately structured, organized, and consistent within subjects at grade levels. This thinking is consistent with the use of course tools to implement the standards.

Contemporaries of Levin, James Strong and his team (Stronge, Ward, Tucker, & Hindman, 2008) studied the relationship between teacher quality and student achievement. They examined 85 Grade 3 classrooms and looked at the achievement levels of 1936 students. In comparing the practices of the effective with the ineffective teachers, Stronge and his colleagues found several distinctions, and they closely align to the best practices addressed in this chapter. Effective teachers (a) provide more complex instruction with greater emphasis on meaning than memory, (b) use a broader range of instructional strategies and a variety of materials and media, (c) employ multiple modalities and a greater range and of assessments, (d) make more differentiated assignments, and (e) ask more high-level questions—in fact, seven times more than their less effective colleagues.

Chapters 3 and 4 will examine popular and widely referenced best practices that are the "menu" for writing teams to insert into their unit plans.

Chapter 3	Chapter 4	

✓ Multiple Levels of Thinking
✓ Goal-Setting
✓ Organizational Patterns
✓ Questioning and Cueing
✓ Similarities and Differences
   – Categorization
     – Comparison
       – Critical Attribute
         – Metaphor
           – Analogy
	✓ Math Problem-Analysis
	✓ Vocabulary Knowledge
	✓ Delivery Strategies
	✓ Recognition and
	   Reinforcement
	✓ Continuous Monitoring
	   With Feedback
	   (. . . a.k.a. Checking
	     for Understanding)
		✓ Basic Assumptions in the
		   Implementation of Unit Plans
		   – The Use of Data
		   – Differentiation
		   – Student Options or Choices
		   – Literacy Standards
		   – Dividing Reading Into
		     "Do-Able" Chunks

MULTIPLE LEVELS OF THINKING

Central to the new content standards as well as the 21st century skills is each student's ability to process information at various cognitive levels, ranging from a reasonable command of necessary facts through the critical evaluation of information. With repeated practice in working at the upper levels of thinking, students become proficient at processing information for themselves, rather than having to be led by the teacher or textbook. Experience has shown that the levels set forth in Bloom's *Taxonomy* provide a familiar and appropriate template to ensure that students are required to think and to process information at multiple levels in every unit plan. Simplified, the *Taxonomy* is useful on three levels when students are learning a new skill, concept, or idea. Notice the placement of the check-boxes in the three divisions that follow:

   1. To be successfully ☐ **introduced to it** and to ☐ **learn about it**, students must process at the KNOWLEDGE and COMPREHENSION levels;

2. To ☐ **solve problems without cues or prompts** and to ☐ **determine how the individual components of the concept interact** to comprise the whole, students must think at the APPLICATION and ANALYSIS levels, respectively; and

3. To ☐ **create something new** and to ☐ **determine the worth or validity** of a concept, students must think at the SYNTHESIS and EVALUATION levels, respectively.

As this example shows, it's not Dr. Bloom's labels that make a checklist for unit planning—it's the bold print that shows the definition or "business end" of each level. Hence, the bold print items form a check-box. It is suggested that each unit plan contain an assortment of activities at the various levels of Bloom. Table 3.1 is one of our Bloom training templates.

One of the most common missteps in working with Bloom is to use one of several published lists of verbs—as if the verbs themselves provide the level of thinking. For example, the verbs "list" or "name" are always linked to KNOWLEDGE. But if "list" or "name" is attached to a task such as "List three reasons why gene splicing may be racially biased," that is actually an EVALUATION task. The verbs "compare" and "contrast" are commonly linked to ANALYSIS or SYNTHESIS. But if the student is to compare or contrast the wolf in "Little Red Riding Hood" with the one in "The Three Little Pigs," the task is really at the COMPREHENSION level. The business end of the Bloom tasks are actually *beyond* the verb. Once teachers get this, the verb lists go where they belong—in the wastebasket.

GOAL-SETTING

Too often, student goal-setting is little more than a feel-good exercise or altruistic gesture with no real intent that students be accountable for actually working toward the goals. In many cases, they are whole-class goals without any individual student accountability. The research is clear that students apply themselves best when they make an investment in their learning and feel a sense of control. The best-practices research confirms that students who make *individual* connections to the goals of each unit by setting their *own* academic/content and personal goals attain higher levels of achievement than those who do not. This individual goal-setting falls within the "active student involvement" and "connecting prior and subsequent learning" criteria. And what could be more "constructive" than setting and monitoring one's own goals?

Based on the unit standards and individual student needs, teachers help each student set at least one *personal* and one *academic* goal for that unit. To model for what is expected of students (another best practice), the teacher models goals that he or she has for himself or herself for this unit by posting the goals for all to view. Throughout the unit, the teacher monitors progress on his or her goals—and allows time for students to monitor their own goals. Again, to model, the teacher makes specific comments about what he or she has done to achieve those goals, and sets a plan for a student to become stronger with the goal areas.

Table 3.1 Bloom's *Taxonomy of Educational Objectives*—Training Example

*= Some taxonomies switch these final two columns.

Knowledge	Comprehension	Application	Analysis	Synthesis*	Evaluation*
Basic Definition - file and retrieve - recall from memory - give literal detail	**Basic Definition** - paraphrase, translate, explain - summarize given information - solve problems using given cues, prompts, or formulas - make verifiable predictions	**Basic Definition** - solve problems *without* cues, prompts, or formulas - locate information without assistance - form and "test" hypotheses	**Basic Definition** - divide a concept, idea, or object into component parts to determine how *each part works together* to comprise the whole - analyze XYZ for error(s)	**Basic Definition** - rearrange or combine ideas, objects, or information to create an original process or product [not necessarily new to the universe, but new to the student]	**Basic Definition** - make a judgment about the value, merit, or worth of an object, idea, or concept *using a valid set of criteria*

Although most teachers are familiar with the levels of Bloom, we find it useful to begin with a "utility" example just to establish common understandings among team members.

Knowledge	Comprehension	Application	Analysis	Synthesis*	Evaluation*
Utility example; e.g., name the three branches of government	**Utility examples;** e.g., (1) summarize "Cinderella" (2) assemble these data into a bar graph	**Utility example;** e.g., decide how much flagstone is needed to make an oval patio	**Utility example;** e.g., identify the parts of a lawnmower and explain how it works (Brian Davis, Washington Local Schools; Toledo, Ohio)	**Utility example;** e.g., reassemble the lawnmower parts as a go-cart (also Brian Davis)	**Utility example;** e.g., choose the best *Harry Potter* movie in terms of technical quality; storyline; and moral lessons taught

(Continued)

Table 3.1 (Continued)

Knowledge	Comprehension	Application	Analysis	Synthesis*	Evaluation*
To make sure team members understand the developmental flow across the levels, we offer a simple academic example, relatively familiar to every teacher. However, this is not to suggest that every topic is to be addressed at ALL SIX levels. The intent is that students work at tasks across a variety of levels and that there be a balance among the levels.					
Academic example: e.g., list the steps to how a bill becomes a law	**Academic example**: e.g., explain to a younger child how a bill becomes a law, giving relevant examples	**Academic example**: e.g., formulate a series of action steps to repeal or amend a specific rule in the school or city ordinance	**Academic example**: e.g., examine a current bill being proposed as a law; which portions are objected to—and why—by Democrats, Republicans, and special interest groups	**Academic example**: e.g., write a bill that could become a law for an important social issue (e.g., use of cellphones in school; the four-day school week; etc.). Address the various implications to all stakeholders	**Academic example**: e.g., decide the merits of a law or a bill currently in the news (e.g., health care; abortion; income tax; etc.) in terms of cost-benefit; equity (who is positively and negatively affected); and overall impact
⇧	⇧	⇧	⇧	⇧	⇧
Students thinking at these two levels are working "inside" the material given by an author or the teacher; activities are situation-specific, have a limited number of correct answers, and yield relatively low rates of transfer.		Students working at these four levels are working "outside" the material given by an author or the teacher; they are applying or extending what they have learned to new situations. They are constructing meaning for themselves by producing a different application than occurred in the classroom with the teacher. Even if the activities are situation-specific, the rate of transfer to other situations is much higher than when limited to "inside" the classroom material.			

To get started with students, the teacher discusses *personal goals* and offers samples such as bringing materials to class, completing homework on time, or not interrupting another speaker. These are specifically tailored to the individual student, and students may want to work on something that has not been evident to the teacher. *Academic goals* are content-related and connect specifically to the standards for the unit. Examples might include using correct math vocabulary to describe an operation, making personal connections to a fictional character, or making a personal distinction between liberal and conservative political views. Of course, the goals can also be more content-specific such as identifying and explaining moon phases or writing a mathematical expression for filling a swimming pool. In the beginning, the teacher may list a few goals from which students choose, but as time goes on (except for very young students), the objective is for students to set their own goals.

Each student records his or her goals in a notebook or journal, establishes a game plan for working toward their accomplishment, and then monitors progress throughout the unit. This should be done regularly (e.g., once a week) so that students know they will be accountable for the goals. At the conclusion of the unit, each student determines a "grade" or rating that represents the level of accomplishment—documented, of course, with evidence of progress.

Table 3.2 is a sample rubric for goal-setting and monitoring devised by teachers.

Table 3.2   Goal-Setting Rubric—to be completed at intervals and at the end of the unit

CATEGORY	0	1	2	3
Development of goals— personal and academic	I did not develop goals.	I developed personal and academic goals, but they were not specific or realistic for me.	I developed personal and academic goals that were "kind of" specific and/or somewhat realistic for me.	I developed both a specific academic and personal goals that are realistic and will help me be successful.
Evidence of progress in meeting goals	There is no written evidence or record supporting my actions towards completing my goal.	There is little written evidence supporting my actions towards completing my goals— _____. The steps I have taken to complete my goals are _____.	There is some written evidence supporting my actions towards completing my goal—it is _____. The steps I have taken to complete my goals are _____.	There is substantial written evidence supporting my actions towards completing my goals—it is _____. The steps I have taken to complete my goals are _____.
Progress toward reaching the goals	I paid no attention to these personal and academic goals.	I have made little progress towards these personal and academic goals.	I have almost achieved these personal and academic goals. ☐ I will keep one or both of these goals.	I have achieved these personal and academic goals. ☐ I will keep one or both of these goals.

Even if students do not completely accomplish their goals, the deliberate act of working toward them and monitoring their progress calls forth the desired accountability. We refer to this as "seeing if the needle moved." Reflecting the new content standards and the 21st century skills, students see that a significant part of what happens to them is the result of their own behaviors and attitudes.

. . . And from those who REALLY know. . . .

When some of our math teachers questioned the practice whereby students set and monitor their academic and personal goals as a waste of time, I had to share a different viewpoint. This reflective practice encourages students to take ownership of both their academic and personal growth and helps them gain a better understanding of themselves and what they need to do to succeed. It can be rewarding, empowering, and enlightening for students and teachers alike!—**Evelyn Jones, math teacher, East High School, Youngstown City Schools**

SAMPLE STUDENT GOALS	
Personal	**Academic**
1. Bring materials to class.	1. Write three complete sentences in my journal.
2. Come to class prepared.	2. Bring in one news article a week dealing with unit topic.
3. Cooperate with things the teacher asks me to do.	3. Self-check math problems, and write an explanation for errors found.
4. Turn in homework at least 80% of the time.	4. Ask a peer to review my notebook, and I will insert missing items.
5. Add to discussions three times a week.	5. Relate unit topics to my own life experiences.
6. Avoid interrupting another who is speaking.	6. Apply the math to work problems on my own re: ___.

SPECIFIC SAMPLES for STUDENT GOAL-SETTING

"ALL ABOUT ME" (Grade 2 MATH)

Academic/Content Goals

- Learn to collect information from my friends.
- Graph my friends' birth weight, length at birth, time-of-day born.
- Make numbers easier in my head to add and subtract.

Personal Goals

- Get facts about my birth.
- Measure things at home to see how long they are.

"TICKLE YOUR FUNNYBONE" (Grade 3 ENGLISH LANGUAGE ARTS)

Academic/Content Goals

- Tell why people like movies and stories that make them laugh.
- Underline words in what I read that the author uses to make me laugh.

Personal Goals

- Don't interrupt someone else when he or she is talking.
- Look at and listen to other people when they talk.

"CYCLES AND PATTERNS OF THE EARTH, MOON, AND SUN" (Grade 7 SCIENCE)

Academic/Content Goals

- Explain how the moon's appearance looks different due to changes in the positions of the Earth, moon, and sun.
- Explain how eclipses occur.
- Explain how tides are related to the moon's position.

Personal Goals

- Participate in class discussions on assigned topics.
- Work as part of a group to analyze data and create hypothesis.

"INTRODUCTION TO SOCIAL STUDIES" (Grade 8 SOCIAL STUDIES)

Academic/Content Goals

- Distinguish primary from secondary sources.
- Compare information given in a primary source and a secondary source.
- Locate a relative's home using GoogleEarth, including surrounding sites.

Personal Goals

- Keep my notebook up-to-date.
- Wait my turn before speaking out.

"GEOMETRY—TRANSFORMATIONS" (Grade 8 MATH)

Academic/Content Goals

- Explain my steps to problems using math terms and new vocabulary for rotations, reflections, and translations.
- Describe a sequence of steps to achieve congruent figures.

Personal Goals

- Justify my reasoning using math terms and vocabulary.
- Participate in class activities to develop understanding of various terms.

"FEAR OF THE UNKNOWN" (Grade 10 ENGLISH LANGUAGE ARTS)

Academic/Content Goals

- Explain why *Animal Farm* was so popular when it came out, including how its message still has an impact today.
- Make a list of figurative language that I can use in my writing and speaking.

Personal Goals

- Avoid interrupting others while they are speaking.
- Accept other people's opinions without getting angry.

ORGANIZATIONAL PATTERNS

When students process new information, they use the mental "circuitry" that they have built inside their heads and have made work for them. Depending on the structure of the concept or idea, students select the corresponding circuit. It may be *time sequence (first___, then ___, next, ___, etc.); cause-effect (if ____, then ___); compare-contrast (A has ___, ___, and ___; while B has ___, ___, and ___; but they both have ___, __, and ___);* or any of several other organizational patterns.

Seasoned authors use similar patterns to organize their writing. Again, depending on the content, authors decide what organizational pattern will most effectively communicate their message. An author's style (i.e., sentence patterns, language, use of imagery to create mood, and tone) is the external "skin" or wrapping of the piece. But the internal structure or organization of the text is its "bones"—the skeleton that supports the style to comprise the whole piece.

Thus, since organizational patterns impact how students *process information* as well as how *authors present it,* an essential best practice is for teachers to use the appropriate organizational pattern to communicate the information *they provide.* To more fully understand the significance of organizational patterns, some background information might be helpful.

Fiction. In fiction, the most prevalent internal structure or organization is the sequential narrative, or the "story." There is at least one character in one or more settings involved in a plot of some sort. There is usually a beginning, a point of crisis, and a resolution or denouement. The chief purpose of most fiction is to entertain, although much of it enlightens and informs as well. Some fiction authors use variations of the time sequence include foreshadowing (looking ahead) and flashback (looking behind).

Nonfiction. But in nonfiction, students encounter several different organizational patterns. And although nonfiction *can* be entertaining, its primary purpose is to inform or persuade. One of the chief requirements of the Common Core standards in English Language Arts as well as the 21st century skills is that students experience an abundance of on-level nonfiction. This does not mean textbooks—in which terms are defined for the students, and any number of reading aids are provided—but *authentic* nonfiction such as speeches, essays, technical manuals, trade books, scientific articles, political tracts, editorials, and op-ed pieces. In fact, the Common Core sets forth Literacy standards that require teachers of science, social studies, and technical subjects (including math) to provide teaching-learning activities involving nonfiction and require students to use specific reading and writing skills.

NOT Word-for-Word! Those who promulgated these new standards fully acknowledge that many students are not capable of *actually reading* (fully comprehending) on-level nonfiction. But they insist that school districts expose all students to high-quality, on-level material using the necessary adaptations and accommodations to help them internalize the information. Understandably, teachers of English as a second language and special needs students strenuously object to the "on-level" provision. But if they look closely at the wording of the requirement, they will see that students are not required *to read* on-level material *word-for-word.* This loophole allows every student to experience the richness and power of, for example, *Ideas and Opinions* by Albert Einstein without the obstacle of having to read it word-for-word. (See the section on Questioning and Cueing later for further details about abridged reading.)

Drilling Down. Let us be clear: this is not to suggest CliffsNotes or otherwise dumbing-down Einstein's incredible genius and predictive insights. Students are shown how to look for and identify the organizational pattern (or "bones") of the piece as a way to understand the author's overall intent and the structure of his or her rhetoric to convey the message. Second, every student is guided through strategically selected portions of the work, differentiated by the student's reading proficiency. This enables every student to directly experience the author's message as well as his or her style and tone. Teachers give synopses and paraphrases of key passages to help every student understand the "big picture" of the piece. Most importantly, students are shown how to develop and answer comprehension and analysis questions about the meaning of the piece and then experience guided searches through the work to locate answers. As students learn this "drilling-down" technique, they come away not only with information about the selection at hand, but also with the skills needed to approach any nonfiction text with similar success. Let's be perfectly honest: Most of us have not read the Bible, Torah, or Qur'an word-for-word and end-to-end, but we can certainly access them effectively because we have learned how to drill-down to discover their messages.

Analyzing the Organizational Pattern or the "Bones" of a Piece

We will examine several of the most frequently used organizational patterns. Not surprisingly, they are precisely the same thinking processes students use to analyze various passages and—eventually—prepare their own organizational patterns when writing. Drawing on their personal "circuitry," students learn to look for specific cue words or phrases that tip off the organizational pattern.

Chronological Sequence. One of the most popular and easily recognized patterns is chronological sequence. Authors typically use this pattern to present events or ideas in a time order, or *first, then, next,* and so on. In most cases, the final item is cumulative of those preceding it (e.g., the events leading to the Iraq War). An example of a passage in which the organizational pattern is the chronological sequence is shown here. Although vocabulary and the sentence structure are fairly difficult, the "chronological sequence" is clear. Students should be shown—and provided practice—to recognize signals like those in the boxes shown.

FOLLOWING THE RESOLUTIONS BY THE CONTINENTAL CONGRESS TO OPPOSE THE KING OF ENGLAND, REFUSE TO PAY HIS TAXES, AND DEMAND THEIR INDEPENDENCE, THE AMERICAN COLONIES WERE HEADED TO WAR. KING GEORGE DECLARED THE COLONIES IN A STATE OF REBELLION AND THEN SENT MORE SOLDIERS TO BOSTON TO DISARM THE COLONISTS AND ARREST THEIR LEADERS. ONCE HE WAS TOLD ABOUT A HUGE STASH OF GUNS AND AMMUNITION IN CONCORD, THE BRITISH GENERAL (GAGE) SENT A DETACHMENT OF TROOPS TO CONCORD TO SEIZE AND DESTROY THESE WEAPONS. BUT COLONIAL SPIES HAD HEARD ABOUT GAGE'S PLAN AND HAD THEN MOVED THE ENTIRE ARSENAL TO A SECRET LOCATION AHEAD OF THE REDCOATS.

Cause-Effect. Another well-known pattern is cause-effect. Information is presented as "here's this thing" (effect) and "here's what caused it." (cause)—the *effect* first. When the *cause* is presented first, the format is more an "if-then" pattern. Following is a sample, again with signal words boxed.

YOU CAN USUALLY SEE A RAINBOW DURING A RAIN SHOWER WHEN THE SUN IS OUT OR IN THE FINE SPRAY OF A FOUNTAIN OR WATERFALL. ALTHOUGH OUR SUNLIGHT APPEARS TO BE WHITE, IT IS ACTUALLY A BLEND OR AGGREGATE OF COLORS—ALL THE COLORS OF THE RAINBOW. WE SEE THE RAINBOW OF MULTIPLE COLORS DUE TO THE FACT THAT MILLIONS OF TINY RAINDROPS ACT AS MIRRORS AND PRISMS ON THE SUNLIGHT. FOR A RAINBOW TO APPEAR, THE SUN CAN BE NO HIGHER THAN 42°, OR NEARLY HALFWAY UP THE SKY. IF THE SUNLIGHT IS STRONG, AND THE WATER DROPLETS VERY SMALL, THEN A DOUBLE RAINBOW MAY APPEAR. THIS HAPPENS BECAUSE THE LIGHT IS REFLECTED TWICE IN THE WATER DROPLETS. BUT IN THE SECOND RAINBOW, THE COLOR BANDS ARE FAINTER AND IN THE REVERSE ORDER—AS IF TO MIRROR THE FIRST.

Compare-Contrast. One of the most effective organizational patterns—but also one of the most difficult to decipher at times—is likenesses and differences, or compare and contrast. Some authors list all the qualities of item A and then all those of item B. Others list a quality and then describe that quality in item A and then item B. Rarely does an author oblige the reader by presenting the proverbial Venn diagram showing the contrasts in the outer portion of the circles and the comparisons in the area of convergence. A sample passage is given here, and the signal words are boxed.

MANY PEOPLE THINK SPIDERS ARE INSECTS, LIKE BEES. ACTUALLY, THE TWO CREATURES ARE FROM DIFFERENT FAMILIES: THE SPIDER IS AN ARACHNID, WHILE THE BEE IS AN INSECT. BOTH HAVE EYES, BUT THE SPIDER'S EYES ARE SIMPLE, WHILE THE BEE'S EYES ARE COMPOUND. THE SPIDER HAS NO ANTENNAE, WHEREAS THE BEE DOES. BOTH ARE ARTHROPODS AND INVERTEBRATES. BOTH HAVE MULTIPLE, JOINTED LEGS. THE SPIDER AND THE BEE ARE BOTH COLD-BLOODED AND HAVE EXOSKELETONS. THE SPIDER HAS EIGHT LEGS, WHILE THE BEE HAS SIX. THE SPIDER HAS TWO JOINTED BODY PARTS—A HEAD AND THORAX. BUT THE BEE HAS THREE BODY SEGMENTS—A HEAD, A THORAX, AND AN ABDOMEN.

Note to the Reader: Additional information about compare and contrast is included further along in this section with Similarities and Differences.

"How To." Much of the nonfiction read by students in technical subjects uses the "how-to" pattern, or a step-by-step procedure. It is the most direct—but not necessarily the easiest to comprehend. Most authors do not offer an enumerated list but offer explanatory prose, usually rich in descriptive detail. Look at the following example. Rather than boxing cue words, we have inserted numbers, as a student might do.

WHEN PAINTING WOOD, THE MOST IMPORTANT STEP IS TO [1] THOROUGHLY SAND THE WOOD TO A SMOOTH FINISH. ALL BURRS AND ROUGH SPOTS MUST BE REMOVED, AND THE SURFACE SHOULD BE SILKY SMOOTH TO THE TOUCH. AFTER [2] CLEANING THE WOOD, ONE SHOULD [3] GIVE IT TWO COATS OF PRIMER. THIS NEUTRAL COLORED PAINT SOAKS INTO THE GRAIN AND SEALS IT. ONCE [4] DRIED, THE WOOD IS READY FOR [5] TWO MORE COATS OF THE FINAL COLOR.

Persuasion. Throughout the 21st century skills as well as newer standards in Science and Social Studies and the Common Core in Math and English Language Arts runs the thread of persuasion. Students are expected to detect persuasion in what they read and hear, to evaluate it in terms of the supporting evidence, and to write and speak in ways that will reasonably and fairly persuade others. Most legitimate persuasive text includes a position, a rationale, valid supportive evidence or argument, and an acknowledgement of the opposing point of view. The following passage has boxed cues as an example.

SCIENTISTS HAVE WARNED US THAT IF WE DON'T CONSERVE ENERGY, IT MAY RUN OUT. MOST PEOPLE DON'T MEAN TO WASTE ENERGY; THEY JUST HAVEN'T THOUGHT ABOUT WHAT THEY COULD DO DIFFERENTLY TO CONSERVE IT. THERE ARE SEVERAL STEPS THAT EVERYONE COULD TAKE IMMEDIATELY WHICH DON'T COST A GREAT DEAL AND WHICH WILL ACTUALLY SAVE MONEY AS WELL AS ENERGY. FOR EXAMPLE, HOMES USE MORE FUEL TO KEEP WARM THAN THEY ACTUALLY NEED BECAUSE SO MUCH HEAT IS LOST THROUGH LEAKY WINDOWS AND DOORS. INSTALLING STORM WINDOWS AND WEATHER STRIPPING WILL SAVE OVER $100 EACH YEAR IN HEATING COSTS . . . IN ADDITION, ANY GAPS OR OPENINGS AROUND THE WINDOWS AND DOORS SHOULD BE TIGHTLY CAULKED . . . THE THERMOSTAT . . . TURNING OFF LIGHTS, . . . [ETC.] CRITICS OF CONSERVATION FEEL THIS IS AN INTRUSION INTO INDIVIDUAL RIGHTS, BUT THEY SHOULD STOP TO THINK THAT IT'S NOT ABOUT EACH OF US; IT'S ABOUT WHAT'S BEST FOR THE PLANET.

Problem-Solution. Another major priority in the list of 21st century skills (as well as the new content standards) is the ability to correctly identify problems and to devise valid and reasonable solutions. Prior to these new requirements, students were typically given problems to solve for which the teacher (or the textbook) already had solutions. This naturally led to *memorized* problem-solving behavior, and students never really had to identify and solve problems authentically.

The following sample also contains a viable solution. But in life, many passages will either not propose a solution or—more challenging—pose unsatisfactory or invalid ones.

DURING THE CALIFORNIA GOLD RUSH OF 1849, MANY HOPEFUL PROSPECTORS HEADED HOME AFTER ONLY A FEW WEEKS. IT WAS NOT THAT THEY HAD GIVEN UP FINDING GOLD, IT WAS THAT THEY HAD NO CLOTHING. THE FABRIC, THREAD, AND BUTTONS THAT WERE SATISFACTORY, EVEN STYLISH, IN THE EAST WERE NO MATCH FOR THE RUGGED ROCKS AND COARSE, THORNY UNDERBRUSH THAT MADE UP THE CALIFORNIA WILDERNESS. ONE OF THOSE HEADING WEST WAS A BUSINESSMAN WHO THOUGHT THAT THE PROSPECTORS MIGHT NEED TENTS. SO HE BROUGHT WITH HIM BOLTS AND BOLTS OF CANVAS AND RIVETS TO MAKE ALL SIZES AND TYPES OF TENTS. BUT WHEN HE SAW WHAT WAS HAPPENING TO THE FLIMSY TROUSERS AND COATS WORN BY THE PROSPECTORS, HE HAD A BRILLIANT IDEA. WHY NOT USE THE TENT MATERIAL TO MAKE TROUSERS AND JACKETS? AND THE RIVETS THAT HE USED TO FASTEN THE TENTS TOGETHER WOULD MAKE IDEAL "WELDS" TO KEEP THE MOST STRESSFUL PARTS OF THE NEW TROUSERS FROM TEARING AWAY. AND WHY NOT SEW IN HEAVY-DUTY LOOPS AND POCKETS ? THAT WAY, A MINER'S TOOLS WERE ALWAYS WITH HIM ! THE FIRST OF THESE REVOLUTIONARY PANTS WERE CALLED "OVERALLS," AND THE FABRIC BECAME KNOWN AS "DENIM." RATHER THAN CHINA OR GLASS BUTTONS, "OVERALLS" WERE FASTENED WITH METAL RIVETS AND HOOKS. THESE OVERALLS—AND THEIR COUSINS THE "JEANS"—LASTED FOR MONTHS IN THE RUGGED CONDITIONS OF THE WEST. THE HEAVY DENIM WAS ALL BUT WATERPROOF, AND ITS COURSE WEAVE ACTUALLY "SHED" DIRT AND DUST. CLEARLY, THE YOUNG TENT-MAKER KNEW EXACTLY WHAT WAS NEEDED TO KEEP THE PROSPECTORS FROM GIVING UP AND GOING HOME. BY THE WAY, HIS NAME WAS LEVI STRAUSS. SOUND FAMILIAR?

Processing Information

In our work with schools, we long ago discovered the tremendous value of using these organizational patterns to show students how to process the information in the text, in speeches, or in media. These processing skills are themselves identified as best practices, but NOT in isolation. They work only when used in the context of actual fiction and nonfiction material. In our work with teachers, we actually take them through simulations of each processing skill and show them how to connect each to the materials students will actually use in the unit plans.

Summarizing. One popular method by which to determine student comprehension or understanding of text (or presentations in any media) is their production of a summary. Contrary to some popular formulas, the summary is not "the 5 Ws" as if all text is fiction or presented as a narrative news account. Indeed, an *effective* summary reflects the organizational pattern of the text and includes *only* information provided by the author—without editorial comment.

Note-taking. When teachers require students to take notes on text, lectures, PowerPoints, and media presentations, it must be remembered that these too have their own internal logic or organizational patterns. Teachers are urged to arrange their presentations to reflect the appropriate organizational patterns (e.g., cause-effect, compare-contrast, chronological sequence) and inform students of those structures as the material is presented. If students can be taught to use these patterns in their note-taking, they are provided another important path in their mental "circuitry" to process information, allowing them to more fully internalize the author's or presenter's message.

Graphic Organizers (a.k.a. Visual Organizers or Nonlinguistic Representations). A third method for presenting information, as well as for students to demonstrate mastery of it, is the visual or graphic organizer. It is a pictorial rendition of information that features key terms or concepts and shows them in their strategic relationship to each other. In effect, it displays the "organizational pattern" of a discussion, text, or presentation. The idea is that teachers not only use appropriate graphic organizers to present information, they teach their students how to devise the correct graphic organizer to demonstrate that they have constructed meaning for themselves. To ensure their deep-level understanding, it is also important that students can label their diagrams with annotations or explanatory labels.

. . . And from those who REALLY know. . . .

*Many of my students enter eighth grade not reading on-level. So the requirement of the Common Core that ALL students were to read on-level text seemed impossible! But I helped my students see that the author typically uses a certain structure to organize his or her work. The most often used include compare-contrast, cause-effect, chronological sequence, "how-to," and problem-solution. Together, we discovered signal words and phrases for each pattern that "set us up" for the author's message. For example, words like first and then and next combined with "time order" tell us to look for a chronology of events. Or when we see two opposite concepts in the topic or title (like protagonist and antagonist), and then we can highlight terms like on the other hand or unlike or whereas, we know that the information **before** those terms goes with (say) protagonist, and the information **after** goes with antagonist. Each pattern has hints like that for students to discover in advance of their reading.*

Another advantage of recognizing an author's organizational pattern is that it helps students structure their summaries—a requirement in the Common Core for the nonfiction they read. We also use the pattern to give and take notes and to sketch graphic organizers to show we know the relationships among details in the text. My students may not be able to read passages word-for-word, but they now have a valuable coping tool to unlock the most important points in an author's message.— **Lisa Perry, English teacher, P. Ross Berry Academy, Youngstown City Schools**

On the following pages, Table 3.3 shows how "organizational patterns" works with summary, note-taking, and graphic organizers. Together, they provide an efficient suite of skills to help students make meaning for themselves—and that's the basis of constructive learning.

QUESTIONING AND CUEING

One tenet common to the 21st century skills, the Common Core standards in Math and English Language Arts, and the Literacy Standards for Science, Social Studies, and technical subjects (including Math) is that students construct meaning for themselves to show mastery. This is in contrast to filling in blanks, circling answers in a word bank, matching, and similar literal or reflexive responses that reflect the teacher's or the textbook's meaning. Students not only answer questions that construct new meaning, but also they learn to devise questions at various levels of thinking and to convert back-and-forth among the levels.

Questioning Happens. It has been reported that questioning accounts for as much as 80% of the exchanges between teachers and students in every classroom on any given day. In a perfect world, the majority of these questions would focus on **academic content**. *Teacher-initiated* questions would determine what students know and understand about the subject matter, and *student-generated* questions would be to drill down beneath the surface of the content and extend their understanding. But in actuality, a large proportion of questions exchanged by teachers and students are geared to **classroom logistics**—and this is unavoidable if both parties are to fully understand each other and make their relationship productive. For example, teachers must ask questions such as:

"Where is your assignment?"

"Who is your partner?"

"Where are you supposed to be?"

"What about the directions did you not understand?"

"How much more time do you need?"

Similarly, students typically ask—

"Scott's absent—what about his part?"

"Can we finish after lunch?"

"Did you say it had to be in ink?"

"What do we do if the printer won't work?"

"How long does it have to be?"

"Is this for a grade?"

Many "questioning" experts consider these managerial and logistical exchanges as time lost. But in our experience—if properly handled—they effectively *support* and *enhance* the quality of content questioning. How? Transparency and clarity in directions and procedures actually prevent wasting time, resources, and opportunity to learn. Anticipating logistical questions and addressing as many as possible *in advance* helps to minimize the extent to which they interrupt the flow of learning. Naturally, it is impossible to anticipate every nonacademic question, but they can be "contained" to a time before or after— and not interrupt—the session devoted to academic questions. The key is to make sure the majority of time, effort, and resources expended on "questioning" are focused on students' mastery of content, not clarifying logistics.

Structure of Organizational Pattern	Format for Summary • = sentence	Note-Taking	Visual/Graphic Organizer
Specific Detail → General Topic: detail or example detail or example → thesis idea detail or example (key concept) detail or example e.g., show students a series of congruent figures in isolation and in context, including a description for and use of each; lead up to the concept of congruence	• synthesis of details or examples that support thesis • thesis idea	• —— • —— } thesis idea or • —— key concept	
General Topic → Specific Detail: thesis idea → (key concept) detail, example detail, example detail, example detail, example e.g., start with the Salem Witch Trials followed by several details of what, how, where, and why; include results	• thesis idea • synthesis of details or examples to support	thesis idea } detail (key concept) } detail } detail	
Chronological Sequence topic (secondary) e.g., the events of the Renaissance in Europe in the context of the political, economic, artistic, scientific, etc., events happening at the same time	• event or cluster of events • synthesis of lead-up events • other contextual events happening simultaneously	Historic event > event > event > event Economic event > event > event > event Political event > event > event > event Social event > event > event > event	timeline flowchart

Table 3.3 (Continued)

Structure of Organizational Pattern	Format for Summary • = sentence	Note-Taking	Visual/Graphic Organizer
Nonfiction Narrative Sequence • setting (time, place) } presented • character(s) } as a story — 1st or 3rd person point of view • conflict e.g., present the discovery of sulfur matches as a narrative; include settings, key people, mishaps and failures, and the final success	• plot scenario, setting, character(s) • resolution and "message"	setting ——— ———	character ——— ——— ———
Problem/Solution: problem (puzzlement) (quandary) } various facets • how • when • where (etc.) } criteria for solution (each facet) ——— ——— ——— } solution of "best fit" e.g., present a quandary (e.g., the class's pet gerbil bites); ask students to identify the facts of the problem, identify the criteria for a solution, pose several solutions, and then apply the criteria to select the best one	• synthesis of problem, including various facets • criteria for solution, and solution of "best fit"	problem solution criteria best solution • ——— • ——— • ——— • etc. ☐	Problem Criteria Solution (with various for viable of facets) solution "Best Fit"
Persuasion/Argument: • takes a position • remains neutral; helps reader make a choice — may or may not take a position controversial issue ⌐ position → support #1 / position → support #2 e.g., present the issue: should the U.S. bring democracy to third-world countries? Offer both perspectives: yes, they'll be better off because. . . . and no, not every culture benefits from democracy because. . . .	• synthesis of issue • alternate positions • indication of support or neutrality	issue • ——— • ——— • ——— ↑ ⇧ ↑ position #1 ——— ——— position #2 ——— ———	☐ — (with rationale) or ☐ — (with rationale) ↑ ☐

Structure of Organizational Pattern	Format for Summary ● = sentence	Note-Taking	Visual/Graphic Organizer
Descriptive/Sensory sensory details ● visual ● auditory } from a sensory "picture" ● etc. e.g., present the setting of Chicago's meat processing plant as found in The Jungle by Upton Sinclair; use only words and no pictures	● topic ● key sensory details ● overall effect	visual auditory tactile ___ ___ ___ ___ ___ ___ ___ ___	sensory details object

Compare/Contrast:
 	
Sample A   Sample B   by feature
                              A   B
___ ___   ● ___ ___
alike ___   ● ___ ___
___ ___   ● ___ ___
             or
topic { ___ ___
diff. ___ ___
___ ___
 	
e.g., compare and contrast ancient Greece with ancient Rome, including social, economic, military, philosophical factors of the day, and the impact each has had on life in the U.S.
	● topic
	● "alike" examples
	● "difference" examples
		A both B
		● ___ ● ___ ● ___
		● ___ ● ___ ● ___
		● ___ ● ___ ● ___	

(Continued)

Table 3.3 (Continued)

Structure of Organizational Pattern	Format for Summary • = sentence	Note-Taking	Visual/Graphic Organizer
Cause–Effect: Topic { casual factors — effects } may be 1:1 (single) or multi e.g., show students the drawing of a box that holds a cup of sand, then make two sides bigger to show how the change in measurement impacts the volume	• topic • synthesis of causes-effects • multiple or chaining (if applicable)	causes effects • ___ • ___ • ___ • ___	single (1:1) multiple
"How To" topic { steps in sequence (secondary) } or (may vary) e.g., explain how to devise a research plan to guide an action research project; use an example (e.g., which drinking fountain in the school has the greatest amount of bacteria?), including drafts and final copy	• topic (what, why) • synthesis of steps, procedures • variations, options (if applicable)	Steps checkpoints product 1. ___ 2. ___ ✓ 3. ___ ✓ 4. ___	timeline flowchart

82

Plan for Effective Questioning

Many of the most insightful and thought-provoking content questions are spontaneous and inspired by the discussion. But the questioning research is clear that unless higher level and constructive questions are planned in advance (and written down!), they are far less likely to occur. Teachers get busy with other details, and unless they just happen to remember those brilliant questions that occurred to them in the shower—or a student's comment happens to trigger a flash of insight—they never get asked.

Mostly Recall. Over the years, we have scripted thousands of lessons, and our findings are consistent with the research: the overwhelming majority of teacher-generated questions are focused on the recall of information and are limited to literal-level thinking. Understandably, teachers want to make sure that students have the basic level of information needed to proceed with the discussion. And the research does say that the more students know about a topic, the more it tends to hold their attention. But the familiar "Q-and-A" typically involves only 10–20% of the most capable students answering the teacher's questions, leaving the majority of students virtually *uninvolved* or mindlessly copying the right answer—grateful not to have been put on the spot.

Higher Level. Questions designed to help *every* student—not just those eager to answer—obtain a deeper understanding will promote an even greater interest in the concepts and topics among all students. Surprisingly, many students who may not know the literal details can process information at higher levels and think about content topics in creative, constructive ways. In so doing, they actually internalize the detail they need after-the-fact in the context of the problem they solved, decision they reached, or creative application they made. But they must be provided questions that give them an opportunity to do this level of processing.

> ! *Lesson Learned*! An example of this was suggested by a parent whose fifth-grade son had failed a test on the states, capitals, and topography of the United States, even though they had carefully rehearsed the information together at the kitchen table. The parent (who was not a teacher) took a map of the United States, cut it into sections that she thought were logical regions, and then used AAA books to gather notable information about the regions she had selected. She created a "treasure hunt" of things for the student to find about each region, including famous places to visit and things to see. As they went along, she asked her son to make connections and comparisons among the regions. The parent asked that her son be given a similar test again, just to see if the plan worked. Skeptical, the teacher agreed. The boy knew most of the topographical information, all the states and their capitals, and noted all sorts of interesting tidbits about every region. To the teacher's credit, she replaced the original F with the later score of 92%. The research is full of similar anecdotes.

In our scripts, far fewer questions ask students to make valid *inferences*, and almost none require them to *construct meaning* for themselves, even though these are both key in the Common Core Standards. These questions require students to make connections, compare and contrast details, analyze information, restructure ideas and details, draw valid conclusions, apply knowledge in a different way, evaluate the worth or merit of something, and/ or construct new meaning for themselves. Such questions produce more learning—and more long-term retention—than asking students simply to recall or to recognize.

In our experience, students must be shown how to process information at different levels and how to answer corresponding questions. Thereafter, they must also become proficient at developing questions at these various levels. Many of the academic standards in several states include the requirement that students *answer* various levels of questions, and some stipulate that students must also construct questions at various levels of difficulty. To that end, we have developed three levels of questions for teachers to integrate into their unit plans.

Level I Questions (Literal)

Level I questions ask students to use stored or immediate knowledge. These questions ask for literal or fact-level information that students have read or been given. Level I questions typically deal with the "who, what, when, and where" of things because that's what the author or speaker has provided. If the information given also includes a "why or how," these too can become Level I questions. But if "how" and "why" information is *not given*, it must be inferred, and that requires a higher level of mental processing.

Another way to describe Level I questions is that they address what the author (or speaker) actually writes or says. Sample Level I questions are as follows:

1. What is the standard form of a quadratic equation?

2. Where do earthquakes occur?

3. In *The Legend of Sleepy Hollow*, who is Ichabod Crane's love interest?

4. What are three essential employability skills?

5. What is figurative about *"He is trampling out the vintage where the grapes of wrath are stored?"*

6. What are three needs and three wants for the typical American family budget?

7. How does marijuana affect the central nervous system?

8. What are the units for length in the Metric system and the U.S. Standard system?

Level II Questions (Inferential)

Level II questions ask students to make inferences, draw conclusions, or see implications in the text or the information given. In contrast to Level I questions, these Level II questions cannot be answered only from the literal detail provided in the material. Students must "read between the lines" or think about what the author or speaker may have *meant* by what he or she *said*. This requires thinking beneath or behind what they hear or what is printed on the page and make inferences about the material. In the English Language Arts Common Core, every grade level includes a standard requiring students to identify *implicit* details. Asking and answering Level II questions—where students do not have literal information—forces them to look for connections and relationships among ideas, concepts, and so on. Sample Level II questions are as follows:

---

9. How would one solve a quadratic equation using the quadratic formula?

10. How have specific disasters changed regions in terms of economic, social, and political impact?

11. Why might the headless horseman may actually have been Crane's adversary, Brom Bones?

12. As the economy slowly recovers, several jobs are becoming available. Why are so many unemployed people still not finding jobs?

13. In the *Battle Hymn of the Republic* after the phrase *"As he died to make men holy,"* the hymn has two alternate lyrics. One is *"let us live to make men free"* and the other is *" . . . let us die to make men free."* What is the difference?

14. What are the advantages and disadvantages of buying with a credit card in relation to the family budget?

15. How do performance-enhancing drugs affect the human body over time?

16. How were the measurements determined for the purpose in the design?

Notice the connection between question 1 in the Level I box and question 9 in the Level II box. They both deal with quadratic equations. Similarly, notice questions 2 and 10 (earthquakes and disasters); 3 and 11 (*The Legend of Sleepy Hollow*); and so on. In contrast to Level I questions that deal with *one* concept or skill, Level II questions include *two or more* concepts and involve *relationships* between and among them. Both Level I and Level II questions are *convergent;* that is, they tend to have a limited range of correct answers—and sometimes only one.

Level III Questions (Analytical)

Level III questions ask students to construct meaning *beyond* the given information and to think at the "what-if" or the hypothetical level; in addition,

Level III questions may also ask students to evaluate the material in reference. Students cannot adequately answer—nor create—Level III questions without a firm foundation of background information (Level I) and a sense of the relationships among the concepts involved (Level II). In contrast to the *convergent* nature of Level I and II questions, Level III questions are more *divergent* in that they involve thinking beyond the material and require students to delve into creative *but viable* possibilities. Many Common Core and 21st century standards require Level III–type student mastery. Again, note the connection among questions 1, 9, and 17—all dealing with quadratic equations, but at progressively higher levels. The same with questions 2, 10, and 18 (natural disasters) and questions 3, 11, and 19 (*The Legend of Sleepy Hollow*). The others connect as well.

Sample Level III questions are as follows:

---

17. When using a quadratic equation for real-world applications, how and why would one decide if the real solutions are reasonable?

18. Using EPA criteria, how would you appraise the efforts of countries to take precautionary steps and institute safeguards to minimize disasters?

19. What might the "headless horseman" have actually symbolized when it was written? today?

20. Pretend you are suddenly in charge of schools in Ohio. What employability skills would you require every student to demonstrate to graduate from high school?

21. How can the *Battle Hymn of the Republic* still be relevant among all faiths? What is it about the piece that still speaks to all of humanity?

22. If a family finds itself with less money in a month than its needs and wants, how does it make choices about managing its resources?

23. How might illegal drug use by famous athletes impact student perceptions about whether or not to use drugs?

24. What measurement or calculation errors were made in the design of the ____ that would need to be corrected? What would need to be done to make the structure safe?

Teachers often tell us that Levels I, II, and III remind them of a compressed Bloom's *Taxonomy,* and that's exactly right! But over the years, we have found that it is easier for teachers to think spontaneously at three levels than six. A closer look at the three functional levels of Bloom we mentioned at the outset of this chapter shows the deliberate parallel between the *Taxonomy* and the three levels of questioning. And as with Bloom's *Taxonomy,* it is not necessary to ask students all three levels of questions on the same topic, but the samples we've included show the developmental relationships among the levels.

Don't Be Misled by "Cue Words." Teachers must take care that students are not fooled into looking for cue words. Just as "who" and "when'" questions can be Level I or Level II—depending on the amount of information given—"what-if" questions are not always a Level III. For example, "What if we substituted Splenda for sugar in this recipe? How much would we need?" is a Level I question, since the answer is literal. And for that matter, a "who" question could very well be a Level III; for example, "Who would be the most likely candidates to test the new stem-cell technology?"

When asking questions, the "wait-time" is as important as the question itself in getting students to higher level, more substantive answers. "Waiting"—even briefly—has been proven to increase the depth of student answers and obtain more substantive responses. In addition, "waiting" encourages more student-to-student interaction.

From the earliest grades, students should be shown how to answer questions at all three levels and to distinguish among the three levels in terms of internalizing the information. Being able to answer questions at all three levels about the information reflects a student's ability to comprehend the material at an independent level. The ability to develop questions at all three levels indicates his or her capacity to construct meaning at an even more intuitive level. Additional information on the value and use of questioning is contained in Appendix B: Questioning.

SIMILARITIES AND DIFFERENCES

The best practice known as *similarities and differences* is based on the student's ability to compare and contrast—to see how things are alike and distinct. Students who can use similarities and differences successfully can sort things into categories or classes based on features or attributes that distinguish them from others. This opens up an entire array of teaching and learning channels. Many researchers insist that a student's ability to compare and contrast is the single greatest predictor of how she or he will score on high-stakes tests. Studies show that students demonstrate a deep-level knowledge of things (i.e., people, objects, events, ideas, or concepts) when they can distinguish them from what they are NOT. That is, they can explain how "things" are alike and different, based on common and distinguishing attributes. The key here is to work through several layers, and students need to "mine" them all in order to master this complex best practice. Starting with the most basic level, we suggest that teachers help students develop this skill by working through these several layers.

Categorization

The basic level for looking at how things are alike and different is the mental process of categorization. Categories are mental bins into which students sort things by common attributes. The skill of categorization begins with simpler, more concrete bins such as people, objects, places, and events and proceeds through more complex bins like actions, conditions, principles, or concepts. Students move from (a) sorting given items by category name (b) to supplying additional examples for their "sorts," to (c) creating new categories for sets of seemingly unrelated items. A basic example is shown here.

If students are given a list of PEOPLE. . . .
> e.g., actor, police officer, goalie, guitarist, shortstop, firefighter

They should first (a) sort them into categories. . . .
> e.g., entertainers, public safety workers, athletes

Then, they need to (b) supply additional examples of each category. . . .
> e.g., entertainers (singer); public safety workers (TSA person); athletes (catcher)

Finally, they should (c) create a new category that might fit all or some of the groups. . . .
> e.g., people in the public eye

The same exercise should be provided for OBJECTS, PLACES, EVENTS, ACTIONS, CONDITIONS, and CONCEPTS. What may seem a parlor game is a serious teaching-learning strategy. The level of thinking becomes increasingly more complex, and by the time students are dealing with CONDITIONS, they are distinguishing among forms of government, math processes, literary genres, scientific methods, and economic principles—just as a few examples. Naturally, the items and categories are adjusted developmentally, but they use actual content standards. A complete exercise for training teachers to use categorization is included in Appendix C.

A second-order categorization exercise involves re-categorizing. For example, a list of men who are all presidents can also be "sorted" as living, political party, or served during a war.

The following diagram shows how to help students perform this second- and third-order sort.

Ulysses S. Grant William McKinley Theodore Roosevelt Harry Truman Dwight Eisenhower John F. Kennedy Gerald Ford George H. W. Bush	but they could also be sorted by:		
	living or deceased	political party	served in wartime

⇩

are all Presidents

Comparison

Once students master the capacity to categorize people, objects, events, ideas, or concepts by *common* attribute, they can make deeper-level comparisons and contrasts across categories, noting likenesses and differences. Comparison asks students to examine members of the same category or classification to determine what they have in common. From this comparison also comes several direct or implied distinctions. When facile at the comparison process, students discover how even similar things have differences as well. In addition to the standard T-chart and Venn diagram that are most typically used, students should learn to become facile at multiple comparisons on multiple dimensions, typically displayed as a *comparison matrix.* In Table 3.4 is an example with basic 2-D and 3-D shapes and where they can be found in the environment.

Table 3.4   Comparison Matrix for 2-D and 3-D Shapes

"Shape" as is ⇨ ———— as in the environment ⇩	Square	Rectangle	Rectangular Prism	Circle	Cylinder	Sphere	Triangle	Student Adds Another One ____
birthday party	*"Happy Birthday!" poster*	*place cards*	*gift boxes*	*birthstone ring*	*birthday cake*	*new volleyball*	*Game-Boy remote buttons*	
the circus								
supermarket								
airport								
the farm								
the highway								
[your idea: _____]								

While all of the examples students place in the cells are a form of "constructing meaning," a deeper-level mastery is demonstrated when students add another column and/or another row. Again, the content reflects one or more content standards.

A more sophisticated example could be done with students in the middle grades where they work in pairs or threes to read nonfiction pieces about several different biomes. As a result of reading the informational text, the students capture specific information that will allow the class to build a comparison matrix (Table 3.5) and then make comparative statements as to how some biomes have features in common and at the same time are quite different.

Table 3.5 Biome Comparison Matrix

BIOMES → FEATURES ↓	TUNDRA	AQUATIC	DESERT	FOREST	GRASSLAND
Vegetation					
Animal Life					
Temperatures					
Sunlight					
Average Rainfall					
Another Feature					

When the cells are completed, students note two or three similarities between and among the biomes as well as two or three differences. When students have fully mastered the "biomes" concept, they should be able to add another row on some aspect of the biomes, such as "human impact" on each.

. . . And from those who REALLY know. . . .

We were pretty skeptical about having students record their notes in a comparison matrix (as in the chart below). Our first reaction was to say, "Why don't we just fill it in and hand it out to them? That would certainly save time."

	Political	Economic	Military	Countries Who Have
Communism				
Capitalism				
Socialism				

*But when we tried it with our students, we were surprised when they actually liked it. They really paid attention to the information they were given—some from reading, some from our explanations, and some from the YouTube video we showed. We've used the comparison matrix as a pretest, a note-taking device, a quiz, or a review before the test. The comparison matrix also makes a great format for authentic assessments.—**Audrey Labenz and Nancy Lecorchick, former middle school teachers, Cleveland Municipal School District***

Critical Attributes

The third best practice in similarities and differences is to help students learn a concept by identifying its distinguishing attributes. Some learning theorists call this "concept attainment," and some refer to it as "critical attribution theory." We call it the critical attribute method. It helps students discover a concept by looking at exemplars and nonexemplars and then identify the critical attributes that make it what it is; once they internalize the concept, students can identify additional examples of it and distinguish it from other concepts. It is a strategy where students do the work, and the teacher guides the thinking. It is NOT telling students the concept but having them discover it from several examples and nonexamples.

A very simple example is that students are shown two piles of what appears to be garbage or junk. *Pile 1* contains a used paper plate, a cardboard box lid, a piece of cotton, part of a wooden spoon, and crusts from toast; it is labeled "Biodegradable." *Pile 2* includes a used Styrofoam cup, a wad of aluminum foil, a broken glass bottle, an empty pop can, a piece of vinyl wallet, and a broken plastic brush; its label reads "Nonbiodegradable." Students are asked to identify the attributes of the items in *Pile 1* and those in *Pile 2.* From these two lists, students will see some common or similar characteristics—perhaps color, function, or the fact that they are broken or used. But by process of elimination, the distinguishing or "critical" attribute is that the "Biodegradable" items are natural and have no chemical preservatives or synthetic resins. Hence, they will decay when left to the elements, and their ingredients will blend harmlessly back into the soil. In contrast, the "Nonbiodegradable" items contain synthetic chemicals and resins that will not decay and not return to the soil. Instead, they will simply remain as unsightly garbage, or pollution. Older students will observe that some of these resins may actually be toxic and harmful to the environment.

If they truly understand the concept, students can supply original examples and nonexamples. In the "biodegradable" example, students can then can add another example to each pile, such as a piece of leather belt to the "biodegradable" pile and a piece of plastic pen to the "nonbiodegradable" pile.

The teacher's role is not to tell students the concept but to ask them questions that prompt them to discover answers. Compared with the conventional method of simply explaining to students the underlying facts or definitions of a concept, the critical attribute method requires students to do more than passively listen and take notes. They must construct meaning for themselves. Likewise, the teacher must thoroughly understand the concept so that she can guide student thinking as students ask questions and pose hypotheses for critical attributes of a concept.

[Prior to the Lesson]

a. Determine what the concept is that students are to draw from the examples.

b. Select clear-cut examples of the concept and sequence them from easiest to more complex.

[During the Lesson]

c. Help students determine which attributes fit all of the various examples.

e. Help students determine which attributes do not fit all of the examples— and are discarded.

f. Help students summarize their thoughts as to what the concept must be, defined by its key attributes.

g. Have students give examples and nonexamples of the concept, verifying against the criteria.

[Following the Lesson]

h. Debrief with students on the "critical attribute" process (how it works; how they felt).

i. Ask students to reflect on their thinking and how they used the information in the dialogue to come to their conclusions.

The critical attribute technique is not appropriate to teach every concept. It is most helpful with clear-cut concepts that are distinct from their opposites. More divergent and inclusive concepts such as *loyalty* or *humanitarianism* are difficult to capture in clear-cut examples and nonexamples. Moreover, they tend to be value-laden, and students often confuse *opinion* with those attributes that actually distinguish (say "invasion of privacy" from "terrorism-prevention").

Table 3.6   Content Topics That Might Be Taught With the Critical Attribute Strategy

Language Arts	Math	Science	Social Studies
Figurative Language	Symmetry	Gravity	Imperialism
Critical Analysis	Congruency	Interdependence	Scarcity
Subject-Verb Agreement	Basic Shapes	Conservation of Matter	Socialism
Supported Argument	Rational Numbers	Adaptation	Landforms
Complete Sentences	Types of Angles	Mammals	Primary-Secondary Sources
Fact, Opinion, and Inference	Perfect Squares	Density vs. Volume	Push-Pull Factors
Connotation/ Denotation	Mathematical Properties	Observance Inference	Goods and Services

Specific approaches to using the Critical Attribute as a best practice are included in Appendix D.

Metaphor

"A picture may be worth a thousand *words*, but a good metaphor is worth a thousand *pictures*" (Pink, 2005). Aristotle saw the capacity to think metaphorically as the sign of genius. Understandably, the best practice of metaphor is an important one.

Using and interpreting the metaphor is the ability to understand an *unfamiliar* "thing" by associating with it one or more attributes of a *familiar* but otherwise unrelated "thing." A few examples are as follows:

a. Pink Floyd's students as "bricks in a wall"—a short way to say that schools treat them as if they are faceless props that hold up the building, with no individuality or uniqueness and certainly no capacity to think or feel or present an opinion.

b. Newscasters describing Black Friday shopping as "a jungle out there"— a short way to say that people behave like wild animals to get a bargain; they proceed without restraint or order or consideration for what's fair to others.

c. Economists and politicians claiming that not to address the national debt is "to just keep kicking the can down the road"—a short way to say that the tactic is foolish and cowardly in that it just puts off the inevitable until later on, which may force another generation to cope with it.

Students who can interpret the above metaphors (and eventually create original ones) need little added explanation about the concept or idea in reference. If the metaphor is the "parent" concept, some of its "offspring" (speaking of metaphor!) are the *axiom, proverb, pun, idiom, simile, hyperbole, onomatopoeia, personification, symbolism,* and *analogy.* Although they each have their own figurative "twist," they are all forms of the metaphor.

In our experience, teachers often "expect" students to come to them prepared to understand the metaphor. But if no one *teaches students how to* think metaphorically, they're unlikely to do so with any success. To help students learn this important skill, teachers should begin with expressions they know. The idea is for students to see and explain the image or thoughts created by the statements, and understand what image the words help them see. A few examples are offered below:

Axioms, Proverbs, and Other Sage Advice

1. Before you criticize others, you should walk a mile in their shoes.
2. Some folks are so obsessed by the door that closed, they miss the open window. (Helen Keller)
3. Some days you're the bug, and some days, you're the windshield.

Idioms

1. That announcer really "hit the nail on the head" when he said the officiating was highly suspect.
2. Don't you hate it when adults "paint all us teenagers with the same brush?"
3. No matter how hard it is to pass the test, never "throw in the towel!"

Similes

1. My brother's car is like a sports locker on wheels.
2. The defendant stayed as tight-lipped as a clam.
3. Life is like a box of chocolates. (Forrest Gump)

Additional ideas for use of the metaphor can be found in Appendix E: Teaching the Metaphor for Similarities and Differences.

Analogy

Considered the most advanced best practice in the similarities and differences group, the analogy requires students to identify multiple relationships simultaneously and to employ one or more reasoning skills to identify the one relationship that is being requested. For example, if the concept to be mastered is "symbols," students know that a red cross symbolizes the world-famous medical service, the bald eagle symbolizes America, and the wheel chair icon symbolizes handicap access or parking. This helps them to understand how the yellow ribbon can symbolize soldiers serving in harm's way. Analogies are typically set up as follows:

Wheel Chair : Handicap Access : : Yellow Ribbon : Soldier in Harm's Way

[is to]   [just as]   [is to]

Like the other techniques in the similarities and differences family, the analogy helps students to (a) internalize a concept and (b) use it independently. Learning theorists are convinced that a student's proficiency with analogies will equip him or her to:

a. identify relationships between TWO items, e.g., hammer : nail = *the hammer drives the nail; and*

b. identify distinctions and similarities among PAIRS of information, e.g., the hammer : nail : : the wrench : bolt = *like the hammer makes the nail "do its job," the wrench makes the bolt "do its job"; the key relationship is* **tool.**

Students must begin their mastery of the analogy by examining very simple and obvious examples, such as, for example:

---

green is to *go* as *red* is to *stop*
   that is, green suggests "go," and red suggests "stop"; the key relationship is **color**

curtains are to *windows* as *sunglasses* are to *eyes*
   that is, curtains protect furnishings from the sun, and sunglasses protect eyes from the sun;
   the key relationship is **function**

fish is to *swim* as *duck* is to *waddle*
   that is, fish move by swimming, and ducks get around by waddling; the key relationship is **means of movement**

$\frac{2}{3}$ is to 66% as $\frac{1}{3}$ is to 33%

   that is, 2/3 and 66% are two ways to show the same quantity, and 1/3 and 33% do the same; the key relationship is **equivalent fractions and percents**

These examples show a relationship between the items in the first pair of words that also exists between the items in the second pair. In these simple examples, there is only one obvious relationship between the two pairs. However, most analogies are not so direct. Many involve words that have multiple relationships, making it more of a challenge to identify the *precise* one requested.

In the following set of analogies, this challenge is more apparent if one of the four terms is left blank in each example. To reduce the amount of print and to present the analogies in the format most typically presented to students, we will use the conventional symbols of the analogy—the colon and double colon. The key symbol ⊶ will designate the relationship.

---

coffee : _____ : : chocolate cake : dessert [⊶ an example of]

[answer: beverage]

triangle : 180° :: _____ : 360° [⊶ the number of degrees in the angles of a shape]

[answer: quadrilateral]

_____ : Congress : : House of Lords : Parliament [⊶ part to whole]

[answer: Senate]

While there may be multiple relationships between two words in the first pair, students must identify the one relationship that also exists between the two words in the second pair.

Common "Types" of Analogies Most Likely Encountered by Students

The following are 15 of the most commonly used types of analogy and a very simple example for each. The exact label is not as important as the student's understanding of the underlying concepts. In our experience, content teachers can use several of these "relationships" to help students learn new concepts, just by swapping out the terms. For example, if students understand **cause-effect** in the sample analogy—**cut : bleed :: ignite : burn**—then the social studies teacher can use that to set up the cause-effect relationship between **unemployment : recession : : job growth : recovery,** and the science teacher can make headway with **fault lines in rocks : earthquakes : : cracks in earth's crust : volcanoes.**

As with all best practices, students pass from (1) *labeling* the relationship in a complete analogy to (2) *supplying* a term in a partial analogy and naming the relationship to (3) *constructing* an analogy to illustrate a relationship. The list below represents the most common types of analogies that students encounter; the ⊶ symbol designates the relationship.

1. **Synonyms:** e.g., purchase : buy :: throw : pitch

2. **Antonyms:** e.g., purchase : sell :: throw : catch

(Continued)

(Continued)

3. **Grammar** (i.e., parts of speech; language; parts of a sentence; rhyming words): e.g., it : it's :: you : you'll

4. **Causes and Effects:** e.g., cut : bleed :: ignite : burn

5. **Part-Whole:** e.g., tail : dog :: mane : horse

6. **Actions:** e.g., chickens : roost :: moles : tunnel

7. **Examples or Types of:** e.g., isosceles : triangle :: epic : poetry

8. **Homonyms** (i.e., homophones, homographs): e.g., knight : night :: great : grate and read : read :: wind : wind

9. **Tool-Function** (a.k.a. object/function or object/purpose): e.g., hammer : nails :: wrench : bolts

10. **Location:** e.g., Mount Vernon : Washington :: Monticello : Jefferson

11. **People** (i.e., scientists, entertainers, statesmen): e.g., Fulton : steam :: Edison : electricity

12. **Mathematics:** e.g., 1/4 : $.25 :: 4/5 : 80%

13. **Associations** (i.e., mascots, state flowers, symbols): e.g., buckeye : Ohio :: swastika : Nazism

14. **Characteristics or Attributes:** e.g., athlete : endurance :: artist : creativity

15. **Members of a Group:** e.g., gulls : flock :: cattle : herd

Summary. This chapter has examined several research-based best practices to deliver classroom instruction. Unlike many traditional delivery practices, these—and those in Chapter 4—are equal to the demands of the new standards and the 21st century skills. Together, these two chapters offer a menu of best-practice options from which work teams decide to insert into their unit plans. Some of the practices should be considered for every unit, and others are more effective if used to address particular standards in specific units.

Without an awareness of each best practice and how it answers the more rigorous demands of the new content standards and the 21st century, work teams have no way to strategically insert practices into one or more units. In our experience, every work team claims to use the best practices in their classroom documents. After all, what self-respecting work team would say they prefer to use the "worst practices"? But without a complete understanding of each best practice, work teams just assign any and every "practice" to every unit—sort of like Alice's Cheshire Cat.

"If you don't know where you are going, any road will take you there!"

—The Cheshire Cat in *Alice in Wonderland*

Integrating Best Practices Into Unit Plans 4

"The mediocre teacher tells. The good teacher explains. The superior teacher demonstrates. The great teacher inspires."

—William Arthur Ward, teacher and teacher-educator

In this the second of the two chapters on "best practices," we will present ideas and examples about the remaining list of research-based practices. Knowing how to select and use the best practices is *essential* for teachers to meet the increased demands of the new content standards and the 21st century skills.

MATHEMATICAL PROBLEM ANALYSIS AND PROBLEM SOLVING

Math problem solving means finding the method for solving a problem and obtaining a solution. It is commonly associated with word problems. To find a solution, students draw on their own knowledge of similar situations and experiences and apply it to unfamiliar problems. Through this process, they develop new mathematical understandings and see relationships not previously comprehended. By learning problem solving in mathematics, students acquire ways of thinking, habits of persistence and curiosity, and confidence in unfamiliar situations—all of which will serve them well both in and outside the mathematics classroom. Problem solving is an integral part of all mathematics learning, and so it should *not be an isolated unit* in the mathematics program. Rather, it should become how students work within every unit of instruction. Indeed, the math practices that are part of the Common Core ask students to think about math and include the following eight practices at all grade levels.

The Core Curriculum provides an extensive explanation for each math practice (Common Core document, pp. 6–8), so we are not going into detail here.

1. Make sense of problems and persevere in solving them.

2. Reason abstractly and quantitatively.

3. Construct viable arguments and critique the reasoning of others.

4. Model with mathematics.

5. Use appropriate tools strategically.

6. Attend to precision.

7. Look for and make use of structure.

8. Look for and express regularity in repeated reasoning.

In developing their math units, the work teams will incorporate these practices into each unit plan. As set forth in the Common Core document, the goal is to include at least two of these practices in each lesson throughout the unit. By the end of a unit, students will experience each practice multiple times and thus increase their independence with each.

The Common Core insists that mathematical concepts must be contextualized (or related to life situations) through problems that come from the students' world, focused on money, time, and measurement. Good problem-solvers tend naturally to carefully analyze situations in mathematical terms. They learn by first considering *simple* problems as a "hook" from which to solve more complex problems.

In essence, math problem solving becomes a matter of students finding one of three things:

The START—e.g., how many cookies does Bob have in the FIRST PLACE

The CHANGE—e.g., how many cookies were added, taken away, multiplied, or divided

The RESULT—e.g., how many cookies does Bob have NOW

Traditionally, students were asked to find the *RESULT*. But with the Common Core and attention to contextualized mathematics, students are expected to find the *CHANGE* and the *START* as well. And to do this, they must also understand how mathematics works, not simply how to plug numbers into a formula to come up with a right answer!

Addition/Subtraction. First, students should consider addition and subtraction. To work successfully with contextualized (life situation) mathematics, students need to encounter different ways to illustrate the same addition or subtraction problem. Researchers and teachers use how children understand operations by their approaches to simple arithmetic problems:

> *Bob received 2 cookies. Now he has 5 cookies. How many cookies did Bob have in the beginning?*

To solve this problem, children might count on from 2, keeping track with their fingers, to get to 5. Or they might recognize the problem as using the inverse operation to solve for an unknown and use $5 - 2 = 3$; or, actually writing the number sentence to reflect the problem as $\triangle + 2 = 5$.

Multiplication/Division. After addition and subtraction, students then consider multiplication and division. Through these, students gain a sense of the relationships among the operations and are able to see the similarity of addition to multiplication and subtraction to division. They are also able to recognize that addition and subtraction are inverse operations as are multiplication and division. Students must (a) recognize that the same operation can be applied in problem situations that on the surface seem quite different from one another, (b) know how operations relate to one another, and (c) have an idea about what kind of result to expect. As with the addition/subtraction, the understanding that students need to have is that they can work to find the *RESULT*, the *START*, or the *CHANGE*. Giving students opportunity to find only the *RESULT* limits their understanding of the types of problems they will encounter in real life as well as on high-stakes tests.

Fractions/Decimals/Ratios/Percents. Students' intuitions about operations evolve as they work with an expanded system of numbers. For example, multiplying a whole number by a fraction between 0 and 1 (e.g., $8 \times \frac{1}{2}$) produces a *RESULT* less than the whole number. This is counter to students' prior experience with whole numbers, where multiplication always resulted in a greater number. Students become proficient in creating ratios to make comparisons that involve pairs of numbers. Students know the ratio/proportion in problems such as: *If three packages of cocoa make 15 cups of hot chocolate, how many packages are needed to make 60 cups?*

In our professional development with teachers, we have helped teachers use these ideas to rethink their approach to math problem solving. As a first step, we dissect common problem types to help teachers understand that problem solving involves more than a sequence of steps posted on the board or a colorful, catchy poster. By showing teachers that problems do not always ask for the *RESULT*, we help them see that every problem cannot and should not be approached without understanding what the problem is asking. After years of preaching about the woes in the teaching of problem solving, we found a chart that summarized problem types in mathematics with variations on each type. This chart provided one of those ah-ha moments when we said, "This is what we have been trying to say for years!" The big idea is this: Problem solving is really multiple ways to look at the same problem. We have made further adaptations to the original chart in eliminating "trigger words" from the problems. It is worth noting that a newer version of this table appears in the Common Core Math Standards, with different examples.

> *. . . And from those who REALLY know. . . .*
>
> *As an elementary math teacher, I found that my students were only good at problem solving when the problems asked them to find the "result;" when I started to have my students tell me what they looked for in solving problems, I found that they were looking for "trigger words" and not really reading what the problem was asking! Wow! Then, I started giving them problems that asked for the "start" and "change" as well as the result, and when they found that these were the same problems with a different twist, they felt so smart! They were willing to "talk" through what a problem was asking and they could tell me what was needed to determine a solution—a simple technique that made a huge impact on my students' confidence in math! They are able to look at problems more deeply now than they were in the past.—**Darcy Burgess, Grade 4 math teacher, Jackman Elementary School, Washington Local Schools**

"Problem Solving Made Real" is this chart, and it appears as Table 4.1. We have used the chart with the authors' permission, and we have adapted it as follows.

Table 4.1   Problem Solving Made Real

PROBLEM TYPE	"UNKNOWN" THAT STUDENTS ARE TO FIND		
JOIN (add/multiply)	**(Result Unknown)** Connie has 5 marbles. Jon gave her 8 more marbles. How many marbles does Connie have?	**(Change Unknown)** Connie has 5 marbles. How many more marbles does she need to have 13 marbles?	**(Start Unknown)** Connie has some marbles. Jon gave her 5 more marbles. Now she has 13 marbles. How many marbles did Connie have to start with?
SEPARATE (subtract/divide)	**(Result Unknown)** Connie had 13 marbles. She gave 5 to Jon. How many marbles does Connie have?	**(Change Unknown)** Connie had 13 marbles. She gave some to Jon. Now she has 5 marbles. How many marbles did Connie give to Jon?	**(Start Unknown)** Connie has some marbles. She gave 5 to Jon. Now she has 8 marbles. How many marbles did Connie have to start with?
PART-PART-WHOLE (fractions/ decimals/ratios/ percents)	**(Whole Unknown)** Connie has 5 red marbles and 8 blue marbles. How many marbles does she have?	**(Part Unknown)** Connie has 13 marbles. Five are red, and the rest are blue. How many blue marbles does Connie have?	
COMPARE	**(Difference Unknown)** Connie has 13 marbles. Jon has 5 marbles. How many more marbles does Connie have than Jon?	**(Compare Quantity Unknown)** Jon has 5 marbles. Connie has 8 more than Jon. How many marbles does Connie have?	**(Reference Unknown)** Connie has 13 marbles. She has 5 more marbles than Jon. How many marbles does Jon have?

The chart was adapted from *Children's Mathematics: Cognitively Guided Instruction* by Carpenter, Fennema, Franke, Levi, & Empson (1999).

Common Missteps. We have observed several missteps over the course of 40-plus years each in this business. But we feel that the Common Core standards—combined with the Math Practices—will help to eliminate many of them. Several are described here:

(1) Teaching isolated math skills. Math is never used in isolation, so why teach it that way? Memorization is mistaken for mastery, as reflected in abysmal test scores. One great example is fractions. Students who are enduring their first exposure to fractions are typically taught or told a series of isolated steps as to how fractions work, followed by several pages of computation with fractions. When we ask students about using fractions in their lives, they can list any number of uses in their daily lives. But when we look at the so-called application problems they are to solve, very few actually relate to their real lives, and NONE require the students to construct meaning by *discovering* how fractions work and making their own real-life connection to the concept. One high school math coordinator gave us the term "naked math," and we have used that now for several years as a way to create an image of what we are trying to avoid. Much like "The Emperor's New Clothes," we fool ourselves when we parade the mastery of basic facts (e.g., scores on the "mad minutes" or timed fact tests) as the mastery of mathematics. Many teachers think that because students master computation in isolation that students are fully "dressed" to carry it over to the problem scenarios and fully capable of applying the appropriate concepts and skills. But it is only when students work with math in the context of real-life situations (like money, measurement, or time) that they truly master the concept, not just memorize the facts alone.

A teacher recently reported that she teaches money and measurement only once during the year because she has so much other content to cover. Surely, measurement, time, and money could be the vehicle to help students see several other concepts such as fractions, decimals, and percents. What is more lifelike than money? Classroom questions must use time, measurement, and money to connect the skills and concepts from previous units or chapters and not merely focus on those just learned.

(2) The lack of consistency between the structure of word problems posed on high-stakes tests and those used on classroom tests. Most textbooks and teacher-made tests ask students to find only the final *RESULT* in a problem. By contrast, the high-stakes tests often present the questions so that students are asked to determine the *CHANGE* or the *START* in a problem. Students should turn problems "inside-out" to show they understand them.

When we review high-stakes tests, we find the skills and concepts detailed in the standards, but they are presented in a context that wraps skills together— much like real life. But when teachers present these same skills and concepts separately, without blending them, students are completely stymied. They give up attempting to solve extended response or short-answer items, thinking that these are things they do not know. If we want our students to do better on high-stakes tests, teachers must include problem situations in their teaching, practice, and assessments that integrate and wrap concepts and skills together. This is what is being done in the Partnership for Assessment of Readiness for College and Careers (PARCC) assessments (e.g., measurement, with geometry and with patterns). Indeed, our classroom assessments need to combine skills rather than measure one skill at a time.

(3)   Trigger Words. Another practice that has become commonplace at the lower grades is to teach students what we call "trigger" words or "signal" words that cue them into what operation is needed to solve a word problem (e.g., how many in all, how many are left). While this practice may be a decent first step, we strongly suggest that teachers wean students away from this crutch. We find that students memorize the "trigger" words, and, without actually comprehending what a problem is asking them to do, jump to the computation too quickly.

(4)   Focus only on the correct answer. Many high-stakes tests don't actually ask for the correct answer but ask students to identify what is needed to solve a problem or explain how to solve the problem. In this case, the process one would use to get the answer shows the thinking involved, and that is the real focus of the question. It is more about thinking through what the problem means than calculating the right answer. Many teachers are uncomfortable with these types of questions, and students are even more reluctant, since they are used to going for THE right answer. The key to finding the solution is being able to think through what a problem asks, not just perform a computation. One example of this in the New Common Core is at Grade 6. Students are to understand division of fractions, not by using the algorithm, but by using manipulatives to show an amount, such as $3\frac{1}{2}$ divided by $\frac{1}{4}$. The key is to use a colored half-circle manipulative to show the seven halves and then use another color showing fourths to illustrate the number of pieces one would have. Yes, the answer is the same as if one used the multiplicative inverse, and so on. But this way, students SEE the concrete result, rather than follow an algorithm that does not make sense. Students see that they have more pieces, but they are smaller!

The previous missteps may be related in part to some teachers' discomfort in teaching mathematics. When we talk with K–6 teachers about their teacher-education coursework, they readily tell us that the primary focus was in the language arts/reading area. Most had one course in mathematics. When teachers are insecure with certain concepts, they fall back on those strategies where they are most comfortable—basic drill with facts and the use of cue or trigger words for problem solving. This is because there are clear rights and wrongs. They are less comfortable with the underlying concepts of problem solving and want to avoid it where they can. The real focus in this process is asking students to explain their thinking so the teacher can determine which concepts they are getting—and not. To remedy this, the most successful strategy we see is having students carry on a conversation inside their heads as they work through the problem. If teachers model this strategy, their students understand what they should be asking themselves as they work problems.

In helping teachers to rethink the manner in which they approach this with students, we offer some samples that can be used to develop students' thinking about what the question asks, rather than doing mindless computation. Teachers must realize that with the first attempts, students will be most comfortable with the problems that yield the *RESULT*. Teachers should start with *RESULT* and then there and show students how to turn the problem inside-out to find *START* and *CHANGE*, too. Students will feel so smart! A Grade 3 example is provided here. After working the problem with the students, the teacher asks them what they are thinking and then to turn the problem around.

> *David grew 12 pea plants; Karen grew 17 pea plants. Write a number sentence to show how to find the total number of plants they grew. [This asks for the RESULT.]*

Turned around, the problem looks as follows:

> *David grew 12 pea plants, and Karen grew some pea plants. Together, David and Karen had 29 pea plants. How many pea plants did Karen have? [This asks for the CHANGE.]*
>
> *David grew some pea plants, and Karen grew some pea plants. Together, they have 29 pea plants. If Karen had 17, how many did David have? [This asks for the START.]*

Additional examples of different problem types appear in Appendix F: Math Problem Solving.

VOCABULARY

The 21st century skills and all of the new academic content standards are absolutely loaded with challenging vocabulary. Plus, the Literacy standards for Science, Social Studies, and technical subjects (including Math) require students to efficiently use domain-specific vocabulary and syntax. For example, a few domain-specific or technical words are:

Science: *adsorption, conductivity, natural selection, mitosis, thermodynamic, zygote . . .*

Social studies: *caucus, democracy, embargo, Manifest Destiny, supply and demand . . .*

Math: *binomial, denominator, greatest common factor, median, sine or cosine. . . .*

English language arts: *allegory, connotation, foreshadowing, protagonist, theme . . .*

In addition, there are the newly minted words in daily language, thanks to 24-hour news cycles and social media. An up-to-date speaking and listening vocabulary—and the ability to comprehend new words in print—are essential to a successful life in the 21st century. Students who shrug off expanding their vocabularies need to be reminded of the Dark Ages and even colonial America. Then, only the few who were educated had access to important information. The average citizen had to rely on the grapevine, carefully controlled by the educated elite, to be "informed."

Currently, America's citizens struggle to obtain truly objective information. So much of our language has become politicized, it is difficult to discern the truth from propaganda. Schools must be the place where students are taught how to obtain, use, and interpret language and to understand when it is and is not biased. This is possible only when students have an up-to-date vocabulary and the ability to determine the likely meaning of language for themselves. The alternative—and this seems to be gaining momentum—is to rely on others to decide what is appropriate, important, reasonable, true, and equitable. Students need to realize that a dependence on others actually diminishes their personal freedom, enslaves them to someone else, and makes them vulnerable to manipulation. The vocabulary requirements of the new standards and the 21st century skills make America's classrooms the perfect crucible in which to distill this important competence.

. . . And from those who REALLY know. . . .

It's clear to any of us who've been in this profession for a while that the vocabulary of today's students is certainly not what it was even a decade ago. And that's due to all sorts of things—students don't read as much, many have very few experiences in travel or excursions, and they participate in practically no substantive conversation. So we have to back-fill vocabulary the best way we can. We need to tell them stories of our own experiences and those about the various cultures in our area. And from those experiences, we need to make a big deal about the language and how it works—synonyms and antonyms, figurative language, roots and affixes, and connotative meanings. They need to know (for example) that contract has two completely separate meanings and that in- and im- may or may not add a negative or opposite to the root. Before the Common Core, playing with the language was something students rarely got to do.

*But we're also expected to expose students to quality fiction and nonfiction that's rich in the language of human experience. And from these we can help students learn to use context clues to make reasonable predictions about what the language means. I realize that many students still can't read the texts word-for-word, but with all this focus on language and how it works, they can access and appreciate all kinds of literature more than ever before.—**Kate Colla, English teacher, Volney-Rogers Middle School, Youngstown City Schools***

The reader may remember we have already made the point that the standards require students to *have experience* with on-level text. This does not mean that students must read and comprehend *every word* of the text. It means that they must be exposed to, experience, interpret, and discuss the text through various accommodations and modifications. To deprive struggling students of material that only the most capable can read fluently deprives them of a sizable share of the literary, technical, and informational texts that have and continue to inform the history of humanity and the culture of the world.

None of us can know every word we encounter, but with purposeful and patient work to build vocabulary knowledge, we can learn to make viable predictions about what unknown words are likely to mean and how they impact the overall piece. To this end, several language tools are available that students can be taught to use. These are described here.

Context. Somehow, some misguided soul decided that the best way to grow a vocabulary was list 10 words on the board (or publish them in a workbook), have students look up and memorize the definitions, and then take a test on Friday—oh, and spell them correctly, while they're at it. But the truth is that people with a strong vocabulary did not memorize it; they developed it in the context of life experiences and making connections between familiar and unfamiliar language. Words have no real meaning out of context, can never really be learned out of context, and thus should *never be taught* out of context. Those idiotic word lists yield about as much growth as grass seed thrown on cement. But using context isn't an automatic skill and cannot be mastered through drill and memorization; it must be learned.

At the outset, it is essential that students understand the concept of "context." What to adults may seem like common sense is often bewildering nonsense for the struggling reader. How well a student "gets it" is easily determined. A few prompts displayed on a wall chart—with space at the bottom to add more examples—could be shown to students.

> *"The bowl games for college football are played in the context of the holiday season."*
>
> *"That snowplow in Florida is weirdly out of context."*
>
> *"The Senator insisted that her comments about tax increases were taken out of context."*

Students who get the concept of context will say things like "surrounded by" or "as part of" or "the background for." To check for understanding, teachers should ask students to give additional examples. They should prompt with one of their own examples, such as, *"On the weekends, my rest and relaxation occurs in the context of running errands and cleaning house."* The students' examples may be a bit literal and not necessarily grammatically correct, but their understanding and finesse will gradually mature with use. Once students can provide their own sentences that correctly illustrate *context*, they can move to the actual application of it in a small paragraph. For example:

> *"I worked all day out in the yard raking leaves. When I came inside, I realized I was not only exhausted, I was famished as well. After eating a triple-decker sandwich and piece of chocolate cake, I felt much better!"*

Students should come up with "hungry" and be able to indicate the surrounding phrases and words that helped determine the meaning of *famished.*

> *"The soldiers crept cautiously down the deserted street, looking warily from side to side. They listened sharply for every sound, suspicious of every movement. It was clear they worried about someone appearing with a gun or a bomb."*

Again, students should come up with "like scared" or "fearfully" and be able to indicate the contextual phrases and words that helped determine the meaning of *warily.* In our professional development, we give teachers sample passages to use in training students to sharpen their context clue skills.

Authors often help the reader by including various context clues such as definition, explanation, synonyms, antonyms, or allusions—just to name a few of the most common. Teachers need to show students examples of these and then show them how to create their own examples. To begin, teachers may use samples such as the following to help students make predictions about what the unknown words may mean.

1. **Definition or explanation:** the author includes a definition or explanation of the unfamiliar word. For example:

   a. The roots of the old cedar tree were **sinewy,** or twisted and knotted like thick rope.

   b. Once it was discovered that the boys had eaten infected meat, they had no choice but to take an **emetic,** or a substance that would cause them to vomit.

2. **Synonym:** the author includes another word that means *the same* as the unfamiliar word. For example:

   a. Many of the farmers or their sons became soldiers, and most of the fields lay **fallow** or unplanted for the entire Civil War.

   b. Newspaper apprentices were easy to spot; their cuffs were always **imbrued** or soaked with printer's ink.

3. **Antonym:** the author includes another word that means *the opposite* of the unfamiliar word. For example:

   a. Rather than being glad he avoided all the hassle, Jonathan now **rued** his decision to skip the concert.

   b. The Senator thought her budget amendment was highly **conciliatory** to the opposition, but they actually perceived it as insulting.

4. **Example:** the author includes an *example* or *illustration* of the unfamiliar word. For example:

   a. Rachel's **metamorphosis** from lab partner to prom date was like the caterpillar who became a beautiful butterfly; Sean could not believe his eyes!

   b. The surface of the cave wall was **glaucous** with tiny mushrooms, as if they were clusters of grapes.

5. Some authors use **allusions** to create a particular *image;* these are mythological, biblical, or famous familiar figures or expressions. For example:

   a. Once a man or woman contracts AIDS, fighting even the common cold becomes a **herculean** task for his or her weakened defenses.

   b. Professor Carter, the man who discovered King Tut's tomb, was indeed the **Indiana Jones** of his day.

   c. Students who want to avoid school fights often find themselves having to **turn the other cheek.**

Of course, students need to *verify* in the dictionary or glossary the hunches they form about the meaning of words using context. There is actually an English Language Arts standard in the Common Core that requires them to do so. But the more practice they get at using context to make viable predictions about word meaning, the more successful they will be. Naturally, they cannot check themselves during a test, but if they have had past successes, it will give them well-founded confidence sufficient not to panic when they cannot use any external aids. As students become more and more successful in using context clues, they will no longer be stymied by dense passages with "tough words"—and that's just one less thing to intimidate the struggling reader!

Multiple Meanings. Since they were in kindergarten, students have been asked to distinguish among multiple meanings. They knew that the word *pass* could mean several things: handing off a football or basketball, going on to the next grade level, one car moving ahead of another, getting into a movie for free, or (when they were older) an old-fashioned synonym for flirting. By looking at the sentence in which the word *pass* was being used—the context—they knew which of the multiple meanings was the right one. To test students' proficiency with multiple meanings—as well as to give them confidence that they really do have command of *context*—teachers may ask students to list the various meanings (contexts) of the following words. For each meaning, students give a personal illustration:

   back   cast   drum   flood   hold   left   letter   part   run   trace   yield

To check for understanding, the teacher may ask students to devise three or four sample sentences for each of the words, each sentence illustrating a different meaning of the word. Unlike conventional multiple meaning worksheets that ask students to mindlessly fill in blanks or circle hidden words, this exercise asks students to construct meaning for themselves.

Once the students are facile with the basic words, they can move to a more mature list:

   account   direct   founder   honor   index   justify

   manipulate   perch   relative   saturate   temper   value

Each of *these* words might appear in any content area. They are the words that appear daily in print and media and impact every aspect of adult life. They can be heard every evening in any one of several network and cable newscasts and commentaries, and they regularly appear in newspapers, magazines, and television scripts. But in isolation, they are limited to their dictionary meaning. Their power is fully derived only from the *context* in which they are used.

Connotations. Another tool to strengthen student vocabulary is to recognize the use of "value" associated with many of the words they will encounter in reading and listening. Even though words are ink strokes on paper, many convey a feeling or tone. Some are negative or critical (such as *skinny* or *miserly*) and others are positive or complimentary (such as *slender* or *prudent*). Still others are neutral, with no intended feeling (such as *thin* or *economical*)). Here again, our friend *context* becomes the determining factor. The neutral sense of a word is its <u>denotation</u>, or dictionary definition. The positive or negative feeling or "attitude" in a word is known as its <u>connotation</u>—either positive or negative. Without context, it is often impossible to tell which is which. Students should see several examples of all three types of words and in various contexts, noting that the "attitude" is not always absolute but rather conditioned by the context. For example, words like *criminal, distasteful, horrific,* and *vermin* are negatively charged, irrespective of their context, and words like *angel, commend, flawless, luxury,* and *personable* typically carry a positive connotation at any time.

But there are other words that could be positive, neutral, or negative all in the same passage, depending entirely on the context in which they are used. For example:

a. **Alliance** is *neutral* when joining forces for a common purpose, *positive* in reference to joining forces against evil but *negative* if talking about a network of drug dealers.

b. **Resistance** is *neutral* in the context of physical fitness, *positive* if avoiding a destructive habit and *negative* when stubbornly refusing to compromise.

c. **Eclipse** is *neutral* in the context of solar and lunar, *positive* when an injured soldier's determination to recover overcomes his pain and *negative* when discovering that red ink has overcome a store's profits.

Students' understanding of "connotation vs. denotation" can be quickly ascertained with a few simple examples. Teachers can begin by explaining that although authors and speakers select words that best communicate their messages, they may also include words and phrases that convey a tone or feeling. For example:

> *"Inside the house, it was warm and toasty. Outside, it was chilly, and the wind was fierce and biting."*

If students understand the tone-feeling thing, they can explain that the author is describing the indoors in a positive way and the outdoors as negative. But what if the sentence read:

> *"Inside the house, it was hot and stuffy. Outside, was cooler and windy, but at least it was fresh air."*

Students who get it about tone and feeling will indicate that the attitude about indoors and outdoors is reversed from the first sentence. Students should be able to distinguish the terms "warm and toasty" from "hot and stuffy." They should see that the former is positive and the latter negative.

In many cases, however, there may be no context clues to help students determine a positive or negative connotation. With enough reading, speaking, and listening experience, students will develop sets of basic comparisons. Teachers are urged to use these basics as often as possible, calling students' attention to them, and asking students if positive or negative "feelings" come to mind. A few of these are shown below in Table 4.2. By the way, a great training exercise is to toss all of them in a hat, and see where teachers place them. This is also an excellent way to review parts of speech and syntax, but the key is not to use only one part of speech. If students can use the words in the table to construct sentences that reflect negative, positive, or neutral connotation, chances are good that they can distinguish among these feelings on a test.

Table 4.2 Connotation/Denotation

The Denotation (or Neutral) is. . . .	A Positive Connotation is. . . .	A Negative Connotation is. . . .
direct	assertive	aggressive
female	lady	babe
drink	sip	slurp
indirect	discrete	evasive
enthusiast	zealot	radical

Word Structure. A final technique to "grow" student vocabulary is to give them practice unlocking the meaning of a word by looking for its roots or affixes. As with parts of speech or syntax, the "word-parts" strategy may not ALWAYS work. But students need to be ready for those occasions when roots or affixes <u>do</u> give clues as to the possible meaning of the word. The following words, taken from the SAT list, illustrate how this might work.

bulbous   *root:* bulb   *affix:* -ous = having
so, *bulbous* suggests having the shape of a bulb; what other *-ous* words can students name? What other words with *bulb* come to mind?

equidistance   *root:* distance   *affix:* equi- = the same
so, *equidistance* suggests having the same distance as something else; what other words. . . . ?

indeterminate   *root:* determine   *affix:* in- = not; -ate = characteristic of
so, *indeterminate* means unable to be determined; what other words. . . . ?

multinational   *root:* nation   *affix:* multi- = many; -al = having to do with
so, *multinational* means having to do with several nations; what other words. . . . ?

premeditation   *root:* meditate   *affix:* pre- = before or prior; -tion = state of
so, *premeditation* is a state of thinking about something ahead of time; what other words. . . . ?

circumnavigate   *root:* navigate   *affix:* circum- = to circle
so, *circumnavigate* means finding one's way around a circular path; what other words. . . . ?

Whenever students encounter words with roots and affixes, it is always good to draw their attention to such words and to give them practice identifying the various parts—and other words with those parts. In addition to becoming facile at decoding unfamiliar words, students use their knowledge of word parts to construct words of their own—some real and some nonsense, for a little whimsy.

This activity not only strengthens word attack skills, it bolsters writing and speaking competence as well. Additional word structure strategies are found in Appendix G: Vocabulary.

DELIVERY STRATEGIES

Several of the best practices are collectively referred to as "delivery strategies." That is, they are an assortment of teaching behaviors or techniques used to convey to students the information they will need to master the standards in the unit plan. However, the best-practice delivery strategies are not a one-way broadcast of information. They are interactive exchanges of information, with students playing an active role in the process. Effective delivery strategies include a specific task performed by students to process the information, internalize it, and construct meaning for themselves. The research is conclusive that when delivery strategies are appropriately matched to the content and cognitive demand of the standards—and then implemented with fidelity—they make a positive difference in student achievement.

. . . And from those who REALLY know. . . .

I learned long ago to match the delivery method I use with the content standard. Actually, I use whatever it takes to reach my students. Sometimes I play a role from the literature to get them engaged with me—the way I'd like to see them engaged with a character in fiction or the author in nonfiction. And I know that the real-life connections I'd try to make for students with The Crucible *in 2012 are not those that worked in 2006 or 2000. It's about adjusting and keeping relevant, while holding students accountable for actually digging into text and determining what the author says. I so appreciate that the Common Core wants students to really analyze text and discover the author's meaning, rather than just breezing over it with an uninformed opinion.—**Al Pompeo, English teacher, East High School, Youngstown City Schools***

What makes a delivery strategy effective and appropriate is that it clearly conveys the intended information and actively engages every student in processing the information to construct meaning. Passive note-taking and mindless worksheets are replaced by active responses to process information, followed by the teacher checking for understanding. From each student's response, teachers can tell what he or she knows, does not yet know, or has misunderstood. A few samples of these active responses are provided here:

- Students analyze completed math problems, written products, physical constructions, and so on to discover (a) IF and WHAT errors are present; (b) how they occurred; (c) how they could be corrected; and (d) how they could have been avoided (or what to do differently next time).

- Each student talks with a partner about a specific prompt (e.g., "Give an example of bartering from your life during the last week"; or "Where might we see an example of mean, median, and mode tomorrow afternoon?") and then jigsaw to compare answers.

- Students signal an answer (with hands) or provide an original example on whiteboards; they then collaborate with a neighbor to come up with a combined answer, followed by joining another pair to compare and contrast their work.

- Students work in twos or threes to devise Level I, II, and III questions about what was read or heard and then exchange them with another team to answer. The developers of the questions evaluate the responses.

- Students create a summary or bulleted list of the information heard or read, highlighting the most important sentence.

- Students identify the author's theme or central idea, and note specific text detail to support it.

- Students work in threes to identify literal detail in a text and make inferences, supported with text detail.

- Student note-taking is structured to coincide with the organizational pattern of the material (e.g., cause-effect; compare-contrast; chronological sequence; how-to) and ask students to create a visual or graphic diagram to illustrate the information. NOTE: This coincides with Literacy Standard RH 5 in Social Studies and Science.

These active student responses are combined with effective *teacher* behaviors to become the delivery strategies that are inserted into each unit plan. A few of the most commonly used strategies are discussed here.

Lecture or Explanation. Also referred to as direct teaching, the lecture is a primarily verbal presentation of information on a particular topic. It typically contains technical and abstract information that is new to the listener/viewer, or it may connect the new information to what is already familiar. The most frequent student response to process the lecture is note-taking. But we recommended that some of the active responses listed previously also be considered. The lecture is considered most effective when it:

1. provides information that students **could not internalize or process on their own**;

2. follows a **logical sequence**, beginning with an introduction to set forth its purpose; presenting three or four clearly identified points, and ending with a summary or set of lead-ins to another segment;

3. follows an **organizational pattern** that "fits" the material (e.g., chronological sequence, compare-contrast, persuasion, narrative) (NOTE: Coincides with Literacy Standard RH 5);

4. is **developmentally appropriate** to the students in terms of:

    (a) language, subject matter, and length (i.e., 10 minutes, max for younger students; 20 minutes max for older students)

    (b) examples and illustrations familiar to the audience (including metaphors and analogies)

    (c) humor, interesting stories, anecdotes, and direct connections to the immediate audience

5. is accompanied by one or more clear, pertinent **visuals or graphics**; and

6. includes a **method to check for understanding** among students, including their direct involvement (e.g., stop frequently to ask questions that check for understanding).

If the lecture is delivered in real time, the speaker can see confusion or lack of understanding on the students' faces as it occurs and make immediate adjustments. Recorded material can be stopped to make similar clarifications or check for understanding.

The newest variation to the conventional lecture is the PowerPoint, accompanied by a handout of the verbatim script and visuals in miniature. Although this is a more convenient, usually colorful, and often animated way to package lecture material, the PowerPoint has several built-in pitfalls that violate the effectiveness criteria for best practices.

1. It typically minimizes or eliminates the "live" interaction between teacher and student.

2. It typically makes students passive participants, since they need not actively tune in to the information—it's printed in the handout.

3. Unless the PowerPoint is actually created by the teacher—increasingly less likely, with hundreds of PowerPoint presentations already developed— it eliminates the need for a teacher to genuinely understand the standards or the content and to adapt the presentation to his or her students' needs.

Demonstration. A classroom demonstration is a performance, modeling, or enactment that provides a concrete illustration of (a) an otherwise abstract concept, idea, or principle or (b) a process, skill, or procedure that students are expected to use or apply. In some cases, students learn best by actually <u>replicating</u> the demonstration themselves (e.g., determining the stress and temperature tolerance for various road surfaces), but in others, the <u>observation</u> of a demonstration is sufficient (e.g., the impact of sound waves on glass).

Students who see, participate in, or replicate a demonstration are provided a direct experience with the concept or process and retain a sensory memory of the event. Students construct meaning from the demonstration by making predictions, then observing what happens, followed by verifying or adjusting their predictions, explaining what occurred, and then drawing viable conclusions.

An effective demonstration is carefully planned to:

1. have an obvious relevance to the concept, idea, or principle from one or more content standards;

2. ensure that all steps are visible to the students;

3. include a role for students to make predictions, observations, record data, and make inferences (e.g., take notes, record key terms, make diagrams or sketches, ask questions);

4. provide a debrief session, including why, cause-effect, what-if, and so on to solidify understanding;

5. conclude with a product submitted by students to reflect their mastery of the concept(s) involved in every subject (e.g., prepare a **summary**; create original Level I, II, and III **questions** to exchange with other students; **sketch** what was observed before and after; draw three viable **conclusions**; develop valid **predictions** about "what would have happened if__" or "Next time, if we ____, then ___" reflecting the adjustment of one or more variables; create sample **math problems** that show___).

A predemonstration session may also be in order. It will introduce the activity, determine what students already know and do not know, and introduce key vocabulary they will need to process what they see. Most importantly, it will offer the chance for students to predict or hypothesize what may happen. However, if the element of surprise is important, this session should be deferred until after the demonstration.

Samples. Sample demonstrations we have seen used successfully include the following:

- warm-cold air masses for weather fronts
- gesture-drawing
- translating a prewrite diagram into a composition
- comparing the volumes of solids to derive formulas
- testifying before a Congressional subcommittee

- using Glo-Germs to help students test which soap is most effective against bacteria
- conducting and compiling the results of surveys for voter registration
- shifting the tone in an essay by adjusting the language
- using carnival games to understand probability

Guided Discussion. A staple of every classroom is the free-form give-and-take classroom discussion. In the free-form discussions, the teacher throws out a prompt, and students respond with spontaneity and enthusiasm. Students may or may not thoughtfully articulate their perceptions, and they may or may not listen respectfully to the opinions of other students (which may indeed be divergent) as part of the live exchange. Albeit informal and unstructured, the spontaneous class discussion has always been and remains an important delivery strategy. Its fallibility is that it often becomes a limited conversation between the teacher and the most verbal students, and nonparticipating students become detached from the process.

A formal variation is the guided discussion. It is a more strategically planned and student-led approach to the exchange of ideas. Instead of being the leader, the teacher is the facilitator, and rather than piping up in a free-form exchange across the classroom, the students work in task teams. At the outset, all of the students are given a common set of details about an interesting topic or incident. Once divided into teams, students are assigned a specific point of view and asked to consider a particular dilemma or quandary relative to the topic or incident. As their discussion draws to a close, each team makes its recommendations for resolution—but from each of their assigned points of view.

For example, suppose a device could be installed in every vehicle that would enable the police to put it into neutral to force it to slow down and come to a stop. It would be used to stop vehicles traveling recklessly and/or at excessive speeds, or it would be used to apprehend those thought to be stolen. Students could consider such a proposal from at least four distinct points of view: the highway patrol, the general public, the American Civil Liberties Union, and the trucking industry. Before assigning each group its perspective, the teacher would set the stage by giving the class 1–2 pages of objective information about the concept. This ensures that all students receive the same background information with equal levels of objectivity. Only after the background information is clarified and understood does the teacher provide a problem-solving prompt and assign students into their respective task groups. The groups then hold their discussions and arrive at their respective solutions. In the example of the automatic shut-off, the prompt might be, "What would be the impact of such a system on society's movement from place to place?" Each team will consider the question from its assigned perspective and compile its recommendations from the information provided all of the teams.

Experience has shown that the activity is most effective when it does not exceed two or three class periods, including the debrief. The impact of guided discussion is in its focus and the fact that students cannot rely on their opinions or extraneous information. Reflective of a 21st century skill, the guided discussion gives students an opportunity to use a specific amount of neutral information to arrive at interpretive consensus. Equally important is the experience of seeing that a common set of data may have multiple interpretations and lends itself to diverse opinions—all of which must be understood and respected. Students cannot learn too early that there is rarely one absolutely unimpeachable right choice; rather, the correct decision is often an amalgam of several perspectives.

A guided discussion is effective if:

1. student groups are as heterogeneous as possible, containing a mix of ability, gender, and ethnicity;

2. the information provided the work teams is objective and free from bias; most importantly, it is provided before the perspective is assigned to prevent students from listening to the information with the bias of their viewpoint;

3. students work only with the information provided; they may not obtain additional information to gain an advantage over the other groups [additional information will be provided later on];

4. students remain consistent with their assigned perspective, regardless of how they feel personally;

5. each team prepares a recommendation (or solution) as per the established guidelines; guidelines comprise a rubric against which to judge the viability of recommendation; and

6. students realize that there are multiple valid (albeit diverse) perspectives on the same issue.

Inquiry/Hypothesizing. Some concepts are best mastered by discovery. That is, students learn by "messing about" with information or physical objects, combining what they know with what they predict or hypothesize, then eliminating what is false—all to arrive at a plausible answer or hypothesis. Students must be shown how to make viable hypotheses and then test them. The learning is not as much about arriving at the correct answer as about the creative and critical thinking that is in the inquiry process. Constructing meaning occurs when students discover what is NOT possible or true as well as what IS.

This is not to encourage wild guessing and wasting time and material resources. The teacher models each step to demonstrate for students how to perform legitimate inquiry, including repeated practice. The inquiry/hypothesizing process begins with asking appropriate questions to narrow the focus, then posing possible solutions, testing the most viable ones, and arriving at a likely answer or solution.

1. The teacher introduces a quandary or discrepant event, and then fields questions from students that will enable them to narrow the possible explanations, discarding the irrelevant information; when they feel they have enough information, students develop hypotheses or predictions about the explanation or solution.

2. Rather than rushing to an answer, the intent is for students to eliminate unlikely solutions by asking key questions and arriving at one that is viable. The testing of the solution involves collecting additional information and applying it to the solution to see if it holds up.

3. The results of the test are recorded, and viable conclusions are drawn, verifying or contradicting the proposed answer to the question. If needed, other solutions are proposed, and the process is repeated.

There are several different types of inquiry or hypothesizing techniques that are divided into two general categories—*real time* and *hypothetical.*

Real Time. These inquiry activities are hands-on, direct manipulation of equipment and events to "see what happens." Their advantage is that the students can actually see the results of their efforts and know immediately what worked or did not.

- **Problem Solving:** Students are presented with a problem to solve, including the constraints about materials they may use and conditions under which they must work. They must identify the underlying concepts involved to generate possible solutions, formulate hypotheses about how each solution might work, and test the most likely.

  Examples:
  o Drop an egg from the roof of a building without its breaking.
  o Devise set of negative and positive consequences to reduce discipline referrals in the high school.
  o Build balsa-wood geometric structures to see which supports the most weight.

- **Invention:** Students use their knowledge about a concept to devise a new application.

Examples:

o Devise a set of cardiovascular exercises for children with diabetes, autism, etc.

o Create a set of metaphors to explain difficult math, science, and social studies concepts.

o Develop a software program that helps students keep track of their grades.

- **Experimental Inquiry:** Students observe a discrepant event or something of interest or curiosity. They then apply rules and concepts they already know as the basis for making inquiries about or explaining the puzzlement. Where possible, they repeat the process or test the hypothesis in a different but related situation.

    Examples:

    o Explain how it could be that a beaker containing 1 cup of water still shows a water level of 1 cup when 100 proof alcohol is added to it.

    o Explain why the peace corps' construction of modern, sanitary, air-conditioned latrines in the fields of a third-world country was a miserable failure.

    o Explain why the number 9 is magical in math.

Hypothetical. These inquiry activities are after-the-fact, indirect speculations of what "might be" or "could have been." They are considered vicarious in that they cannot be tested.

- **Systems Analysis:** Students examine various kinds of systems to predict the effect of altering one or more components, hypothesizing viable scenarios of the altered system.

    Examples:

    o Investigate the impact on the ecosystem of raising the temperature each year by 3° Celsius.

    o Consider the effect of replacing the current income tax structure with a flat tax.

    o Alter various literary elements in a short novel or story to see the impact on the entire piece.

- **Historical Investigation:** Students are presented with an historical or scientific event that has continued to be somewhat controversial. They obtain information about the situation; propose viable alternative explanations about why and/or how; decide on the most viable; and then test it to see if it can be supported or refuted by other available evidence or confirmed facts.

Examples:

o Determine why the sinking of the Lusitania by the Germans may have been the fault of the United States, even though they were not in the war.

o Examine the theories about what wiped out the dinosaurs.

o Investigate the mathematics used by the builders of the pyramids.

- **Hypothetical Problem Solving and Evaluating Options:** Students are presented with hypothetical situations (e.g., "Who was the most influential rock group of the '90s?" OR "What is a viable method to have ended World War II—other than the atom bomb?"), and asked to pose viable options. For options, students may devise and use a rating system (i.e., 5, 4, 3, 2, 1) or a set of evaluation criteria or rubric to arrive at an objective decision.

Examples:

o Suggest ways that the Hindenburg disaster might have been avoided.

o Examine an unfamiliar artifact; attempt to determine how and when it was used and by whom.

o Evaluate five Caldecott winners to determine which had the greatest impact on adolescent behavior and attitudes.

Advance Organizer. By no means a recent discovery, the advance organizer was used by Plato, Jesus, and Homer. Labeled the "advance organizer" in the early 1960s by David Ausubel (1962), this delivery strategy is the process of using a parallel situation or a metaphor to create a *familiar* mindset for the *unfamiliar*.

Ausubel based his rendition on the "hook-and-loop" theory about learning. He advanced that human beings are born with a series of hooks or receptors in their brains that are responsible for helping us process information (or loops) as it comes along. For example, there is a "taste" hook that decides which foods we like and don't, and whenever a new food (loop) comes into the picture, our food hook decides how to respond. There's a "danger" hook that tells us not to touch a hot burner when that loop comes by. And there are all sorts of "learning" hooks that help us generalize from one situation to the next—so we don't have to have things retaught each time a new loop enters the picture. Once we know how to use numbers to determine quantities, whenever a new set of numbers comes our way (the loops), we have a math hook on which to hang it and process the information. Examples of the advance organizer are plentiful in every classroom. Some are listed here.

1. Using a personal timeline (or that of a student's life to this point) with key events placed at strategic intervals helps students understand the idea of a timeline in history. It's also an ideal way to help students discern causation from coincidence. For example, the fact that a student was elected to student council in high school is *causally* related to his or

her having become interested in school politics during the sixth grade. However, it may be purely coincidental that the election came one year after he or she decided to take guitar lessons. In this same way, students can come to understand the timeline for the Civil War and which events prior to that war were causes (e.g., secessionism) and which were coincidental (Lee and Grant were classmates at West Point).

2. Bringing in pictures of the San Francisco earthquakes of 1909 and 1989 as an introduction to earthquake waves and how they are predicted and measured.

3. Using a wad of clay, chopped into small pieces, then recombined to prepare younger students for studying the Conservation of Matter.

4. Bouncing a ball off the wall to introduce radar.

5. Holding an agora (or world market) fair to prepare students for a multicultural unit.

6. Using 2-dimensional shapes to introduce 3-dimensional shapes.

7. Using pennies to begin the teaching of money; then moving to the nickel, the dime, and the quarter—in that order.

8. Helping students understand torque by having them open (old-fashioned) pop bottles.

RECOGNITION AND REINFORCEMENT

Among the best practices considered essential for the operation of an effective classroom are recognition and reinforcement—recognition of effort and reinforcement of performance. In our experience, these are instinctive to many teachers (and administrators) and are thus dispensed appropriately—that is, they are legitimate and sincere, not disingenuous or patronizing. But we have also found in too many classrooms (and principals' offices) a shocking lack of authentic positive feedback. Either there is none at all—the reasons varying from "they don't deserve it" to "I'm too busy" to "I never thought of it"—or it is contrived and phony. What's important is that legitimate, encouraging feedback becomes a habit, a genuine reflex.

However it's defined, this feedback cannot be scripted or robotic. But we have had great success in helping teachers (and principals) develop the habits of recognition and reinforcement by adding at least some of the following to their communication repertoires. As you can see from the samples for teachers in Table 4.3, most of them can be mixed and matched, but they all refer to something specific—some directly and some implicitly. The key is that the recipient connects the recognition or reinforcement with a specific behavior, idea, statement, or action. Generic phrases like "Good Job!" or "Way to Go" are just vacuous noise and signify nothing that the recipient can remember to do again.

Table 4.3   Recognition/Reinforcement Habits for Teachers

To students	To fellow-teachers	To other staff	To parents
for EFFORT			
It was so nice to get a journal from you this week. I knew you could do it.	You set a good example for all of us by calling those parents.	I so appreciate your help and support with Marie.	You've certainly done a great job helping Ross remember his notebook.
You're sure giving probability your very best.	That food drive is certainly taking a bunch of work; good for you.	Thanks! Your idea of a weekly memo will make our jobs so much easier.	Whatever you've been doing has sure improved Arla's willingness to participate.
for SPECIFIC ACCOMPLISHMENTS			
Look what your extra work in writing a numeric expression has accomplished. Now you can translate that to solving for an unknown.	That basket of goodies for parent conferences was so thoughtful. Everyone appreciates your hard work.	It's good of you to clean up these shrubs; it makes the entryway look much nicer.	Those notes you sent me about Inga's homework have really helped me to know how I can help her.
You've sure made great progress on distinguishing observation from inference in your science field notes. That must feel great.	What a great idea to dignify the kids' answers even when they're not quite correct. This is something I wish I could do better.	What a great job scheduling the parent conferences and coordinating the refreshments! Do you hire out?	Bravo to you for supporting our efforts here by giving Jamal jobs at home and holding him accountable. His whole attitude has made a definite turn for the better.

So what about principals? Many of the examples in Table 4.3 can be used by principals as well as teachers. Table 4.4 offers additional examples for principals—both for general recognition and for more specific reinforcement. As shown in the table, the more specific feedback refers to classroom performance. Many of the reinforcements are *private*—and rightly so, to avoid embarrassment for the recipient and to prevent resentment by his or her peers. But some need to be *public* recognitions (carefully so!) to validate teachers' efforts and to strengthen the widespread feeling of competence among the entire staff.

This best practice serves the dual purpose of (a) strengthening each recipient's self-confidence as a learner or teacher and (b) in the collective, establishing the overall culture and tone of a supportive learning community. Minimizing the idea of winners and losers and destructive competition among students and staff promotes an atmosphere of productive civility and mutual respect—the very qualities expected in every 21st century workplace.

Table 4.4   Recognition/Reinforcement Habits for Principals

To students	To teachers	To parents
for EFFORT		
I hear from Mrs. Baker that you've really tried hard on your journal writing.	When I came by your door, I heard a discussion on the second amendment; you've really helped those kids think.	You've certainly followed through on helping Ross with his assignments. We know we can count on you to keep it up.
You're sure working harder in math this term. Keep up the good work.	That food drive certainly took a bunch of work; thanks for going to all that trouble.	That was so good of you to try timeout at home. What a huge difference it has made.
for SPECIFIC ACCOMPLISHMENTS		

In classroom management	In teaching techniques	In differentiation or intervention	In assessment and evaluation
Listing the routine for the period (day) is such a great idea. That way, students know what to do next if they finish early.	Thanks for asking me to look at your Level I, II, and III questions on the Renaissance. These questions should help students secure their footing with the facts, make logical inferences, and think hypothetically as well!	It seemed to work well having three different (in level of difficulty) nonfiction pieces about the 1919 influenza epidemic. All the students could be included in the common discussion and offer a slightly different perspective.	I appreciate the chance to view the blogs created by your students on using statistics to influence public opinion. Nearly all of them captured what you included in the scoring rubric.

CONTINUOUS MONITORING WITH FEEDBACK

It's no surprise that continuous monitoring with feedback has been included on everyone's list of best practices. That research has verified what common sense and experience have shown for years: if we monitor student progress along the way, we (and they) have a specific sense of what has been learned and mis-learned; this provides the opportunity to self-correct or to provide immediate and targeted intervention. This increases every student's chances to master enough content and skill to pass the final test. Although waiting until the end of a unit may be more convenient for teachers, it risks allowing confusion to persist and mistakes to become permanent. Since adults—particularly teachers and school administrators—insist that they be given feedback along the way and the opportunity to self-correct, it seems contradictory (even hypocritical) to deny that same consideration to students.

Since the days of Madeline Hunter (1994), teachers have been urged by reformers to check for understanding among all students and to provide them guided practice to determine their level of proficiency before setting them on their own to work independently. If done in a timely manner, these assessments will also indicate any mis-learning and target students who need intervention. For best results, these monitoring practices should be planned-for within the unit itself.

To that end, each teaching-learning strategy in the unit plan format includes not only the teaching behavior or strategy but also a method by which the students process the information and internalize it to construct meaning for themselves. Each of these student responses is a way to monitor their understanding of the material and mastery of the standards involved.

Let's look more closely at the feedback on student performance. If efforts are made to continuously monitor student performance, equal energy must be expended to give students substantive and timely feedback on their level of mastery. This does not mean the casual "good job" or "great" or "nope" or the oh-so-humiliating "someone else"? Students should be given specific feedback about their performance to affirm the right answers or to correct responses that are incorrect or incomplete. In addition, students need direction on what to do differently to strengthen their understanding of the concept or proficiency with the skill. Table 4.5 displays this dynamic.

Table 4.5 Continuous Monitoring and Feedback

Teaching Strategy		Student Response		Feedback
Model how to write a summary, including complete models, partial models, and flawed models.	⇨	(a) Imitate the original models; (b) complete the partial models; (c) identify the criteria for a complete model; (d) correct the incorrect models; and (e) create an original example.	⇨	"This partial model still has something missing; take a closer look." [and later] "Absolutely right on the corrections; you saw that opinion statement right away!"
Demonstrate a scientific or technical (mathematical) process.	⇨	Draw pictures, take notes, summarize, generate questions about the demonstration; make predictions; hypothesize "what-ifs;" replicate the demonstration; identify causes and effects.	⇨	"I'd never noticed that. The water DID turn a slightly greenish color. Why do you suppose that happened? See if you can find out, and help all of us understand."
Assign a reading.	⇨	Create Level I, II, and III questions to exchange with peers; and then answer the peers' questions.	⇨	"Are you sure you mean this to be a Level II? It has only one answer, and it's fairly literal."
Post five sample math word problems already solved.	⇨	Analyze the solved problems to identify (a) whether the answer obtained is correct; (b) the steps taken by the solver; (c) any computation errors; and (d) an alternative set of steps to take.	⇨	"Good job finding the two problems with the wrong answers; you could see the solver's mistakes and explain how the errors were made. Next time, what should he do? Is there another way?"

The best practice of continuous monitoring and feedback may seem to some readers to be as natural and obvious as breathing. But for many others, it represents a change in habit that will need to be planned for and consciously practiced until it becomes automatic. The key to feedback and monitoring is that they be *timely* (immediate to the moment) and *targeted* (specifying what was right OR the error, and what to do next). In addition, it must be sincere and substantive; phony and contrived remarks are completely counterproductive.

Before leaving continuous monitoring and feedback as a best practice, one particularly damning practice associated with it is the tardy return of papers submitted by students. A few rules of thumb should be applied:

1. If these papers do not provide specific practice/applications to help the teacher monitor student mastery, *do not assign them.*

2. If these papers cannot be returned to students *the next day*—with affirming and correcting feedback, *do not assign them.*

3. If students have no opportunity to relearn what they mis-learned or to have clarified what confused them—*replace those papers* with ones that *will provide such an opportunity.*

If scrupulously followed, these rules of thumb will eliminate such malpractices as "busywork," "punishment tasks," and the ubiquitous "check mark for turning it in."

BASIC ASSUMPTIONS

Every district can easily say they've adopted the Common Core, the new Social Studies and Science standards, and the 21st century skills as their new curriculum. But the actual implementation of this new curriculum in district classrooms must be guided by solid *unit plans* that guide the day-to-day classroom instruction using the standards. For a district staff to truly "own" these units and internalize them as a way to do business, they must be written by the teachers who will use them. These unit plans must be strategically developed to address a specific cluster of related standards and use appropriate best practices and delivery strategies aligned to the content and cognitive demand of those standards. But as helpful as they are, the unit plans are not scripts. They are guides that require competent, caring, and creative teachers to animate them and to engage students to construct meaning for themselves. This animation is powered by several basic assumptions. In fact, the title for this section could have been **"Unit Plans Are Terrific, But They Won't Work Unless. . . ."**

1. Teachers use district-level and classroom-level PERFORMANCE DATA to plan and adjust instruction. This topic is the entire focus of Chapter 5. But its importance cannot be overstated. By "performance data," we think of a three-legged stool: (a) *high-stakes test scores,* since (sadly) they have become the measuring stick for school quality across the nation, and it would be foolish and naive to discount them altogether; (b) the standards-based *classroom unit test*—tied to the specific standards being taught in each unit; and (c) the *authentic or performance test*, requiring students to construct meaning for themselves by completing a real-world task to solve a problem or complete an analysis. All three legs will be more fully discussed in Chapter 5.

> **!** *Lesson Learned*! An important lesson learned from experience has been NOT to over-test. In their zeal to be "data-driven," to make all classroom decisions, many districts fall into this trap. Sadly, they spend more class-room time testing than teaching; students spend more energy responding to test questions than to learning the standards! Interventions are based on test scores, not specific weaknesses in skills and standards. Districts cannot expect to see dramatic improvements in student performance overnight. Students and staff need time to become accustomed to the new course tools and the various trans-formations they have brought to the classroom before high-stakes testing is begun in earnest. And then care must be taken not to over-test. It can become like a carpenter who measures a plank again and again, hoping to make it longer. Districts who are sincere about school reform place greater emphasis on authentic student performance than test results.

2. Each *unit plan* includes several strategies to DIFFERENTIATE INSTRUCTION—for remediation as well as enrichment. This does not mean tracking! Even though it follows the section on using performance data to make instructional decisions, differentiation should not be interpreted as using performance results to track students by ability. In our work with dis-tricts, we have helped them move away from assigning students based on test scores. Instead, we advocate keeping all students together for common learning experiences and then providing for their unique needs *within* the classroom in guided and independent practice, working with small groups as needed. [The exception, of course, is the severely challenged student whose needs are best met in a self-contained setting.]

In developing their unit plans, teachers devise as many whole class activities as possible to establish and maintain a sense of community about the classroom. For a shared experience, it is important that all students hear the same oral readings, view the same videos, and hear the same presentations at the same time. Every student plays an important role in the classroom community—so much so that when anyone is absent, the whole is diminished. And the effective teacher (paying attention to Recognition and Reinforcement) continuously stresses that the class is a seamless whole.

In addition, the effective teacher will explain to the group that there will be times each day (or class period) when some students are called away, sometimes to work with the teacher, sometimes to work with an aide, and sometimes to work with one or more other students. Some of these pairings or groupings are based on student interests, some are chosen at random, some are self-selected, and some are for skill needs. But these skills groupings are temporary and used when appropriate. Like every 21st century community, the intent is to integrate students of every ability, interest, and culture to forge a collective respect and interdependence.

In our training, teachers are shown how to differentiate using the following adjustments, in response to need—irrespective of ability. As shown by the black-white contrast in the descriptors, the first letters of these eight differentiation tools make a clear and simple label for teachers to designate differentiation strategies in their unit plans. In fact, our consultants have begun referring to them as TALLDCaPSS—a silly but familiar moniker to remind teachers of the need to differentiate.

Time. Some students need more time than others to complete a task. This is not to suggest removing all time limits; students need to become good stewards of time and not waste it. It means to extend the time when it is clear that a student is making a legitimate effort and simply needs a few more minutes or an extra day.

Assistance. Some students need more direct assistance to understand what is being taught. This help may come from the teacher, another adult, or a fellow student. The effective teacher will know who these students are and make sure that additional help is provided, albeit discretely, so as not to embarrass them. One frequently used strategy for assistance is additional modeling of the desired tasks and asking students to "show me" or "tell me" in your own words what you need to do.

Length. This refers to the number of a) words in a passage, b) pages, or c) problems a student is assigned at one time. For struggling students, coping with fewer items (or shorter passages) at one time makes particularly good sense—especially when checking for understanding. There is no merit to assigning 20 problems when a student doesn't understand how to do five of them. And it certainly makes no sense to assign several pages of text that is well above a student's reading capacity.

NOTE: As we have previously suggested, the standards require ALL students to experience on-level texts, but they do not mandate that students read the entire text word-for-word. The idea is that every student be exposed to the material and discuss its message and impact. For example, if the class is studying Custer's Last Stand, the text of "The Battle of Little Bighorn: An Eyewitness Account by Lakota Chief Red Horse" is several pages in length and includes some Native American vernacular. Many students would be unable to read the account word-for-word, but all of them can read small sections of text and benefit from paraphrases and summations of other sections prepared by the teacher or more capable readers.

Level of Difficulty. In developing teaching-learning activities for their unit plans, teachers are asked to think of alternate tasks—for example, one more difficult for students who need a challenge and at least one less difficult for students who are struggling.

In addition, the alternate activities may use more and less difficult material. The idea is that all students have a task, the accomplishment of which will lead to mastery of a standard. In the "Little Bighorn" example, the students in need of a challenge may be asked to read the original manuscript—part of which is in Lakotan hieroglyphs. Their processing task might be to prepare a study guide for younger students. The tasks for the struggling students might be to (1) scan the published text, finding images and phrases that suggest the battle and subsequent slaughter were due to several misunderstandings that might have been avoided and (2) to devise Level I, II, and III questions for the rest of the class to answer. In math, this can be driven by the types of numbers students are asked to work with when learning a new concept.

. . . And from those who REALLY know. . . .

*After "unpacking" the new standards, I found them to be rigorous and challenging! Since all students are to experience on-level literature (both fiction and nonfiction), teachers must put together activities that will enable students of all ability levels to enjoy the same high-quality material. My colleagues and I use cross-ability groups to process reading passages. We provide struggling students with coping mechanisms to construct meaning from what they read, even if they cannot manage every word. Armed with key details and core vocabulary, they participate in the analysis conversation as equals with stronger readers. Their self-esteem and feelings of accomplishment have brought their mastery to much higher levels than when they were given only what they could handle.—**Nancy Wanyerka, teacher, Cuyahoga Heights Middle School, Cuyahoga Heights Schools***

Concretes. This adaptation refers to the number of models, demonstrations, simulations, or concrete objects needed by students to comprehend what is being taught. Some students will need more concretes than others, and some will need to revisit concretes again later . . . and then perhaps again. For most adults as well as students, a familiar, concrete example can be referenced again and again to trigger a learned memory. A perfect example is the swastika.

Practice. Just as some students need more concrete examples than others, some students need more practice at applying or using the standards to reach mastery. This first-tier of practice—known as *guided practice*—involves close supervision by the teacher, with immediate, substantive feedback. Following successful guided practice, students are ready for the next tier of practice, or *independent practice*. It is this independent practice that teachers hope will cement student mastery. In addition to more or less, some students will need different kinds of practice.

Structure. To demonstrate mastery of the content standards and to become proficient in the 21st century skills, students must construct meaning for themselves. They cannot fill in blanks or select the correct answer, and they cannot mindlessly reproduce memorized answers or solve the same problems rehearsed in class. To construct meaning is to create an original product. It might be as simple as a letter to the editor or as complicated as conducting an original experiment and preparing an analysis of the data. But the specific structure of the product can be differentiated according to the needs of each student. For example, the letter can be set up as bullet points, or it can be written using the voice of a particular interest group. The original experiment might have only three steps and two variables versus ten steps and multiple variables.

Sophistication. In addition to—or instead of—the structure, another way to differentiate the product is to adjust the level of complexity or sophistication required. As with every adaptation, the key to differentiation of both structure and sophistication is to maintain equity for the effort required. At one extreme, for struggling students, the product cannot be so simple that it completely misses the standard or insults students' self-respect. That extreme yields a counterfeit mastery that will not stand up against legitimate measures. At the other end, the product cannot be so elaborate and complex that is requires far more effort than necessary and yields no greater level of mastery than the product being completed by the rest of the students.

A Warning Note About Technology. While the command of technology is a major focus of both the content standards and the 21st century skills, a word of caution is in order. We are seeing an overemphasis on the "techie" part of the requirements, irrespective of academic standards. Districts are rushing out to purchase all sorts of hardware and apps for this and that—without a direct connection to student learning. Requiring students to create a PowerPoint, a blog, a Glogster, a website, and so on are all very important ways to help them master technology. But teachers must be careful that the technological aspect of the product does not overshadow the standards portion. We have seen situations where more time and effort went into the dazzling visuals and the clever sound effects than the topic being displayed. One example was an impressive PowerPoint that showed an inaccurate way to use probability in winning on the carnival midway—it was simply wrong and had to be contradicted. Another was a clever "Glogster" on how the Egyptian Pyramids were built. Although aesthetically well done, it focused only on the use of the pyramids and had nothing to do with their construction.

. . . And from those who REALLY know. . . .

*Working as a high school inclusion team, we developed unit plans that focused on the differentiation necessary to help all students succeed in mastering the Math standards assigned to a given unit. The key for us was sharing the teaching in a true inclusion team so that students felt they had two people to work with and ask questions of during the class—not that one of us was special ed, and only those students on IEPs would ask that teacher a question. Students viewed us as equals in charge of the class. It was also important to note that we had common planning time to develop the unit plans as a team, and we were able to make adjustments in our teaching from first block to subsequent blocks during a day's lessons. One "aha" for us was when we conducted parent-teacher conferences, parents coming to our table did not know which of us was the special education teacher or the general education teacher, just that their child had identified us as the teachers of the class.—**Kelly Cowan and Brent Baumgartner, Whitmer High School math teachers, Washington Local Schools**

3. Students are provided options or choices. Within each unit, students are provided choices among processes and/or products for the teaching-learning tasks as well as how to show authentic or performance mastery. For example, to show mastery of the U.S. Bill of Rights, students may decide to devise a lesson plan for younger children or write a letter to a cousin in England. They may get the information they need about the carbon dating from reading text or listening to an audio recording. In math, they may show mastery of 2- and 3-dimensional shapes by making pencil drawings or using nets to create and label various objects. To process the concept of irony, students may read several short illustrative snippets, or read a complete story by O'Henry (e.g., "The Gift of the Magi").

But whichever choice they make, students are accountable to execute it with fidelity. At the core of both the new content standards and the 21st century skills is the expectation that students take responsibility for their own learning. It needs to begin in the classroom.

4. Common Core Literacy standards are included in science, social studies, and technical subjects (including math) for Grades 6–12. Until districts examine the Literacy standards (actually housed in the English Language Arts Common Core), there is a tendency to overlook them. But it is clear in the text of the English Language Arts (ELA) standards that the Literacy standards are to be authentically taught in social studies, science, and technical subjects, including math. Since many similarly worded standards are also included in ELA, it is strongly suggested that the four departments coordinate their efforts.

A summary of the Reading Literacy standards is shown in Table 4.6. The Science and Social Studies Reading standards are nearly identical, with a few technical differences. The directions for the Literacy standards make it clear that "text" does not refer to textbooks but to scholarly writing about science and social studies. These standards require students to analyze text in terms of technical language; the author's central ideas, purpose, and evidence (facts, judgments, hypotheses); the rhetorical structure of the piece; the use of quantitative and qualitative information; and the comparison and contrast of information from multiple sources. Many of the Math standards are similar, with the addition of listening to and critiquing peer explanations of reasoning; justifying math reasoning orally and in writing; and representing and interpreting data with and without technology.

For Writing, Table 4.7 shows the writing projects required in the Literacy standards for Science and Social Studies, but it also reflects the writing projects required of students in ELA. Since the Writing Literacy requirements for Social Studies and Science are spread across Grades 6–8, 9–10, and 11 and 12, districts can decide how best to distribute the instruction. But since the ELA standards require these writing projects at *every* grade level, there are obvious reasons to coordinate these efforts.

Table 4.6 Literacy Reading Skills

MATH (Ohio Priorities)	SCIENCE	SOCIAL STUDIES
Learn to read mathematical text.	Locate text evidence to analyze content materials.	Same as Science, but includes primary and secondary sources
Communicate using correct math terminology.	Determine the central ideas and conclusions of content text; provide accurate summary of the text.	Same as Science, but includes primary and secondary sources
Read, discuss, and apply math found in literature, including author's purpose.	Follow multistep procedures to carry out experiments, perform measurements, or to complete technical tasks; analyze the results.	Analyze and evaluate the steps in a procedure; determine where the text leaves matters uncertain.
Listen to and critique peer explanations of reasoning.	Determine the meaning of symbols, key terms, and other domain-specific language.	
Justify mathematical reasoning orally and in writing.	Analyze the rhetorical structure used by an author to organize content text, including relationships among key terms.	Same as Science, but includes adding how a source is structured and how sentences and sections comprise the whole
Represent and interpret data with and without technology.	Analyze an author's purpose, including unresolved issues.	Compare the viewpoints of two or more authors on the same subject, including the comparative evidence cited.
Read appropriate text, providing explanations for mathematical concept, reasoning, or procedures.	Integrate quantitative and qualitative information (including multimedia) to address a question or solve a problem.	Same as Science but includes visual information in print or digital text.
	Distinguish among facts, reasoned judgments, and hypotheses, and examine the validity of an author's claims with corroborating or challenging information.	
	Compare and contrast information from multiple sources; synthesizing information into a coherent understanding and resolving conflicting information when possible.	Same, including primary and secondary sources
	Read and comprehend on-level science, social studies, and technical texts (including math) independently and proficiently.	

Table 4.7 Writing Literacy Standards—Projects or Papers

Grade	Argumentative		Informational		Narrative
6	Sci and/or SS	ELA	Sci and/or SS	ELA	ELA
7		ELA		ELA	ELA
8		ELA		ELA	ELA
9	Sci and/or SS	ELA	Sci and/or SS	ELA	ELA
10		ELA		ELA	ELA
11	Sci and/or SS	ELA	Sci and/or SS	ELA	ELA
12		ELA		ELA	ELA

One example of this coordination is that the content teachers take responsibility for helping students select viable and appropriate topics and collect valid information from approved primary and secondary sources. The ELA teachers can then help students organize the information into the final product—typically a paper. A complete summary of the Writing Literacy standards is shown in Table 4.8.

Table 4.8 Literacy Writing Skills

MATH	SCIENCE	SOCIAL STUDIES
research math topics or related problems	Write "arguments" focused on discipline-specific content [includes specific requirements for claims and support; counterclaims; language, styles, and tone; and viable conclusions]	
apply [details of math] readings and use information found in math texts to support reasoning	Write informative/explanatory texts, including the narration of historical events or scientific procedures and processes [includes specific requirements for organization and structure to develop the topic; valid sources; transitions and sentence structures; language, style, and tone; and a concluding statement]	
develop a "works cited" document for research done to solve a problem	Produce clear and coherent writing appropriate to task, purpose, and audience	
	Strengthen writing by using a writer's checklist and/or rubric	
	Use technology to produce and publish pieces	
	Conduct short as well as more sustained research projects to answer a question or solve a problem	
	Gather relevant information from multiple authoritative primary and secondary sources; integrate the information to maintain a flow of ideas, avoid plagiarism, and follow a standard format (e.g., Modern Language Association or American Psychological Association)	
	Draw information from texts to support analysis, reflection, and research	
	Write routinely over extended time frames for reflection and revision as well as shorter time frames for a range of discipline-specific tasks, purposes, and audiences	

In our work with content teachers, we help them include these Reading and Writing Literacy standards right into their unit plans. We also train the content teachers to provide instruction in and measure student mastery of the Literacy skills. It is clear from these standards that 21st century students are expected to locate and process technical information and to write intelligently about it. This is a significant departure from what has been expected in the past.

. . . And from those who REALLY know. . . .

*We're working with our teachers in small teams or one-on-one—whichever works best for them—to fold these Literacy standards into their Social Studies and Science units. At first, they were very apprehensive and had no idea how to address the Literacy standards. The whole notion of "determining the central idea or conclusions of a text, summarizing the key relationships among the ideas" was so scary to them. But once they showed us the kinds of quality nonfiction pieces they wanted their students to read, we were able to talk through how to go about it. In the first place, the pieces could be short—1 or 2 pages were fine. Secondly, we taught them to annotate the piece, pretending they were the student and had to demonstrate the standard. They learned to identify not every difficult word but only those that were essential to comprehension—and then how to show students the use of context. They learned to distinguish the central ideas from those not as essential. And so on. It's truly become embedded "PD." We're finally realizing that this is something very doable that needs to be a part of our instructional practice!—**Brian Davis, director of Curriculum & Instruction, Washington Local Schools**

---

5. Classroom routines and the pace of lessons are strategically designed to prevent loss of time and promote every student's opportunity to learn. The following principles of effective classroom management have been proven to result in more productivity and student engagement.

a. Time and opportunity are set aside to deal with "logistics" questions to prevent interruption of instructional time.

b. During instructional time, student questions are limited to the lesson and related academic issues. However, this includes questions that take the discussion to a higher level.

c. "Bell work" engages students from the time they enter the room; the bell work is related to the unit and used during the day's lesson—this in contrast to busywork and/or fun activities that are unrelated to the lesson. NOTE: Using items from the state's high-stakes tests as bell work is effective ONLY if the content coincides with the day's lesson or the unit at hand. The structure of these released items is useful for helping students think through how to "unpack them" on the high-stakes tests to answer the questions.

d. The pace of each lesson is slow enough for all students to actually process the information being presented but brisk enough to avoid tedium and allow for off-task disruption.

e. The day's schedule is posted, and students move to the next task with less dependence on the teacher.

f. Time and opportunity are provided to accomplish logistics (e.g., picking up and returning notebooks, calculators, and other hands-on equipment; sharpening pencils; and gathering and putting away supplies).

g. "In" and "Out" boxes are located with easy access for picking up and submitting work.

h. Procedures are in place for students to obtain clarity without interrupting the teacher when he or she is engaged with other students (i.e., "ask 3 before me").

i. Models or exemplars of assigned products are posted.

j. Scoring rubrics for completing tasks are posted and used for readiness and planning products.

k. Private work spaces—but within the eye line of the teacher—are available for students who are distracted by noise or movement.

6. Teachers divide assigned readings into "doable" chunks. On their high-stakes tests, students will typically be required to read fiction and nonfiction passages of 350–500 words (Grades 3–6) and 600–900 words (Grades 7–12). Teachers are encouraged to use these lengths to "chunk" reading assignments, giving students practice negotiating this amount of material in one sitting. At the outset, passages may be shorter than this, but students work up to the desired length across the year. Although the following strategies include team and partner reading, teachers are reminded that *each student* will need to develop the *reading stamina* to focus on the 350–500 and 600–900 word passages, respectively, when taking high-stakes tests. Remember, this stamina may take most of the year to develop and only comes with repeated practice and a sense of success.

Prereading (least to most constructive)

1. The teacher provides an **open outline** for students to fill in as they read; students then use the recorded information to construct meaning (e.g., summarize, paraphrase, develop questions, apply to a real-world context).

2. The teacher asks **guiding questions** (i.e., that represent major topics, terms, ideas, concepts); students jot brief answers as they read, including page numbers; students then use the recorded information to construct meaning (e.g., summarize, paraphrase, develop questions, apply to a real-world context).

3. The teacher previews **key concepts and ideas**—highlighting vocabulary, but in CONTEXT; students record relevant information as they read.

4. The teacher provides **"look-fors,"** or direct references to key concepts and ideas (e.g., look for images of war; look for color words; look for words that get repeated).

During-the-Reading: Options for "DOING" the Reading

1. All students read the **entire text**, taking "process" notes [see Processing activities below].

2. Students are divided into three or four teams, and **each team reads a section** of the text—each student reading a portion; after completing a process activity [see below], students will jigsaw to join the ideas from the separate sections.

3. Students **read in dyads or elbow** partners, each reading to the other, followed by paraphrasing or another assigned task to construct meaning.

4. The **teacher reads aloud sections** of the text, and may invite volunteer students to read portions; variations include whole-class **choral reading**, "row" reading, "boys" or "girls" reading, or other creative clusters that will keep all students focused and not embarrass individual readers. The key to these read-alouds is brevity and emphasis. NOTE: This is NOT to suggest reading large sections of text in class as a substitute for students reading on their own.

During the Reading: Options for "PROCESSING" the Text

1. During oral reading, check for understanding at key intervals (main ideas and supporting details; hunches; predictions or details about characters, setting, plot, theme, tone).

2. Students **take notes** using appropriate **organizational pattern** template.

3. Students complete a **directed reading guide** (DRG). [Note: Effective DRGs have no fill-ins; they require students to construct meaning via higher level questions to predict, infer, conclude, evaluate and justify, and so on. The items focus on key terms, ideas, events, or developments, not minutiae.] The DRGs can be divided among the teams and become the agenda for the jigsaw.

4. Students create a set of **bullet points** to represent what was read; these include some literal information but also interpretations, evaluations, and extensions.

5. Students develop **literal, interpretive, and evaluative questions**; these questions are exchanged with others (teams, triads, dyads, individual students) to be answered, including citations to the text.

Postreading (students. . . .)

1. Create a **monologue** to share with the class.

2. Plan a **talk-show** segment—both the host's questions and the guest's prospective answers.

3. **Devise a directed reading guide** for a section of text; this also makes a good activity for teams and a perfect agenda for the jigsaw.

4. Synthesize a section (or a critique of the entire piece) into a three-minute **"talking head"** for CNN or Fox News.

5. Devise **questions to ask the author** (or a person referred to in the text; e.g., John Adams, Marie Curie); could be extended to become an actual interview and include probable answers.

6. Create the **"top ten reasons for ____"** relative to the text concepts.

7. Prepare a **summary** using the appropriate organizational pattern as the structure.

8. Devise a **real-life scenario** to **illustrate** what has been read, featuring key concepts and ideas (e.g., having read about mitosis and meiosis, the student devises a modern-day scenario using students in the classroom or neighborhood to illustrate forming committees with particular characteristics and equipping them with special tools to accomplish specific tasks).

9. Write an **extension** or **next segment** of what's been read, reflecting an understanding of the written piece and maintaining a consistent voice and viewpoint.

10. Devise and then analyze a **scenario that contains *errors*** (e.g., while the new country is still operating under the Articles of Confederation, we join a tavern bull-session where participants are discussing recent Indian raids and thefts from highway bandits. They have decided to call in the army to restore order.). The objective is to find the error and suggest a workable remedy.

. . . And from those who REALLY know. . . .

I work with students in an alternative school, and getting them to read even the most important fiction and nonfiction texts is a major challenge. So I was really disheartened when I read that the Common Core ELA standards expect students to read on-level texts. But then I learned how to divide the readings into smaller chunks—similar in length to items on high-stakes tests. I also began showing students how to read more actively, such as with a partner, listening to me read aloud, doing some choral reading, and LOOKING for certain details as they read. They may not read the entire text word-for-word, but they will know about and discuss and analyze what is IN the entire text. My students are willing to try as long as the reading tasks are doable and they feel some measure of success. That's more than I saw before, and I can build on that!—Selina Cotton, teacher, University Project Learning Center, Youngstown City Schools

Continuous Assessment to Monitor Results 5

Wouldn't it be wonderful if all students mastered everything they were presented? Every student would come to your class prepared and ready for the on-level curriculum you have to deliver!

Yes, it would be wonderful if every student showed up prepared for the on-level standards. However, we know that some students are not ready, and others are able to do more! Teachers are prepared to teach their grade-level standards, only to discover that the students assigned to their classes have gaps in their learning, making it impossible for them to proceed with on-level standards as planned. Not all students master concepts, skills, and processes at the same rate and on the preordained schedule set forth either by state standards or the district curriculum. That is not news to anyone! But the key is how we determine what students know—and don't—and how we address these learning needs. In this chapter, we will address the assessments needed to continuously monitor student performance relative to the standards. The tools are many and varied. This chapter will address use of high-stakes data, benchmark assessments, and formative and summative assessments. As with the other chapters, we have included specific examples from the Core English Language Arts and Math standards, the state Science and Social Studies standards, and the 21st century skills.

THE USE OF HIGH-STAKES TEST RESULTS AS ENTRY-LEVEL DATA

Definition of High-Stakes Tests

A decade or so ago, the tests referred to as "high-stakes" were standardized achievement tests such as Terra Nova, the Iowa Test, Stanford, and the ACT and SAT precollege tests. These are norm-referenced tests in that they are "normed" using students across the country to determine what is considered on-level achievement. By design, normed tests deliberately sort students into various categories along a standard bell curve, expecting half of the test-takers to score below the 50th percentile. But most state tests are mastery tests—criterion-referenced to state content standards—designed with the expectation that all students can achieve mastery. But to maintain a balance of national and state-level expectations, many districts rely on both norm-referenced and state mastery test results to establish their entry-level data.

High-stakes tests measure an individual student's level of proficiency with content and skills considered essential to his or her grade level in comparison to same-grade students across a state or the country. But fierce debate continues as to the validity of high-stakes tests and how sensibly the results are used.

As the name implies, the impact of these high-stakes tests is considerable. Pedagogically, the results should be used to identify (a) trends and patterns of group achievement across time—not only across the district but within each building and classroom and (b) the strengths and needs of individual students and grade levels. But unfortunately, their political impact has nearly eclipsed their usefulness in the classroom. Based on these scores, individual schools and entire districts are literally "ranked" in terms of their overall effectiveness. These rankings are not only tied to state and federal funding, their publication in local media has resulted in dramatic public reaction, including pressure for vouchers, free tutorial services, and state takeovers. We see far too many cases of school leaders feeling so much pressure about their scores that they actually cheat to get higher results.

Long-term test watcher James Popham (2005) worries that in their efforts to be overarching and representative nationally (or statewide), high-stakes tests are insensitive to the specific curricular priorities of a school or district. Earlier, Robert Marzano (2003b) agreed, seeing high-stakes tests as "indirect" measures (p. 57) of mastery, admitting that they have no intention of being criterion-referenced to the district curriculum. A second of Dr. Popham's concerns is that teachers spend more time teaching to these tests than to the adopted curriculum, thereby compromising even the most thoughtfully developed courses of study. Thus, he fears, these tests are really unhelpful to schools who are counting on them to modify their curricular and instructional programs. Marzano would agree, suggesting that when districts overemphasize high-stakes test results as equivalent to the effectiveness of their curriculum and instructional program, they are like exercise buffs who confuse weight with physical fitness—true, the two are related, but they are not synonymous.

So where does that leave us? The reality is that high-stakes tests are now—and are likely to remain—an integral part of life in America's schools. So while the pundits and politicians debate the worth of tests, their validity, and even their morality, those of us working in schools will need to encourage school leaders to use high-stakes test results to their students' advantage as best we can.

Before long, the norm-referenced tests and state-level tests will be joined by—or in some cases replaced by—national Common Core tests and end-of-course exams based on the new standards. Most likely, they will be mastery tests rather than norm-referenced tests. But they will greatly expand the current assortment of high-stakes test results available to, and perhaps required of, most of the nation's school districts. Going forward, we will refer to both norm-referenced and state tests as high-stakes tests. Another coming change is the opportunity for online testing, including the advantage of instant scoring. This immediacy of test results will allow teachers to provide more timely and targeted corrective help within the school year.

Common Missteps With Data From High-Stakes Tests

Before we discuss HOW to take advantage of high-stakes test results, let's take a look at what **NOT** to do. Over the years, several misuses of high-stakes test scores have become so commonplace, they are often overlooked or, worse, perceived as an acceptable use of data.

- **Use only one year of data at a time.** Because each year brings changes in staffing, materials, and often "the next new thing," many districts dismiss prior years of data as irrelevant. But with the advances in technology, prior years of data and different forms of the tests can be extrapolated to display comparable results in terms of key content standards. This enables district leaders to see any patterns or trends in grade levels and skills that may be predictive of current and even future data. In addition, these data offer strategic points for intervention. There's certainly no need to allow a negative pattern to persist if it can be rectified.

- **Focus only on the overall number of students who achieve a passing score rather than what individual student results might mean.** Because parents, the community, and many state departments of education place so much emphasis on the percent of students who pass and fail, districts may fall into the trap of looking at this summary number as their level of success, rather than examining what students actually know. In doing so, they fail to disaggregate their data by subgroups and skill areas, and thus overlook drilling down to the individual student. Overall group scores—as with single ratings of any kind—mask the granularity of individual skill strengths and needs, the types of errors made, and specific distinctions that comprise achievement gaps among subgroups.

- **Collect data but fail to use it to drive instruction.** Many districts simply "measure and move on." Although it is tempting to feel that "all the slicing and dicing in the world won't raise the scores," the fact remains that behind those scores lay enormous amounts of useful data to be mined. Districts often ask principals to compile data notebooks, and indeed, may even ask teachers to keep a data notebook. But what is done with the volume of paper generated is little more than a cursory review in order to track or tier students. The data are then filed and not used to determine students' instructional needs. Teachers should be shown how and then expected to use these data to make instructional decisions.

- **Place students who fail into Tier III.** In their zeal to comply with Response to Intervention (RTI), many districts place students who fail the high-stakes test into Tier III groups as a nearly permanent assignment. These Tier III students are taught a remedial or below-level set of expectations. Even though they are not identified as special needs, they are rarely expected to master the on-level content standards. Although the defenders of this practice feel it is more humane and less frustrating for lower functioning students, Tier III students are still required to take the high-stakes tests. So the net effect of this tracking is that these students are never prepared with on-level work and practically doomed to fail the on-level tests. This practice is exactly the opposite of what was intended by the RTI tiering of students to determine appropriate instruction. It is the blending of students across tiers that allows for struggling students to see good role models and different ways of thinking about something.

Strategies for Making Better Use of High-Stakes Test Data

Every fall, students come to the classroom without essential learnings in place, and teachers must determine how to help them achieve the greatest success possible. While they wrestle with how to help students master grade-level standards, teachers must also cope with other factors that continue to impact classroom success and contribute to learning gaps, including attendance, discipline, individual education programs, and the contents of 504 plans. However, it is this total picture of the student that helps us know what is needed. California State University's Victoria Bernhardt (2002) has developed several protocols for schools and districts to use in compiling data on their current status and for use in determining school improvement goals. She suggests collecting various types of data on students and the school environment and intersecting the data so planning teams can better see root causes and secondary relationships.

Indeed, looking at specific high-stakes data from various tests, one can garner more quality information about individuals and groups of students in terms of their learning and the gaps that may exist. But it is necessary to look at more than the overall score, or even the subtest scores. The types of errors made and patterns within concepts should also be examined; in addition, comparisons should be made between how the skill is tested and how it is taught. In the area of student achievement, data that inform classroom instruction must be made available to teachers, and teachers must be trained to use the data productively. In our experience, it is not that the content or skills haven't been taught; it is that they are taught one way and assessed another. For example, figurative language at Grade 6 is actually included in three different Core Standards—not just one: Reading Literature, Reading Informational Text, and Language. So it requires multiple contexts for teaching and testing.

RL 6.4. Determine the meaning of words and phrases as they are used in a text, including figurative and connotative meanings; analyze the impact of a specific word choice on meaning and tone. **[would be assessed in FICTION passages]**

RI 6.4. Determine the meaning of words and phrases as they are used in a text, including figurative, connotative, and technical meanings. **[would be assessed in NONFICTION passages]**

L 6.5. Demonstrate understanding of figurative language, word relationships, and nuances in word meanings. **[would be assessed in BOTH fiction and nonfiction passages]**

a. Interpret figures of speech (e.g., personification) in context.

b. Use the relationship between particular words (e.g., cause/effect, part/whole, item/category) to better understand each of the words.

c. Distinguish among the connotations (associations) of words with similar denotations (definitions) (e.g., *stingy, scrimping, economical, unwasteful, thrifty*).

In one of our districts, the high-stakes test questions about figurative language asked students to interpret the meaning of a metaphor in a poem by (a) selecting the phrase that best conveys the meaning and (b) selecting the impact of the metaphor on the tone of the poem. But when the teachers explained how they teach figurative language, they indicated that they give students several examples of figurative devices and have students label or identify what figure of speech was used. In addition, they reported having students use figurative language in their writing. When the teachers analyzed the test results in conjunction with how figurative language was taught, they concluded that they were not taking their teaching to the level required in the standards. They needed to have students interpret figures of speech in context and have students analyze both fiction and nonfiction pieces having figurative language to determine the impact on the tone of the pieces. While it may sound quite simple, it is this level of analysis that allows teachers to determine what students need to be more successful in mastering the standards.

If teachers are to be held accountable for drilling down through this level of analysis, they must be provided the data in a functional format and shown how to make use of it. So let's look at moving from the numbers on the page to analyzing the instruction and providing opportunity for students to address the standards in the true spirit in which they were written. Teachers need to see principals as part of the team in this process, not as the judge on whether teachers are doing the right things for students. Nancy Sharkey and Richard J. Murnane (2003) support this view and offer three recommendations: (1) Provide adequate technology and software to make the *data quickly and simply accessible* to every teacher—both by the student and as class summaries that will help teachers know how to plan more efficiently. (2) Use professional development to *prepare teachers and themselves to interpret the reports* that are generated and to translate them into classroom activities; nothing is more frustrating than to be given a pile of numbers and expected to "do something with them" without any training. (3) Provide adequate time and opportunity for teachers to consider their own students' data and to *work with colleagues* to interpret the reports and to translate the data into classroom applications.

Table 5.1 offers a format to show the precise level of competence in a specific standard for each student in the classroom. It provides an ideal forum for teachers to analyze and discuss test results in the context of their own classroom teaching. By extension, it offers this same granularity for an entire grade level, building, and district. This sample uses the figurative language standards mentioned earlier.

Part I: Looking at the Data is a report compiled by the principal, an instructional coach, or a central office person. The data are clustered in a way that teachers can focus on: the standard, the concepts or skills involved in demonstrating that standard, and the questions that relate to that standard. There is also an elaboration of what the test questions ask students to do and what level of thinking is required. It is important to identify the students who struggled with the questions and the errors they made as well as those students who were successful with the questions. After these analyses, the teacher team reviews and discusses the teaching that has taken place for these standards.

To use ***Part II: Working With Teachers***, the teacher team discusses the results and completes the information requested. They start by looking at where (and how many times) these standards are placed in the district curriculum and pacing guide and what teaching strategies are used with these standards. They

Table 5.1   Part I: Looking at the Data

GRADE LEVEL: 6th		SUBJECT: Reading			
STANDARDS: Figurative language					
RL 6.4. Determine the meaning of words and phrases as they are used in a text, including figurative and connotative meanings; analyze the impact of a specific word choice on meaning and tone. **[would be assessed in FICTION passages]**					
RI 6.4. Determine the meaning of words and phrases as they are used in a text, including figurative, connotative, and technical meanings. **[would be assessed in NONFICTION passages]**					
L 6.5. Demonstrate understanding of figurative language, word relationships, and nuances in word meanings. **[would be assessed in BOTH fiction and nonfiction passages]**					
a. Interpret figures of speech (e.g., personification) in context.					
b. Use the relationship between particular words (e.g., cause/effect, part/whole, item/category) to better understand each of the words.					
c. Distinguish among the connotations (associations) of words with similar denotations (definitions) (e.g., *stingy, scrimping, economical, unwasteful, thrifty*).					
Skills/ Concepts Involved	**What the Test Items Asked Students to Do**	**Level of Difficulty** Literal, interpretive, constructive	**Students Who Are Struggling** (Number indicates the error made)	**Predominant Mistakes** Based on error analysis	**Students Who Are Successful**
Figures of speech Connotative meanings Technical meanings Relationships between words [in analogies]	(1) Interpret the meaning of a metaphor in a poem; select the phrase that best conveys the meaning (2) Select impact of the metaphor on tone of the poem [other test items would address these other parts of the standard]	Interpretive Interpretive	Juanita (1) Mark (1) Terrell (3) Sasheen (2) Brittany (3) Sam (3) Marco (2) Nathan (2)	1. Identified literal meaning 2. Misinterpreted negative connotation as figurative 3. Selected opposite tone (mournful rather than fearful)	Labelle Hailey Lucas Dionne Heather Kami

discuss how students demonstrate mastery and what level of thinking students are to use. Finally, the teachers discuss what is needed going forward to help students attain the level of mastery described in the standards as well as what will be needed to address all levels of RTI, including students with special needs. By outlining these key pieces of information, teachers are writing their plan for going forward in the classroom.

If we want teachers to actually change what they do in the instructional process, they must first articulate what is needed to change understanding for students. There is no substitute for the principal, coach, or central office person to facilitate the conversation and take notes on what is discussed. It is critical that the team develop strategies for what will be done to solve the problem of deficiencies: how will they alter their instruction, making notes directly on the unit plan and/or the curriculum map? Once these ideas are committed to writing, the documents are shared with all teachers who are responsible for implementing the additional instruction that would be needed for a group of students. Next, the team determines how to monitor the implementation, using the principal or other designated person to help teachers hold themselves accountable for changing what happens in classrooms. There will be some areas where professional development is needed to change what we have traditionally done with instruction. Again, the principal or a designated person must be at the professional development, and specific follow-up actions for the teachers involved must be specified. Table 5.2 shows how the dialogue around the data sample above might be captured.

Table 5.2   Part II: Working With Teachers

GRADE LEVEL: 6th				SUBJECT: Reading	
Current Status					
Curriculum Map/Pacing Guide Where in the school year this is taught	**Teaching Strategies Used**	**What Students DO to Demonstrate Mastery**	**Level of Difficulty** Literal, interpretive, constructive	**Going Forward—We Need to . . .** Keep doing what we are doing if a strength; adjust to ___ if an area of weakness	**RTI/Special Needs Students** What changes are needed for students who missed this
1st Quarter; October 4th Quarter; May	Teacher gives several examples of figurative devices; asks students to offer other examples Student expected to USE figurative language in writing	Label device Create examples Use figurative devices in own writing	Literal Constructive Interpretive Constructive	Stop obsessing about label and interpreting out of context Have students analyze fiction and nonfiction for figurative devices (and connotation) to determine impact on the tone of the piece	Use familiar "figures of speech" in sports, the news, songs; help students grasp impact by removing the devices to see how it sounds now. Practice finding tone and connotation in everyday language.

Tables 5.3 and 5.4 display a math example.

Table 5.3 PART I: Looking at the Data

GRADE 6 MATH					
6.NS.3 Fluently add, subtract, multiply, and divide multidigit decimals using the standard algorithm for each operation.					
Skills/ Concepts Involved	What the Test Items Asked Students to Do	Level of Difficulty Literal, interpretive, constructive	Students Who Are Struggling (Number indicates the error made)	Predominant Mistakes Based on error analysis	Students Who Are Successful
Problem solving Computation with decimals Unit cost	**Problem 11** Students are given a table of prices for purchase of multiples of items; student must determine amount of money needed to purchase items that are not multiples of the items listed in the table; students must show or explain their work	Extended response Constructive	Ben (1) Sharon (2) Tyra (2) Amy (1) Jon (1) Ray (1) Tyson (1) Alicia (1) Juan (2) Dennis (3)	This is an extended response item (4 points); students lost points if they did the following: 1. Provided the cost of each item in the table but did not take into account the number of each that was needed 2. Had major flaws in the explanation 3. Provided only an accurate total but showed no work and gave no explanation	Canon Kayleigh Mason Jenna Riley Cooper Megan Trevor
Estimation Problem solving Computation with decimals	**Problem 42** Students are given a unit price and then asked to estimate the approximate cost of buying multiple items at that unit price (e.g., $24.68)	Multiple choice Literal	Ben (2) Sharon (1) Tyra (1) Amy (3) Jon (3)	This is M-C; students missed this question if they did the following: 1. Estimated the cost of one item rather than multiple items 2. Added the cost of one item and the number needed 3. Estimated the cost of one item incorrectly, therefore, estimate for multiples would be incorrect	Canon Kayleigh Mason Jenna Riley Cooper Megan Trevor Ray Tyson Alicia Juan Dennis

Part I: Looking at the Data (Table 5.3) was prepared by the principal from the high-stakes test results, and then the teacher team met to discuss **Part II: Working With Teachers** (Table 5.4) and what is needed for these students going forward. While a teacher cannot go back and reteach standards from the

Table 5.4 PART II: Working With Teachers

Curriculum Map/ Pacing Guide	Current Status		Level of Difficulty	Going Forward—We Need to . . .	RTI Tier II, III, or Special Needs Students
	Teaching Strategies Used	What Students DO to Demonstrate Mastery	Literal, interpretive, constructive	(Keep doing what we are doing if a strength; adjust to ___ if an area of weakness)	What changes are needed
This standard is in the curriculum map for second quarter	Teacher uses SmartBoard to demonstrate how to multiply and divide decimal numbers and decimal numbers with whole numbers; each operation is done separately; students practice computing problems on worksheet. Teacher focuses on placement of decimal point in final answer so students understand the idea of decimal.	Students solve shopping scenario problems where they compute with money (e.g., Joe wants to buy 5 balls that cost $3.99 each; calculate the total spent. Kayleigh needs .5 yards of ribbon to make a bow for her hair. If the ribbon costs $1.99 per yard, how much will she spend?) We use one operation or the other, but not both in the same problem.	Literal—with some application	We need to incorporate two-step problems that require students to use both multiplication and division in the same problem. (Constructive) Students need to use various strategies to solve and explain how they solved problems involving decimals. For example, Becky drove 75 miles in the last hour and a half by driving at a constant speed. Students should be able to compute how many miles in total Becky will drive if she drives for another half hour at the same speed. Becky has driven for an hour and a half already, which is the same as driving for 1.5 hours. So she drove at a speed of 50 miles per hour ($75 \div 1.5 = 50$). If she drives for another half hour, she will have driven for a total of 2 hours ($1.5 + 0.5 = 2$). Therefore, Becky will have driven 100 miles ($50 \times 2 = 100$). We also need to have students practice writing an explanation for how they solved the problem; it can be done with numbers, pictures, and/or words. We have not been focusing on estimation with decimal numbers, especially rounding of money. Students need to round the cost of a single item and estimate the total cost for multiple items.	Use manipulatives or concrete items that work with decimal numbers that are "user friendly"—.25, .5, .75, .33. Make the numbers that students work with "manageable" so that students have a sense of approximately what the potential solution might be. Offer fewer problems and extra time to complete.

previous year, many of the grade/course standards build on what was in previous years, and teachers can use this as an opportunity to remediate skills or concepts that were missed or mislearned. In addition, the Grade 6 teachers should examine what went wrong for their students—by focusing on the "Predominant Mistakes" column—and make adjustments in the current year's instruction to be sure that teaching-learning activities are taken to the level that students need to master the standard.

The level of teacher discussion in *Part II: Working With Teachers* will direct the team to examine instructional practice for what needs to happen in the classroom for the next quarter. Let's say that the teacher team determines that they need to develop problems involving scenarios where students must use multiple operations with decimals. It is essential that the problems used do not cue students as to what operations to use. Students must learn to look for what a problem is asking, rather than looking for cues or key words that "tip them off" as to what is needed to solve the problem. If students learn to think mathematically, they will be better prepared for these types of questions.

Another key is to focus on the correct level of instruction. There may be teachers who are not comfortable working beyond the lower level problems. As a grade-level team, teachers need to discuss the contextual instruction and how that will look, even modeling for each other in the work session what they might do with students in their classes. These team meetings should be held throughout the school year to enable the continuous modification of instruction and assessment, based on previous activities. But at least one or two meetings should definitely occur prior to the start of school to permit the teams to (a) analyze the entry-level or baseline data assembled on the students they will have this school year; (b) examine the standards that will be addressed in the first quarter; and (c) determine what adjustments and modifications they will need to make in their instruction. Then as the other meetings occur, the teacher team can focus on the standards that are coming up in the next quarter.

Reporting of test results varies from state to state, but most indicate the benchmark and/or standard for each item on the test. This permits a drilling down per item to identify the skill or concept being assessed as well as the distractors and what diagnostic information they reveal. By looking at individual student reports as well as grade-level or class reports—all within the context of the standards—teachers gain valuable information on where their students are missing the mark. In one case, we witnessed teachers looking at a measurement question that involved conversion among measurement units. Students were asked to calculate the area of a figure whose measurements were given in feet and convert the final answer to square yards. The error that more than 70% of the students made was in converting square feet to square yards; they knew how to find area. But the mistake they made was using 3 square feet in one square yard rather than 9 square feet in one square yard. This type of information helps a teacher understand where students' thinking has a gap. Indeed, if students really understand area, they understand that it is length times width, and so a square yard would be 3 feet by 3 feet, or 9 square feet. However, if the only thing students understand is the strict linear measure of 3 feet to a yard, they will make the error that these students made. Again, it is about teaching for the deep-level understanding of what area represents rather than being able to use algorithms for quick calculations.

Teachers examine data of the students from past years to determine curriculum areas of strength as well as weakness. This also allows the team to see where, over time, their students have mastered specific standards and where they have struggled. With this level of analysis, the grade-level teams can better align standards in the pacing guide or curriculum map to spend more time where the students were unsuccessful, and less time in the areas of strength.

As the initial or entry-level data are sorted, it is critical that this be done by class clusters that display the scores of the students assigned to each teacher for the coming year. This allows teachers to discover the specific skill strengths and weaknesses of this year's class of students. If these data are then subjected to several deep-level analyses, teachers will have even more granular information to better meet their students' needs (March & Peters, 2007):

- If teachers examine the items missed—and specifically, which distractor was chosen—they can determine the types of errors made and thus gain an insight into instructional needs. The stem and the correct response set forth the concept being assessed, and this allows a comparison between the way the concept was assessed and the way the course tools have suggested it be taught. In addition, careful scrutiny of how students perform on short-answer and extended-response items allows a teacher to see specifically where students need assistance, not only with the concepts and skill of the standard, but also with the level of cognitive demand required for mastery. If students have had exposure to concepts only at a lower, recall level, they are not prepared for higher level questions. Hence, they don't even attempt to answer these more challenging questions when they see them on high-stakes tests.

- If teachers similarly analyze the items with correct answers, they gain insights into what certain clusters of students appear to understand. These strengths can be used as a foundation to remediate weaknesses.

- If teachers examine the scores of the more capable students in comparison to the strugglers, they can identify where both groups missed the point, where both groups did well, and which students need specific remediation and/ or enrichment. One important consideration is that when a majority of more capable students miss a concept, it may well have been mistaught.

- In keeping with the intent of the Response to Intervention (RTI) process, students are assigned to one of three levels for intervention, depending on the severity of their needs. However, these interventions should be skill- or concept-specific and fluid, not permanent assignments as a veiled form of tracking.

Since high-stakes tests are not going away, let's make the most effective use of their results to help our students perform better. Districts often worry more about what is on the test than about how and what they teach! They see little connection between what they teach and what is tested. But lately, several teachers with whom we are working have made a significant discovery about the new standards: "If we teach the new standards and get students to master them at the right level of rigor, our students will do fine on the high-stakes tests!" Yes!—and hooray for their epiphany that the new standards are a great opportunity to renew themselves while they increase their students' academic performance.

But to truly capitalize on the new standards—and the new course tools developed by grade-level teams to implement them—teachers must begin the year with a full picture of their students' high-stakes test scores. Admittedly, students come to each school year with different sets of skills and multiple learning difficulties. But with so much data available on each student's prior test performances, there should be no more mystery about how to differentiate instruction to meet the needs of individual students.

. . . And from those who REALLY know. . . .

*Our district wanted principals to be more engaged with teachers about the data from the high-stakes state tests. We decided that having principals work through the data and have discussions with teachers about areas where students scored poorly as well as areas where the did well was critical to this process—there was no substitute for the dialogue that **took place**. The conversations centered around having teachers determine what the tests were asking students to do, compared to what we were doing instructionally with that standard. The building teams looked at which students did well versus who did not, to see if for a particular standard there were certain students **and how many** missed it, how many of the questions related to a **particular** standard did the students not do well, and what the predominant errors were that students made. **During** these dialogue sessions, teachers talked about where the standard fell in the curriculum map, the materials **and activities** used to teach that standard, as well as the degree of congruence between the test and their own classroom instruction. We had many "a-ha" moments, and our principals were able to lead the process and help teachers determine what additional actions might be needed to overcome areas of weakness.—**Brian Davis, director of Curriculum & Instruction, Washington Local Schools***

DISTRICT BENCHMARK ASSESSMENTS

The purpose of districtwide or common benchmark tests is to monitor student progress toward mastery of a prescribed chunk of the adopted curriculum at a specific point in time. In addition, these assessments indicate how closely the adopted curriculum is being implemented in each classroom. Coordinators of the National Center for Research on Evaluation, Standards, and Student Testing, Joan Herman and Eva Baker (2005) insist that well-designed benchmark assessments can contribute to student learning as well as measure it.

While some districts devise their own quarterly, semester, or annual benchmark tests, many have contracted with online assessment firms for this process. The advantages of using a firm include their access to nationally validated item banks and their production of sophisticated reports to assist with the analysis of their data. Districts who do their own benchmark tests may not have the capacity to generate timely and thorough reports, nor be able to manage longitudinal records of performance trends. In our experience, districts have had mixed results with their benchmark efforts. But from these various successes and missteps have come some valuable lessons.

. . . And from those who REALLY know. . . .

*As a teacher leader in my previous district, our Grades 5–8 math teachers worked with an electronic data management system with validated test items coded to standards. From this item bank, we created our own quarterly benchmark tests aligned to the units taught for a given quarter. The tests were administered to students online, so the data were immediate. The data reports allowed us to analyze how students were doing on individual standards as well as what errors they made so that we knew where we needed to intervene and remediate. Teachers had quarterly meetings to analyze and discuss the data with other teachers at their grade levels as well as analyze results in relation to the units plans taught for a quarter and subsequent opportunities for instruction. Student results allowed teachers to make instructional decisions about revisions to the curriculum maps and unit plans in terms of time spent and strategies used.—**Kelly Dever, coordinator of Achievement and Accountability, Green Local Schools**

FORMATIVE AND SUMMATIVE CLASSROOM ASSESSMENTS

The tests and assessments that have the most direct and immediate impact on teachers are the ones they use to assess student mastery as part of classroom instruction. Even before the terms *formative* and *summative* were in vogue, the most successful classroom teachers continually monitored student performance throughout their instruction on a unit. That's now called **formative** assessment, since it informs the teacher about student mastery at given points and targets any mis-learning or the need to provide enrichment. At the conclusion of the unit or chapter, the effective teacher administers a paper-pencil test and/or requires a performance assessment to determine each student's final or cumulative level of mastery before beginning the next unit. That's now referred to as **summative** assessment, since it represents a summation or summary indication of mastery.

While some districts use common classroom assessments at a grade level or within a course—for quality control and consistency—others allow teachers the flexibility to construct their own tests. Either way is appropriate, but the key is to construct them correctly and to use their results immediately and effectively.

In planning for their formative and summative assessments, each grade-level team must make several important decisions—many of which are made during the clustering and mapping stage:

1. Which standards are best assessed by traditional paper-pencil tests and which are best assessed with an authentic or performance assessment?—and which need to be assessed by BOTH to ensure full mastery?

2. For those standards to be assessed with paper-pencil tests, which would be best assessed with multiple-choice vs. extended or constructed-response items?—and which should be assessed using BOTH types?

The most difficult part of this process is being sure to honor not only the **content** of the standard but—more importantly—the **cognitive demand** as well. Granted, the information in this section is a bit overwhelming! But developing effective formative and summative assessments of the new standards (as well as the 21st century skills) is one of the most important aspects of transforming the curriculum in any district. Overlooked or poorly done, these assessments can undermine the entire process and jeopardize its success—not only in the short run but for years thereafter.

For example, as shown in Table 5.5, a standard on how a poem's form or structure contributes to its meaning appears in most grade levels of the Common Core English language arts standards. At Grade 7, the standard expects students to "Analyze how a drama's or poem's form or structure (e.g., soliloquy or sonnet) contributes to its meaning" (Common Core ELA Grade 7; Reading Literature; RL 7.5; Common Core State Standards Initiative, 2012a).

Table 5.5   Analyze How Structure Contributes to Meaning

"January" by John Updike		
The days are short. The sun a spark Hung thin between The dark and dark. Fat snowy footsteps Track the floor, And parkas pile up Near the door. The river is a frozen place Held still beneath The tree's black lace The sky is low. The wind is gray. The radiator Purrs all day.	1. *Read this poem about January by John Updike. How does the poet's form or structure contribute to his message?*	**Sample Student Response:** The poem uses short lines and one-syllable words. He uses words like *short, dark, thin, snowy, frozen, lack, low,* and *gray;* it "feels" like cold. He uses "wintery" images like the sun as just a *thin spark, snowy footsteps, parkas piled up, a frozen river, held still,* the bare tree described as *black lace,* a *low sky* and *gray wind.* At the very end, is a twist of warmth—*"the radiator purrs all day."*
	2. *How would the "message" be different if the author used longer lines and more adjectives to describe winter? Or what if Mr. Updike used a short story or letter instead of a poem?*	**Sample Student Response:** The longer lines and more adjectives would make the poem longer. It wouldn't communicate the same feeling of cold and bleak. A short story would miss the point. It would have more details and complications that wouldn't be as sudden or quick as this poem. The letter could work if it had the same short, quick images of cold.
	3. *Suppose you were paid to write a poem about your first day in seventh grade? What form would you use? We've studied sonnet, soliloquy, narrative, and ballad so far. Choose one of these and say WHY.*	**Sample Student Response:** I'd use a sonnet because it's only 14 lines, with 10 beats per line and a definite rhyme scheme to follow. I like the idea of 3 quatrains and a 2-line conclusion to develop the theme of being totally blown away that first day. It was a new building, we had to change classes, and I didn't know anyone. I can express my frustration and terror in the first 12 lines and then come back with a surprise twist in the last two! (March & Peters, 2007)

With the old content standards, students read samples of different forms of poetry and drama and discussed the content. What was important was the literary analysis—not the mechanics or structure. With the Common Core English Language Arts standards, there is an equal emphasis on the *format* an author selects and its relationship to the *message* he or she intends to convey. Students must determine the impact of the structure on the message and explain how the same message would come off differently if couched in a different genre. Indeed, the medium is part of the message

FORMATIVE ASSESSMENTS. The most common <u>definition</u> of formative assessment is the interim or interval measure of standards mastery; the most common <u>function</u> of formative assessment is to inform instruction. Put another way, formative assessment is checking for understanding or determining whether and how well a student "gets it"—or *doesn't*. It has become known as "assessment FOR learning" and provides valuable diagnostic information for going forward.

Robert Marzano (2003b) reminds schools that high-stakes tests are *indirect* measures of their district's academic program and that their own local tests should be a *direct* reflection of the taught curriculum. Dylan Wiliam and his colleagues (Leahy, Lyon, Thompson, & Wiliam, 2005) feel that various "fine-grained assessments" should be embedded throughout instruction, blurring the distinction between teaching and assessing. Using questions at different cognitive levels as "range finders," teachers can determine students' understanding and misunderstanding of the content. Although they advocate modeling as a means to establish expectations, Wiliam and his teammates caution teachers not to include in their assessments the exact scenarios, examples, or problems already used in class. Instead, they need to help students construct their own meaning by applying their skills to unrehearsed materials, just as they would face in life. Jay McTighe and Ken O'Connor (2005) also insist that teachers include formative assessments throughout their units to monitor student performance and to provide learners with specific, constructive, and timely feedback. These formative assessments may be informal as well as formal, and their purpose is instructive, not punitive. For the effective teacher, these ongoing assessments also indicate the need to adjust instruction, redivide students into alternate groupings, and/or provide direct intervention. Drawing on this principle of embedded assessment, Larry Ainsworth (2006) urges districts to connect their formative assessments to standards-based instructional methods. His advice includes making sure students receive immediate and specific feedback, that interim or formative tests are aligned with other district and state tests, and that results are used to differentiate instruction. Respected assessment specialist Lorrie Shepard (2005) worries that formative assessment is being "hijacked" by commercial test publishers who develop convenient tests that are taking time away from instruction. Shepard cites the results of several research studies to support such classroom practices as reciprocal teaching, metacognition, the folly of teaching for the test, substantive feedback, eliciting prior knowledge, sharing performance criteria (a.k.a. rubrics) in advance of students doing the work, the importance of extending meaning, and the impact of student self-assessment. Assessment expert Jan Chappuis (2005) agrees with

Shepard about the importance of students using the results of formative assessments to self-monitor and self-correct. This promotes student ownership and higher levels of engagement.

Formative assessment can be oral questions, the observation of student work, a pop quiz, a 1:1 conversation, or a written test. In many cases, teachers preassess students at the outset of a new unit to determine what they already know—and don't know. This permits a more sensible use of instructional time going forward and enables differentiation from the outset.

During the unit, teachers continually assess students' progress toward mastery. With some standards, formative assessments test each student's gradual progress toward mastery. But in many cases, the formative assessment actually tests lead-up or enabling skills as *requisites* to the actual standard. It is mastery of these enabling skills that leads to mastery of the actual standard. Here is a sample Grade 2 Math standard from the Common Core:

> 2. MD.10   Draw a picture graph and a bar graph (with single-unit scale) to represent a data set with up to four categories. Solve simple put-together, take-apart, and compare problems using information presented in a bar graph.
>
> The enabling skills would be picture graphs (what they are and how they are used), including the single unit scale; bar graphs (what they are and how they are used—and the fact that both graphs can be used to display the same information); data sets with up to four categories; "put-together" problems; "take-apart" problems; and "compare" problems. By the end of the instruction, students will be expected to pull together these enablers to demonstrate mastery of the entire standard.

Throughout the unit, teachers continually assess students' progress toward mastery of unit standards. If students cannot apply the skill or concept to an unfamiliar but real-world scenario, problem, or situation, they really have not mastered it—and by "mastery," we mean they can apply the skill or concept independently. But with the Common Core standards being so much more complex than prior standards, their mastery requires an integration of skills and deeper-level thinking than before. Here's an example. Formerly in Ohio, each literary element had its own standard and, hence, would be assessed alone. In addition, most required fairly low levels of cognitive demand, requiring one and sometimes two steps for mastery. Look at the 2002 Grade 6 standards here:

> R.6.1. Analyze the techniques authors use to describe characters including narrator or other character's point of view; character's own thoughts, words, or actions.
>
> R.6.2. Identify the features of setting, and explain their importance in literary text.
>
> R.6.3. Identify the main and minor events of the plot, and explain how each incident gives rise to the next.
>
> R.6.5. Identify recurring themes, patterns, and symbols found in literature from different eras and cultures.

The comparable Common Core standard is considerably more complex:

> RL 6.5. Analyze how a particular sentence, chapter, scene, or stanza fits into the overall structure of a text and contributes to the development of the theme, setting, or plot.

The Common Core standard *integrates* the literary elements, asking students to analyze an *intact work* in terms of how the author's structure actually develops the literary elements to make the whole. Note that it does not include characterization per se, but its mastery will require the student to take characterization into account. The formative assessments would involve each literary element, but they would also need to involve dealing with the overall structure of a piece and how that structure or pattern brings the elements together to communicate the author's overall message. In keeping with the researchers' and our own recommendation that the formative assessments include new and authentic pieces of literature—just as would be required of students in real life—formative assessment should ask students to apply the entire standard in a different context.

Summative Assessments. In contrast to formative assessments, summative assessments are the final or end-of-unit measures of mastery. If formative testing is wet clay—to be reshaped and reconfigured as needed—then summative assessments are baked clay, or considered as finished. The intent of summative tests is a final measure of mastery at the conclusion of a specified interval of instruction. In the current vernacular, summative assessments are referred to as assessments OF learning. Typically, these are cumulative tests that are given at the end of a unit. However, some districts administer end-of-quarter benchmark assessments.

Summative assessments typically take two forms. One form is *the traditional paper-pencil test and the second is the performance or authentic* assessment. The technical and structural details of both will be further discussed later in this chapter.

Dylan Wiliam and his colleagues (Leahy, Lyon, Thompson, & Wiliam, 2005) feel summative assessments are a matter of quality assurance—a verification of mastery. They also suggest that teachers make certain students fully understand the criteria for mastery from the outset. Jay McTighe and Ken O'Connor (2005) feel classroom assessments fall into three categories—summative, diagnostic, and formative. Teachers should use summative assessments to frame meaningful performance goals, show criteria and models in advance, encourage self-assessment and goal-setting, and allow new evidence of achievement to replace old evidence. Lynn Olson (2005) summarizes the comments made by keynote speakers at the 2005 Invitational Conference on Assessments, sponsored by Educational Testing Service (ETS). She indicates that President of ETS, Kurt Langraf, is convinced that teachers use assessments as an accountability hammer rather than a diagnostic tool to strengthen student learning. Other specialists at the conference included James Pellegrino, Susanna Navarro, Charlotte Danielson, and Lorrie Shepard. Essentially, they agree with Langraf, fearing that teachers see assessment as the means to grade and classify students rather than to determine what they know and what they still need to know. They all agree that teachers need professional development around how to construct and analyze tests for themselves. In so doing, teachers are more aware of what the standards expect and how to better-align their instruction accordingly. Lorrie Shepard (2005) insists that valid summative assessments—while they focus on the standards—also elicit prior knowledge, assess the students' capacity to extend meaning, test the level of transferred knowledge, and ask the student to self-assess.

COMMON MISSTEPS IN ASSESSMENT

Benchmark Test Missteps. While benchmark testing is a focus in many districts, there are some common pitfalls that we have observed as people attempt to integrate this component into their assessment programs.

• *Testing occurs too frequently.* Determining when to administer benchmark tests is a major decision that a district must make. However, sometimes it is made with little thought as to what other testing is occurring simultaneously. Indeed, with assessments such as DIBELS, Rigby, state-level diagnostic tests, unit tests, high-stakes tests, and now a benchmark test, what time is actually left for teaching?

• *Selection of test items is haphazard, and items are often invalid.* This misstep is three-pronged. *First Issue:* As mentioned earlier, many districts have contracted with assessment companies who have purchased validated test item banks. Because the items are coded to a standard, many districts assume they automatically match both the *content* and *cognitive demand* of the standards. When the items are below the cognitive level of the standard, the district gets a false positive of their students' level of readiness because the items are easier than those on the high-stakes tests. For example, a popular item selected for Grade 5 Reading benchmark tests is to give students a sentence that contains an unfamiliar word in italics—but that is contextually rich. The prompt asks students to identify the most likely definition for the unfamiliar word from among four synonyms. The students are not actually required to use and/or identify the context clue(s) involved. But the Common Core standards for Grade 5 Reading (actually, there are two in the Grade 5 Language strand) expect students to use context clues (such as cause-effect and compare-contrast) to determine the meaning of words and phrases. In addition, students are to use context to interpret figurative language. The fact that students are now expected to use context within passages—not single sentences and not for targeted words—makes the test items described earlier out of sync.

This is not always the fault of the assessment company; it may be the selection of easier items by the district. Those developing the benchmark tests must be trained to analyze the potential test items to assure alignment to the standard being measured. Some of these items may be appropriate for **formative assessment** to determine if students have certain enabling skills, but not appropriate for the **summative** or the final benchmark tests.

Second Issue: When selecting items from an item bank, there may be multiple items for a particular standard; in many cases, these items are variations of the same question, and if districts are not careful, the same question is asked three or four times with the names and/or numbers changed. For example, *"Jane had 8 marbles, and some were given to her. She now has 11. How many were given to Jane?"* followed by *"Jim had 3 trading cards, and Frank gave him some others. He now has 11, how many did Frank give to Jim?"*

Third Issue: When some staffs write their own benchmark tests, they use items previously used on end-of-unit tests. When districts do this, they are not measuring whether students truly understand the concept being assessed, but rather if students can answer a set of questions or solve a specific type of problem that has been "rehearsed." They know only that the students can do this one thing. When districts write their own tests, we see failure to observe rules of valid test construction.

- ***The benchmark assessment is not coordinated with other events taking place in the district.*** Coordination of benchmark assessments is frequently left to individual departments without regard for the schedule of other departments. Problems arise when all of the teachers need to use the computer lab for their testing, and they cannot all get into the lab at the times needed. Giving separate tests in all of the subjects is not only a challenge for the teachers—taking time away from instruction—it can create in students "test weariness." They simply do not care or are too tired to try.

- ***A major issue reported by teachers is that students simply are not motivated on these benchmark assessments.*** Many teachers have reported that while benchmark assessments are important to the adults in the district, the students "frankly don't care!" In response, teachers have sought methods to get students motivated to participate with integrity. Some have offered "points" for effort on these assessments, while others have offered students other perks such as a free homework pass or opportunity to have some "down time" later. While this feels like bribery, students must have an incentive to do their best work. The trick becomes finding what that will be. We caution against giving "points" that count toward the grade, as the grade needs to represent *mastery* not *compliance.* This is a difficult issue, to say the least; as with all high-stakes tests, the results of benchmark tests are far more important to adults and the school community than they are to the students.

Formative and Summative Assessment Missteps. Although the objective in using formative assessments is to determine what students know and do not know about specific standards just taught, there are some pitfalls that threaten the effectiveness of formative assessments. By contrast, summative assessments are to assess as much of the unit content, concepts, and skills as possible. Developers must be strategically selective and choose items that generalize to the entire array of standards in a unit. As with formative assessments, there are pitfalls in summative assessments as well.

- *"Grading" formative assessments.* Remember, these assessments are to check for understanding, not to determine mastery. If grades are attached to doing well and/or doing poorly, students will misunderstand the intent of the formative measures and perceive them as actual tests. The intent is for students to indicate where they are on the learning continuum.

- *Overtesting.* At times, districts become so zealous about formative assessments and collecting data, they actually test too much. In fact, they spend more class time testing than teaching. The cycle of assess > teach > assess > reteach > reassess becomes so continuous that little or no new learning can occur. Worse, there is no opportunity for students to actually USE what they have learned or apply their skills to problem solving or other life-related tasks.

- *Using the same scenario or material to check for understanding as was used in the direct teaching for both formative and summative assessments.* If formative and summative assessments are to be legitimate, they must use scenarios, texts, or problems that are new and unfamiliar—NOT those used in the unit instruction. Understanding is demonstrated only when students apply what they have learned to new situations or problems.

- *A lack of congruence among the standard, the method of teaching, and the assessment prompt.* Without careful planning, many teachers fall into the trap of teaching the standard according to the instructor's manual or their own personal preference without regard for the cognitive demand of the standard or the method of assessment. There must be congruence between the way a concept or skill is *assessed* and the way it is *taught* for both formative and summative assessments. For example, look at these standards from Grade 9 English Language Arts and Social Studies Literacy.

RL 9.6 Analyze a particular point of view or cultural experience reflected in a work of literature from outside the United States, drawing on a wide reading of world literature.

Literacy Standard for Social Studies: RH 9.6. Compare the point of view of two or more authors for how they treat the same or similar topics, including which details they include and emphasize in their respective accounts.

Table 5.6 shows lack of congruence, while Table 5.7 shows congruence.

Table 5.6 Lack of Congruence

Teaching Method	Assessment
Teacher gives students passages; students identify 1st or 3rd person point of view.	Students are given excerpts from the anthology and asked to identify 1st or 3rd person point of view.
Students determine the impact of changing point of view from 1st to 3rd person.	Students are given short-answer prompt to compare 3rd person with 1st person in the case of a car accident.
Students identify the impact of culture on a character's viewpoint.	

Table 5.7 Congruence

Teaching Method	Assessment
Teacher explains that point of view is no longer about 1st and 3rd person; with the new curriculum, it's more about viewpoint.	Students are given an excerpt from two essays about the origins of the Israeli-Palestinian conflict, one by an Israeli and one by a Palestinian author. The test prompt asks students to analyze the piece to suggest how the authors' own cultural perspective may have impacted his or her work.
Teacher gives students brief passages from world literature (Europe, Africa, the Mideast, Asia, and South America) and helps them relate the author's perspective in the literature to the culture in which he or she lives.	
Students practice identifying text details that reflect cultural distinctions and hypothesize the impact on the authors' thinking.	
Students try to decide how a text written in Scandinavia might be different if written by a citizen of Chile, etc.	
Teacher helps students consider the respective impacts of different world authors and genres on U.S. literature—past and present.	

Clearly, the point of view in the ELA standard is *viewpoint*—not 1st and 3rd person. Secondly, the ELA standard speaks to the impact of culture on writing and specifically requires students to experience world literature. The Literacy standard calls for two authors and implies comparison. The teaching methods shown and the assessments are both discrepant from the standards, and culture is not assessed at all.

With the development of course tools as described in previous chapters, grade-level teams will have made sure this lack of congruence does not happen. The teaching methods for each unit will be strategically congruent with the unit standards, and the formative assessments—observations, quizzes, and paper-pencil—will be accurate and valid measures of the content as well as the cognitive demand of the unit standards.

- *Too many items—too long a test for both formative and summative assessments.* In an effort to be thorough, some districts give too many of the same problems or redundant test questions just for additional points. Psychometricians tell us that to achieve a valid measure of a standard, one must use a minimum of three items (ideally, five). Since time may not permit assessing *every* standard in the unit with three different items, developers should take care to focus on those standards that are the most important and the most likely to be needed in subsequent units.

- *All of the items for one concept are clustered together on the formative or summative assessment.* Test-makers tell us that test items measuring the same concept should *not* be clustered together for two reasons: (a) if they are too similar they may actually "contaminate" each other and give away the answers, and (b) students stop paying attention to what is being asked by the item and answer them all the same way—even if there are differences in the stem. On commercial and high-stakes tests, items related to a standard are distributed throughout the test. This *does not mean* that when several questions are asked about the same passage or graphic that they are spread around the test, but rather that several questions are asked about multiple passages. Questions that deal with a single passage or graphic should be clustered near it—and with as few as possible turns of the page.

- *The constructed-response items are all placed at the end of the test.* This is probably true more for summative assessments rather than formative assessments. Although it is more convenient—especially with online scoring for multiple-choice and hand-scoring for essays—the short-answer and extended-response items should be mixed throughout the test. Students who experience test fatigue rarely have the stamina to tackle any essays when they are placed at the end of the test.

- *The summative assessments are all paper-pencil, with no authentic or performance assessments.* Although the performance or authentic assessments take more planning to develop and to grade, leaving them out of summative assessment is a mistake. Nearly all of the new Common Core standards in Math and English Language Arts, the 21st century skills, and many of the new Science and Social Studies standards are performance-based. That is, their independent mastery is most fully demonstrated by a constructive task or series of tasks used in solving real-life problems.

Again, with the careful development of the course tools for each subject and grade level, the work teams will have developed formative and summative assessments that are congruent with the standards in each unit. In total, all of the assessments for each unit will be accurate and valid measures of the content as well as the cognitive demand of the standards.

One mystery that continues to bedevil teachers is the "disappearing standard." Even when a standard has been thoroughly taught, and students have shown mastery on quizzes or tests, on the high-stakes test, they fail to use it successfully. In our experience, this is because the students have only been asked to fill in blanks or select from multiple choices rather than to actually use the standard in an authentic or real-world situation. Moreover, teachers tend to assess one process at a time (e.g., one type of math problem at a time; one type of sentence), while high-stakes tests mix up their test items, requiring students to determine which of several processes they must use.

STRATEGIES FOR MAKING BETTER USE OF ASSESSMENT RESULTS

While many districts struggle with the issues outlined in the missteps, some are having a great deal of success with their assessment efforts. Coordinators of the National Center for Research on Evaluation, Standards, and Student Testing, Joan Herman and Eva Baker (2005) offer several recommendations if assessments are to be effectively constructed and the results actually used to improve student performance. The following features characterize effective assessment efforts and serve to guide the process forward:

- **There is alignment between the tests and what is taught in class-rooms.** Although an end-of-year benchmark test should include a valid sampling of all the content taught across all four quarters, quarterly or midyear tests should reflect only the content taught within those respective time frames. The benchmark assessments reflect the curriculum—not the reverse.

- **The items included—even if they are from nationally validated item banks—accurately measure the content and the cognitive demand of the standards.** Even though the items are nationally validated, it is necessary to examine them to be sure they are a strong content and cognitive match to the standards. Finally, the developers use valid test construction techniques to ensure the diagnostic value of the tests. When tests are validly constructed, the wrong answers (in multiple choice) and missing points (in extended response) tell teachers where students are making mistakes, allowing for intervention to address specific needs.

- **The scheduling of the benchmark assessments is coordinated with other major activities in the district to minimize their disruptive impact and thus enhance their effectiveness.** If tests in the four core contents are to be taken on the same set of computers, careful scheduling is essential. In addition, the schedule must be practical and "student-friendly" to prevent students from becoming oversaturated and test-weary, which may negatively impact the results.

- **The time spent testing is not excessive to interfere with instruction.** Careful scrutiny of the testing and teaching schedules is needed to ensure that only the *necessary* tests are administered and that they are *not redundant* (e.g., a unit test given the week before a quarterly benchmark test measuring much of the same content). In addition, the results should be immediately available for use by teachers to adjust instruction. Central office and building-level coordination make sure that the placement and timing of every test is part of a larger plan, and the testing augments rather than interferes with teaching.

- **In addition to measuring student performance, a major purpose of the assessments is to monitor the implementation of the adopted curriculum.** The primary purpose of assessment is to measure student performance. But these tests also allow principals, coaches, and curriculum staff to determine the degree to which the adopted curriculum is being implemented with fidelity and to pinpoint schools and classrooms where this is not the case. Indeed, through their review of each teacher's weekly planning, principals, coaches, and curriculum staff ensure that the curriculum maps and unit plans are being followed; and through time spent in the classrooms, they also determine the quality of instruction—all of which are further validated in students' test results.

- **The data from these assessments are used to make instructional decisions.** The timely and standard-specific review of the data from these assessments helps grade-level and content teams compare students' test performance with the content addressed, the type of instruction, and the practice provided in the classroom. These deliberations are also the foundation of annual revisions and edits to the course tools.

- **The assessments are workable for all students.** Districts that are successful with assessments maximize the fairness of the tests by making them accessible to students with special needs and students for whom English is not their primary language. All students are given a fair opportunity to demonstrate their learning.

- **Meta-analysis:** As they develop formative and summative assessments for each unit plan, developers are encouraged to plan time for students and the teacher to carefully review the results as a form of meta-analysis. Students need an opportunity to review their graded tests (both traditional and performance or authentic) to see both their mistakes and their successes and to reflect on any patterns that may help them on subsequent assessments. Teachers will have provided substantive and timely feedback on students' work to reinforce what they are doing well and to give them direction for improvement and growth. This activity also links directly with the students' review of their own goals, both during the unit and at its completion. And with the pilot of the units and the collection of "green ink," the overall quality of each unit—both the delivery strategies and the assessments—will be considerably stronger.

. . . And from those who REALLY know. . . .

Although we administrators always insist that teachers use test results to adjust instruction, we don't always provide what they need to do that. Just giving them tables of scores isn't enough. I found a system that reports test results by the concept tested as well as individual items. For example, for the concept of measures of central tendency: mean/median/mode, suppose there were several test items. With the right kinds of reports, teachers will know not just that 18 of the 25 students failed to master the entire concept, but that 22 of the 25 scored well on mean—plus, which 8 students missed median, and which 11 missed mode. Better yet, we know what type of error each student made! This level of granularity is absolutely necessary to determine not only what each teacher needs to do but where an entire grade level needs to revamp that grade's curriculum. And if the concept is also weak in the grades prior to and following (say in every school), it's my job to see that it becomes a districtwide priority. I was able to bring grade-level teams together to examine quarterly test results in just such detail. That enabled us to make adjustments at each grade level and in those classrooms where there was a specific need.

*But even more importantly, the system we used enabled the teachers to select test items that were truly aligned with the standards—not just in content but in cognitive demand as well. Trust me; every superintendent knows the pain of having to report poor test results to a board and to the citizens. But with so many item banks now available, there's no longer any need to alibi that the tests don't match the curriculum. In fact, if students are being tested with items that aren't aligned with the standards, and if the standards aren't used to drive classroom instruction, THAT superintendent will know REAL pain.—**Walter Davis, superintendent, Woodridge Local Schools**

DESIGN OF ASSESSMENTS: TRADITIONAL TESTS AND AUTHENTIC ASSESSMENTS

The design of valid, standards-based test items—both traditional paper-pencil and authentic or performance-based—is based on several key points. For benchmark, formative, and summative assessments, the design can well mean the difference between valid results and undetected testing errors. If left uncorrected, flaws in test design or construction will compromise a district's assessment results from the outset and continue to jeopardize the validity of reports and interventions thereafter.

Years ago, teacher-training programs included test construction as one of the required courses to graduate. That requirement has been all but dropped. Most people justify its removal with the advent of electronic test item banks and the fact that the textbook companies now publish their own tests. In essence, the industry has attempted to "teacher-proof" the assessment process. But in so doing, they have effectively removed from the equation the people who make the most important contributions to student success—or failure. In our experience, this is an enormous mistake. Although we realize that nationally validated test banks may provide far more valid assessment items than the average teacher can develop, teachers are still the ones who select the test items from these banks. Thus, they need to know the rudiments of good test construction to be able to select—as well as develop—validly constructed items that assess not only the content but also the cognitive demand of the standards.

The other key point is the number of standards assessed at once. Testing experts advocate that **for each standard assessed, students should be given three to five test items**. When district development teams want the tests to be no longer than a class period, it limits the number of standards that can be included on one test. Including too many standards on one test forces districts to limit the number of test items per standard to one or two, weakening the test's validity and diminishing the students' opportunity to show mastery.

. . . And from those who REALLY know. . . .

For too long, we assumed that teachers knew how to create valid test items and were regularly doing so. But the closer we've looked at the tests they create, the new standards, and the structure of the new high-stakes tests, the more we know we need to rethink things. For example, I knew we needed to actually show teachers how to develop valid 2- and 4-point constructed items. [That's what the state uses.] So we provided [professional development] on test construction and test interpretation—particularly aligned to the content standards. Actually, we embedded the work right into the construction of the classroom tests. Working in grade-level teams, teachers developed common unit assessments to go with each of their common unit plans. We gave teachers templates for the 2- and the 4-point items, based on the test items from the state achievement test. We also showed them how to model the correct answers for the students, provide partially complete answers for the students to correct, and ways to help students determine what the prompt is asking and how to supply each part. As part of the scoring, teachers are expected to perform item analyses to pinpoint each student's precise error and determine what remediation is in order. Our principals were included in the training, expected to oversee the implementation of these grade-level tests and to facilitate the interpretation of the results. That has invested the process with an importance that otherwise may have been overlooked.— **Lora Garrett, former director of Administrative Services, Cuyahoga Heights School District**

Traditional Paper-Pencil Tests

The valid construction of multiple-choice test items and short essays (now being called extended or constructed responses) is neither random nor automatic. The original research was that of Margaret Fleming and Barbara Chambers (1983), and it has since been cited by recent assessment specialists such as Richard Stiggins (in Chappuis, Stiggins, et al., 2004) and ourselves (March & Peters, 2007).

Paper-pencil tests are typically called "traditional" because they are so familiar to anyone who has ever been a student. Paper-pencil tests have consisted of matching, true-false, multiple-choice, fill-in, and essay questions. However, the most recent generations of high-stakes tests (both norm-referenced and mastery tests) have consisted of multiple choice and 2-, 3-, or 4-point essays. We advise districts to be sure that their own paper-pencil tests are limited to these formats. From the humblest quiz to the important benchmark test, if students develop good test-taking skills with these formats, their chances of doing well on the high-stakes tests increases dramatically. In classroom tests, there is little merit to including matching, true-false, elaborate essays, or fill-in when students will rarely, if ever, see them on high-stakes tests.

There are several "rules of thumb" underlying effective paper-pencil test construction, many of which have been promulgated from the research of major national testing companies, including ETS, the College Boards, McGraw-Hill, Stanford, and Pearson. They have determined that for the most valid results:

a. Single test session should last no longer than 45 to 50 minutes.

b. The number of items should not exceed 30 to 35.

c. To fully assess a skill or concept, the student should see at least three (ideally five) test items; doing the math, this means that ideally, a single test should assess only 7 to 10 standards.

Given these parameters, it is easier for the formative tests to "pass muster." They are typically given during one class period and do not attempt to include too many standards at once. But for the end-of-unit summative assessments—particularly for units involving 12 to 15 standards—or benchmark tests, developers have to make the important decision of which standards to include. Once that has been determined, developers must consider which multiple-choice items to include as well as which extended-response (short essays) are appropriate.

Multiple-Choice Items

Typically, multiple-choice items are used when students can demonstrate mastery by distinguishing the correct from incorrect answers to reveal their understanding about the skill or concept involved. Unfortunately, many teachers believe that multiple-choice items are confined to literal or memory-level bits of information. But multiple-choice items can also assess inferential or higher-order knowledge. The following research-based recommendations are key considerations in constructing valid multiple-choice questions.

❖ The **stem** should be a **complete thought** or sentence that gives direction to the item. Students should not be forced to use the distractors to know what they are being asked.

Incorrect	Correct
Seahorses are a. unusual in that they swim upright b. small fish with a head like a horse c. forced to eat frequently because of their very small stomachs d. the only animal where the male carries the fetus	What feature about a seahorse most distinguishes it from other animals? a. backbone is actually made of muscle b. female carries the eggs c. male carries and delivers the unborn fetus d. stomach is very small, requiring it to eat constantly

Two helpful reminders about this rule are (a) any word or phrase that begins every distractor should be brought into the stem and (b) if you can't cover the distractors with your hand and get a solid 2-, 3-, or 4-point essay, the stem is not complete enough!

❖ The item must reflect both the **content and** the **cognitive demand** of the standard being assessed. For example, in California, one Grade 5 Earth and Space Science standard is: "The solar system consists of planets and other bodies that orbit the Sun in predictable paths."

Incorrect: this prompt asks only for identification of facts	**Correct:** this prompt asks students to make an inference based on a predictable phenomenon
Which of the following is a true statement? a. During the day, the earth gets 10 hours of sunlight, and at night, it gets 10 hours of moonlight. b. Earth's axis is tilted at a 35° angle. c. It takes 425 days for the earth to make one revolution around the sun. d. The earth turns once on its own axis every 24 hours.	If you stood all day and night in one location looking up at the sky, why do the sun, moon, and stars appear to change position in the sky? a. Changes in the earth's temperature cause clouds to hide everything in the sky. b. During the daytime, there are no stars or moons. c. Earth makes one complete rotation each day. d. The sun's gravity pulls the stars and moon in its path.

❖ The **distractors** should be **parallel** in structure.

Incorrect	Correct
Which of the following is an example of figurative language? a. heavily congested breathing b. finally getting housework under control c. killing your enemy with kindness d. at a brisk pace along the highway	Which of the following is an example of figurative language? a. breathing so hard, everyone could hear b. getting caught up with housework c. killing your enemy with kindness d. trotting along the highway

❖ The **distractors** should be **diagnostic** so that the incorrect answer gives the teacher a clue as to what it is the student does not understand. In the **Correct** figurative language example above, consider the distractors. The second column indicates the diagnostic value of the distractor.

a. breathing so hard, everyone in the room could hear	*this choice is a loud sound, but it is still literal*
b. getting caught up with housework	*this choice is a colloquialism—not actually figurative*
c. killing your enemy with kindness	*this choice IS correct*
d. trotting along the highway	*this choice is highly visual, but it is still literal*

This would be a great time to go back to the section on Entry-Level Data. One of the columns in Tables 5.3 and 5.4, "Looking at the Data" and "Working With Teachers" respectively, drew teachers' attention to the errors in the multiple-choice items: who picked which incorrect distractor? This information tells us what students don't understand, and it gives direction to the reteaching needed for each student. Typically, two or three students select each distractor. Naturally, if a large majority of the class (including the more capable students) chose letter b in the sample above, there is confusion between figurative language and colloquialisms. The concept of "figurative language" may need to be retaught to the entire group. Commercial test-makers are careful to make sure their distractors are diagnostic, and it is just as important for teachers or teams of teachers to do the same.

❖ The **distractors** should be listed in **alpha** or **numeric order** to prevent inadvertent "patterns" of correct answers—the most typical being "b." The **Correct** examples above have alphabetized distractors. Math distractors should be in numeric order, unless the question is asking students to select items from least to greatest.

Constructed or Extended-Response Items

The second test format used by high-stakes tests—and recommended for inclusion on classroom tests as well—is the short essay. It is also known variously as *extended response, constructed response,* or *short answer.* The idea is to ask students to construct meaning for themselves. Typically, these questions are worth 2, 3, or 4 points and are scored using a rubric. Such questions typically ask students to formulate a response when given a scenario or set of circumstances—a response that would require them to apply concepts they have learned.

The secret to an effective constructed response item is the prompt, for it is in the prompt that the scoring criteria are embedded. Naturally, the prompt also depends on the point value of the item. The value of the item depends on what is required of students in the given prompt. The prompt should clearly indicate how the item will be scored.

Sample 2-point prompts

Gr. 4 [students have read a brief passage]
Using details from the selection, give two reasons why Luis's brother decided to send the cat as a package. [Response must include two reasons.]

Gr. 6 [students have read a brief passage]
Explain why the author mentions Andre's pet spider as one of the "treasures" in his final paragraph. Support your answer with specific details from the selection. [Response must include (1) why the author mentions the spider and (2) passage detail to support that reason.]

Sample 3-point prompts

Gr. 5 [students have read a brief passage]
Describe how Julia feels after the hot dog–eating contest and 2 reasons why she feels this way. [Response must include (1) how Julia feels and two reasons (2) (3) she feels that way.]

Gr. 7 [students have read a biographical passage (silent pictures; Al Jolson)]
According to the dictionary, the word "talkie" entered the English language in the early 1900s. Explain what a "talkie" was, how the film industry helped introduce this word into the English language, and give the name of the "talkie" that brought an end to the silent era. [Response must include (1) what a "talkie" was; (2) how the film industry brought the word into the English language; and (3) the name of the "talkie" that brought an end to the silents.]

Sample 4-point prompts

Gr. 4 [students have read a biographical passage]
Use the selection to explain how John Chapman collected and prepared apple seeds.

Use the selection to infer how John Chapman planted and cared for apple trees.
[Response must include (1) how John Chapman collected apple seeds; how he (2) prepared the apple seeds; (3) how he planted apple trees; and (4) how he cared for the apple trees.]

Gr. 5 [students have read a nonfiction science passage]
What are four characteristics of lions that make them good hunters? Use both literal and implied details from the selection in your answer.
[Response must include four characteristics that make lions good hunters *actually listed in the passage.*]

Gr. 10
In the late 1800s, a population shift among African Americans began in the United States. Known as the "Great Migration," this pattern of shifting population accelerated as a result of World War I and continued throughout the 1920s. Describe the population shift involved in the "Great Migration." Explain how this migration produced an important change in the domestic affairs of the United States during the first three decades of the 20th century. [Response must include a description of the population shift (**2 pts**) and an explanation of how this migration impacted U.S. domestic affairs for the first 3 decades of the 20th century (**2 pts**).]

. . . And from those who REALLY know. . . .

*As a staff who works with academically challenged students, we have always understood the importance of formative and summative assessment to help us know exactly where our students are and what they need next. But since our state achievement tests require every student to write 2- and 4-point constructed responses (in addition to answering multiple-choice questions), we've focused considerable energy on including both 2- and 4-pointers in our unit tests. With the primary students, teachers ask them to "give me two reasons why . . ." or "tell me two of your favorite foods and why you like each." These are recorded on the board or chart paper in a format similar to the way they will learn to write them later on. For the older students, teachers model how a 2-point and a 4-point response should look, what makes each "worth" its respective points, and how to "fix" responses that are missing points. We're trying to develop thinking and responding habits that will enable our students to demonstrate mastery on any paper-pencil test they encounter.——**Lydia Brown-Payton, director, Mollie Kessler School**

Begin at the Primary Level! Many primary teachers consider the discussions about paper-pencil tests irrelevant to them. But even at these lower grades, teachers can help students learn to select from among options and to explain why they did not choose the other answers. Moreover, these young ones can respond to essay questions by drawing pictures and diagrams and/ or giving verbal explanations. As soon as possible, they should represent their thoughts in writing—even if it's nonsense or scribble early on. It builds for them the conviction that what they write is an important way to express themselves. They also learn to operate within basic time limits and to check their work. These are all lead-up skills to prepare not only for paper-pencil classroom tests but for the high-stakes assessments that will so heavily impact them.

Authentic or Performance Assessments

Authentic or performance assessments ask students to complete holistic, real-life tasks to demonstrate independent mastery of specific standards. The intent is for students to construct meaning for themselves solving a problem or completing a task that extends what they learn in the classroom.

Some of the most popular include writing an original short story or poem, constructing a model, negotiating a new treaty, devising story problems, creating a "business" plan to produce widgets, conducting an original experiment, collecting raw data and placing it into interpretive tables, designing a new approach to solving a problem, error analysis, or performing an original dance or dramatization. While these products are creative and unique to reflect each student's personal style, each follows a set of guidelines that are based on the standards they are intended to measure.

. . . And from those who REALLY know. . . .

One of the scariest things for me as a high school social studies teacher in an urban district was doing authentic assessment with my high school students for the first unit of the new school year! It was so gratifying to watch how seriously the students in my classes approached the assigned task; an assessment that required them to write a letter to a person in authority about some aspect of school safety that they would like to see implemented. While the spelling and grammar were not perfect in the first draft, and the structure of a formal letter needed work, the thinking displayed by the students was amazing! They had indeed learned what was in the unit and better yet, were willing to attempt a task they had never done before without fear of failing! What a great moment for them and for me!—Christopher Patrone, social studies teacher, Chaney High School, Youngstown City Schools

---

We urge districts to strategically plan their assessments to include a balance of traditional and performance or authentic assessments. The complementary strength of the two is best seen in Table 5.8.

Table 5.8 Balancing Paper-Pencil Assessment With Authentic Assessment

Paper-Pencil Assessments Are . . .	Authentic/Performance Assessments Are . . .
(1) selective and representative, indirectly measuring key standards addressed in the unit to imply a wider mastery; students respond to these items in ways that closely parallel classroom practice.	(1) holistic projects or tasks that provide *direct* measures of mastery; students apply skills and concepts learned during *unit* to solve problems, complete projects, create original products, etc. outside the unit.
(2) both formative and summative; the formative measures check for understanding during the unit; the summative measures (a.k.a. the unit test) determine mastery at the end of the unit; the content of the test items are similar (but not identical) to those addressed in class.	(2) more summative than formative; they are intended to show independent mastery of standards and the ability to apply what was learned in a different, real-life context; this level of application is beyond the examples and scenarios addressed during classroom instruction.
(3) teacher-developed or published items with an exact answer (or limited range of acceptable answers) that correspond to a scoring key; some extended responses may be creative but are still fairly convergent, and the product is basically paper-pencil.	(3) student-constructed with a wide range of options to complete and more than one right answer (albeit within guidelines); evaluated with a rubric devised from the unit standards and typically result in a concrete display or product, although some may be displayed on paper.
(4) designed to approximate high-stakes testing (e.g., Iowa, SAT, tests used for No Child Left Behind) by including multiple-choice and extended response items and by being timed; students have limited options and must respond to all items.	(4) designed to approximate real-life situations (i.e., problems to create, products to develop, processes to complete), including more flexible time frames; students have options for completing the assessment tasks and are encouraged to be creative.
(5) typically completed during class time as "on-demand."	(5) may be completed during class as on-demand or accomplished cumulatively over time; may be completed outside of class.

Authentic assessments are largely student-controlled with a wide range of options for completion and several correct answers. But as shown in the example above, the finished product must observe specific guidelines corresponding to the standards it measures. In most cases, the authentic or performance assessment is a culmination of the unit activities and assesses a student's independent mastery of at least one of the standards addressed during the unit plan. In many cases, one assessment may measure more than one standard.

Some teachers are tempted to assign groups to complete the authentic or performance assessments. And these tasks do involve the types of collaborative problem-solving and creative use of resources set forth in the 21st century skills. However, EACH student must demonstrate independent mastery of the standards called for in the task. Care must be taken that if the project is expanded to involve more than one student, there must be a way to assess the independent mastery of EACH as an individual.

The research base for authentic or performance assessments began in the latter part of the 20th century. Linda Darling-Hammond and her colleagues (Darling-Hammond, Ancess, & Falk, 1995) advocated that report cards and diplomas be awarded not on test grades and time spent in classrooms but on "exhibitions" of competence. These "exhibitions" show students' independent mastery of standards or skills in an authentic display of problem solving or creation of an original piece. David Niguidula (2005), an education consultant from Rhode Island, helped research the effectiveness of digital portfolios as an assessment tool in the mid-1990s. He integrated work samples from high school English classrooms as digital displays of mastery. Rhode Island is a leader in using portfolios to prove students have met the state standards required to graduate from high school.

Just after the 1993 adoption of the National Council of Teachers of Mathematics math standards—which placed a greater emphasis on conceptual and contextual problem solving than computation—determining alternative means of assessment became a hot topic. Lesley College's Jean Moon and Linda Schulman (1995) published one of the first books about using holistic performance assessments to complement traditional paper-pencil tests, just as constructivist math was to complement the algorithmic approach. They are among the first math reformers to advocate talking and writing about math and solving open-ended problems that do not include all of the information.

In the assessment handbook published by Richard Stiggins, Judith Arter, Jan Chappuis, and Stephen Chappuis (2004), a chapter is devoted to performance assessment. The authors discuss complex *performances* such as playing a musical instrument, carrying out the steps in a science experiment, speaking in a foreign language, repairing an engine, reading aloud, and working productively in a group. They also address complex *products* such as a term paper, a lab report, or a work of art. Both types of performance assessment are evaluated using a rubric that corresponds to the objectives or standards assessed.

Describing a five-year project on differentiating authentic assessments for middle school students, assessment researchers Tonya Moon, Catherine Brighton, and Carolyn Callahan from the University of Virginia and Ann Robinson from the University of Arkansas (2005) find that as a nation, more emphasis is placed on "test prep" than assessments that help students construct their own meaning. Among their guidelines for authentic assessments are the following: (1) focus on essential (not peripheral, even if easier to measure) content; (2) help students develop issues in depth and see connections with other issues; (3) require students to complete their authentic assessments in the classroom or other school facility and on school time (to avoid the distortion that results from outside help); (4) focus on a holistic product or performance, not a single right answer; (5) emphasize students' strengths to encourage even the strugglers; (6) make success criteria clear from the outset, use examples, and include student input as much as possible; (7) allow students multiple avenues and various options to demonstrate mastery; and (8) include scoring that is focused on the task.

From William Carey College in Mississippi, Pokey Stanford and Stacy Reeves (2005) describe the relevance of alternative assessments in the context of every classroom. Central to these assessments is a fair and relevant rubric (i.e., "a set of criteria that outlines expectations for the completed product" [p. 18]). Rather than applying the rubric at the end of the assessment, they insist that it be used throughout the instructional process to give students a focus from the outset as well as frequent feedback as they go along. This helps teachers better know what other guidance or instruction each student needs. Classroom instruction should be directly linked to the scoring rubrics to ensure that teachers will be working toward the alternative assessment throughout the unit, and not just at the end.

Doug Reeves (2001) writes that classroom tests should consist of a balance between paper-pencil multiple-choice items *and* performance assessments. According to Reeves, these performance assessments should be evaluated with user-friendly rubrics based on the academic standards and that students themselves should have an everyday familiarity with the rubrics as a means to help them understand the standards and their expectations for mastery. Another important feature of the performance assessments requiring students to write extended responses is their predictive value of success on the high-stakes tests. Reeves cites studies that indicate a clear connection between performance measures and higher scores on the high-stakes tests. Some **sample authentic or performance tasks** (excerpted from March & Peters, 2007) and updated to reflect the new standards are listed here.

Math

[Elementary] Prepare an expense sheet showing dollars, expenses, subtractions, carrying balances forward, etc. using figures supplied by the teacher [hint: the teacher should create three or four scenarios, place them in a hat, and draw one per student]. [assesses Math Common Core 4 NBT 4; 4 NBT 5; 4 MD 2]

[Intermediate] Design a blueprint for the redecoration of your bedroom [include the flooring; e.g., carpeting; tile; walls; e.g., wall paper, border, paint; allow for doors, windows, and other unusual features]; use correct scale, include designated shapes, and show proportions [option: may also include costs and a virtual three-dimensional view of the proposed product].

[assesses Math Common Core 4 MD 1; 4 MD 2; 4 MS 3]

[High School] Devise a rubric to analyze a variety of problem situations involving measurement computation (e.g., volume, area, rate, money, distance) to discover possible errors in (a) labeling, (b) conversions, (c) accuracy of computation, (d) viability of estimate, (e) accuracy of measurement, and (f) the viability of the solution; show samples to illustrate each possible error. [assesses Math Common Core NQ 9.1; NQ 9.2; NQ 9.3]

Language Arts

[Elementary, Gr. 2] Compose a narrative that recounts a well-elaborated event or short sequence of events; (a) include details to describe actions, thoughts, and feelings; (b) use temporal words to signal event order; and (c) provide a sense of closure. Use correct capitalization, punctuation, and spelling, including commas and apostrophes. [assesses ELA Com Core W 2.3 and L 2.2]

[Intermediate, Gr. 5] Prepare a museum display of an important 20th century event (e.g., the Hindenburg, the Lindberg kidnapping, the Lusitania, the first moon landing, the assassination of J.F.K.). Interpret relevant information presented in diverse media and formats (e.g., visually, quantitatively, orally) and explain how each contributes to the event being displayed. Compare the various accounts (visual, quantitative, and newscasts of the event), and show a coherent understanding of the three, by displaying parts of each medium in the display. Indicate if there were any discrepancies among the three media. [assesses ELA Com Core SL 5.2 and RI 5.7]

(Continued)

(Continued)

[High School, Gr. 10] You have been asked to give testimony to Congress about a controversial issue. Prepare a written argument in support of one position or the other a controversial topic. Write your argument to support your claims based on an analysis of the topics in relevant texts, using valid reasoning and relevant and sufficient evidence, including a–e below [W 10.1]. In compiling your material, delineate and evaluate the argument and specific claims in each text, assessing whether the reasoning is valid and the evidence is relevant and sufficient and identify false statements and fallacious reasoning [RI 10.8]. The following guidelines will be used to evaluate your written testimony [a–e from W 10.1 and f–j from L 10.1 and 10.2]:

    a. Introduce precise claim(s), distinguish the claim(s) from alternate or opposing claims, and create an organization that establishes clear relationships among claim(s), counterclaims, reasons, and evidence.

    b. Develop claim(s) and counterclaims fairly, supplying evidence for each while pointing out the strengths and limitations of both in a manner that anticipates the audience's knowledge level and concerns.

    c. Use words, phrases, and clauses to link the major sections of the text; create cohesion; and clarify the relationships between claim(s) and reasons, between reasons and evidence, and between claim(s) and counterclaims.

    d. Establish and maintain a formal style and objective tone while attending to the norms and conventions of the discipline in which they are writing.

    e. Provide a concluding statement or section that follows from and supports the argument presented.

    f. Use parallel structure.

    g. Use various types of phrases (noun, verb, adjectival, adverbial, participial, prepositional, absolute) and clauses (independent, dependent; noun, relative, adverbial) to convey specific meanings and add variety and interest to writing or presentations.

    h. Use a semicolon (and perhaps a conjunctive adverb) to link two or more closely related independent clauses.

    i. Use a colon to introduce lists or quotations.

    j. Spell correctly.

Social Studies

[Elementary, Gr. 3] Make a list of two goods and two services that the third grade could produce to sell to other students at lunchtime. Say why you think each of the four would be popular with the consumers. Select one good or service, and explain how it could be "produced" by your class to sell; include each step in the process, and decide on a price. [assesses Ohio Social Studies/Economic Strand 3.17 and 3.18]

[Note: During the unit, students will have addressed basic economic terms and factors of production, including actual school-based goods and services such as homework help, running errands, crispy rice squares, and pencils.]

[Intermediate, Gr. 6] Draw from each of four hats one world government. The four hats will contain monarchies, theocracies, dictatorships, and democracies—all of which were studied during the unit. For each of the four governments drawn, prepare a graphic that displays the dominant type of government (and its attributes), including citizens' liberties and responsibilities. Include in each of the four visuals an indication of how the positive features of the other types of government *might be* successfully integrated—and why this would be an advantage. [assesses Ohio Social Studies/ Government Strand 6.10]

[High School, World History] You have been asked to prepare a table or chart that will be featured in a news special (e.g., *60 Minutes*) about the Enlightenment. Use what has been addressed in the Enlightenment unit about the dominant thinking *before* and *during* the Enlightenment and those ideas that are *still impacting* life in the 21st century, specifically in the areas of scientific thought, religion, political rule, and economic systems. Include specific examples—including people and locations—of ideas, beliefs, and practices that distinguished the "before" from the "during." [assesses Ohio Social Studies/History Strand WH 5; WH 6; WH 7]

[Note: During the unit, students will have spent time completing various comparison matrices about the events of the Enlightenment and their origins; most likely, the student will use a similar template to the one presented below.]

	Pre-Enlightenment Thinking	Enlightenment Thinking	Still Relevant Today
Scientific Thought			
Religion			
Political Rule			
Economic Systems			

Science

[Elementary] Conduct an original [but guided] experiment re: [unit topic]; record observations, make inferences and predictions, test the predictions, and note results. [PS 2.1.a, b, c]

[Intermediate] Create a realistic representation (e.g., an annotated model, a picture, or a poster) of how an imaginary canyon developed in your backyard; include both (a) slow-moving changes on the earth's surface (e.g., erosion, weathering, mountain building, deposition) and (b) rapid processes (e.g., volcanic eruptions, landslides, earthquakes); explain the progression of the changes and how they resulted in the canyon and its features. [ESS 4.1.c, d]

[High School] Create a timeline that demonstrates the development of an earlier theory (e.g., continental drift, the greenhouse effect) into a current theory (i.e., global warming, plate tectonics) by plotting the development or use of various technologies (e.g., submersibles, satellite imaging, advances in photography) to account for the changes; use yarn, for example, to include descriptive (explanatory) annotations. [Environmental Change/Human Impact on the Environment]

. . . And from those who REALLY know. . . .

One of the BEST techniques I've added to my "best-practices" inventory is to include an authentic assessment in every unit plan. I've always tried to keep my students actively engaged—which for 12th-grade English is no small feat. But the idea of using these authentic projects to measure mastery of standards has been great! For example, we read The Epic of Gilgamesh, *one of the oldest surviving works of literature, written in Mesopotamia on cuneiform tablets between the 13th and the 10th century BC. From the outset, I tell students (and frequently remind them) that they should be on the lookout for a 3- or 4-line passage that particularly interests them. When we finish the epic, each student creates a replica of a cuneiform tablet using TerraCotta Sculpey and a stylus made from wooden skewers. Each student's tablet uses the Cuneiform alphabet and captures the 3- or 4-line verse previously selected, followed by his or her name and the date. I take the tablets home to "fire" in the oven. Each student's tablet is accompanied by a two-page paper to be displayed next to his or her artifact in the English Hallway Showcase. The paper will include an explanation of Cuneiform, the Mesopotamian culture from which Gilgamesh was taken, and the personal significance of the 3- or 4-line passage on the student's tablet. This task measures student mastery of 3 content standards—2 Writing and 1 Language.*

*Authentic or performance assessments such as this one are direct, holistic measures of student mastery. The KEY has been to make sure the task is an actual and valid measure of one or more unit standards. If this alignment isn't there, then the tasks are just so much busy work—interesting and creative, perhaps, but of little value to determine mastery.—**Cindy Lambrecht, English teacher, Whitmer High School, Washington Local Schools***

Homework and Grading—Two Critical Issues for Success 6

"Education is the most powerful weapon which you can use to change the world."

—Nelson Mandela

HOMEWORK

Definition. Homework, by its very name, suggests that students practice what has been learned in the classroom in a setting away from school. Notice the word "practice" in the previous sentence; homework is to be an opportunity for students to gain a level of comfort or independence with concepts and skills that have been taught. It is not an indicator of mastery, and it should not have disproportionate influence over the grade.

However, in many districts, homework falls under academic freedom, and very little attention is paid to how it is handled—what it is, how it is used, and how it impacts the student's course grade. Rarely does a district adopt guidelines that speak to consistency in the quality of homework, the type of feedback required, or the impact of homework on a letter grade.

In the context of the new standards, each district must decide what will be the purpose of homework. Hopefully, it will not be used as punishment or to determine mastery. But it definitely should help teachers determine where to focus their instruction in the next lesson. It is suggested that homework be used to check students' *understanding,* provide additional *practice,* and help teachers determine what and with whom *reteaching* is needed. Properly constructed, homework is an extension of unit activities and thus must be directly related to one or more standards. Homework should yield helpful information about a student's level of understanding, providing students have done their own work. In some instances, the homework may be deliberately structured as a group effort, and as such, it is not intended to determine individual understanding.

Common Missteps With Homework

Current research as to the impact of homework on student test performance reveals more questions than answers. Critics cite several abuses and misuses of homework as well as troubling inconsistencies across districts and even within the same building. But other school reform studies have clear proof that, when done correctly, homework will positively impact student achievement. But several troubling issues need to be resolved if the "done correctly" is to prevail:

• ***The "what" that is assigned as homework.*** Sitting in classrooms, observing the instructional process, we often see teachers who assign content questions or math problems for homework. These questions and problems are assigned without regard for which standards they address, but to finish what was begun in class or to provide additional practice.

In some instances, teachers assign the easiest problems or questions for homework so that students will feel successful. But if students never apply their skills at a more rigorous and challenging level, the teacher (and students) get an inflated sense of mastery.

One of the more destructive homework practices we have observed lately reaches a whole new level of dysfunction. Actually, it's in-class seatwork that's been mistakenly labeled as directed reading or guided reading but serves the same purpose as homework. Teachers have compiled pages of actual or paraphrased text passages, filled them with blanks and literal-level questions, hole-punched them as work packets, and use them to torture students. Students simply copy words from the actual text to fill in the blanks or supply literal answers, turn the page, and repeat the process. It is a mindless copying exercise. Students never actually process the information, never actually comprehend what they read, and never apply it to real-world problem solving. Worse, teachers are almost completely dissociated from the entire exercise, except to drone through the packet page by page providing the correct answers—still without helping students to actually process any of the information, without determining the students' level of comprehension and without showing students how to use what they've read to solve problems. It's an astounding exercise in compliance that has virtually no academic benefit.

• ***Homework as filler for double periods or block schedules.*** Homework has often become the "filler" for double periods or "block schedules" in schools where teachers have not been trained to use these extended time frames successfully. We have observed in far too many cases that the second half of these longer sessions is devoted to beginning homework—as if it were a study hall.

The intervention, enrichment, or other differentiation that is supposed to be going on during this additional time is nonexistent. Especially troubling is when nearly half the students finish the assignment (even those dreadful packet pages!) within a few minutes, many times by simply dividing the questions amongst themselves and copying from each other. Even if the teacher is working with the other half of the class, the half that finished quickly spend the duration of the period socializing. Looking at the numbers, even if this "socializing" occurs three of the five days, if it happens four times a day, that's 12 times each week, for as much as 30 minutes, or six hours per week. That's 20% of the total instructional time. Multiplied by the 36 weeks of the whole school year, that's 216 hours lost each year, or 36 days!

- *Homework is "graded" and is included in calculating a student's grade.* Many teachers tell us that if students do not receive "something" for doing the homework, they are not motivated to do it. Therefore, the infamous "point system" has been instituted in many classrooms and includes homework. The stumbling block here is that if homework—as practice—is to show teachers what students understand and where they need help, why should it be accompanied by points? They become a reward for "compliance" or a penalty for needing help. We have observed situations where failure to complete homework has actually lowered a student's letter grade, even if a student's test performance shows mastery of the designated standards. In other cases, completing "busywork" outside of class—work that may or may not relate to the unit of study—has been allowed to raise a letter grade, even if legitimate mastery has not been demonstrated. If a district is moving towards standards-based grading, awarding grades for homework really does not make sense.

- *No constructive feedback on the homework assigned.* Another issue is the lack of constructive feedback on homework. Students are given no affirmative or corrective information by the teacher as to what they did well and where they messed up. They get a "check" if they complete the work and a demerit if they did not. Used in this manner, homework can scarcely serve any purpose—other than a vestige of "power over." Without actually reviewing the student's work, the teacher has no sense of what each student knows and does not and has no indication of the type of assistance needed by each student to demonstrate mastery. If students do not have a sense as to the status of their understanding, they continue to make the same errors, assume they are moving along at an appropriate rate. Worse, if they continue to receive demerits without explanation, they simply give up!

- *The overuse of isolated drill and the volume of homework.* Many parents complain about the volume of homework assigned. One source of these complaints is the number of the same items assigned. How many grammar drills are necessary, or how many math problems are needed to show the same level of understanding? It is the "what" in relation to the number that appears to be out of sync. How much repeated practice is sufficient? A second concern about volume is the perceived lack of coordination among teachers, resulting in excessive amounts of homework in any one night.

- ***The way homework is used in class.*** All too often, completed homework is the basis of the next day's lesson, during which the teacher supplies the correct answers. This practice provides a disincentive for students to have done the work themselves. The entire class period is spent redoing the homework on the SmartBoard or having students put the questions up on the whiteboard. When the teacher spends a major chunk of class time reviewing the homework, he or she sacrifices instructional time that should be used to focus on new content and/or more specific student needs.

- ***Awarding extra credit for doing homework.*** This is probably the practice that inflates grades more than any of the others! Extra credit for doing *later* what was expected *in the first place* sends students the message that they need not do what is required at the time it is required because they can hustle around at the last minute to do other homework that will earn them points to offset those they've lost. If homework is so expendable that it can be ignored or postponed until later, it surely cannot be taken seriously.

- ***Students copy the homework from each other.*** When the homework is overdone, meaningless, or if it has no bearing on their learning, students find ways to beat the system. In our research, we have seen many instances where students copy each other's answers, making the exercise even more meaningless. Indeed, with the use of technology, students have so many ways to accomplish this! They divide the work—each doing so many items—and then "tweet" their answers to other students in their network.

If they do nothing else, the above practices certainly oblige districts to define their position on what is the purpose of homework, anyway!? Is it to (a) check student understanding; (b) teach students responsibility; (c) make students accountable for something; or (d) a way to accumulate points toward the grade or credit of some type? And how consistent are homework practices in the classrooms across the district, within the same grade level, or in the same building? Clearly, these issues have been at the heart of any homework discussion we have had with teachers and administrators.

Collectively, the case against homework in its current state is compelling enough to disallow it altogether. In the homework research, there are equal numbers of studies that find *a positive impact* on student performance as those that find *negative impact* as those that *no impact at all*. It is really a matter of "what" homework is and how it is used that separates these studies.

Strategies for Making Better Use of Homework

Probably the most important decisions to be made about homework center on the purpose, the feedback provided, and the extent to which a district regulates its use. In our work with teachers, the subject of homework never fails to arise—whether as a measure of mastery or a method of practice. There is so much emotion about homework and whether students do it or not, teachers act almost as if doing it poorly or failure to do it at all were a personal affront directed to them. Therefore, the penalties associated with "not" doing it seem to drive the discussion! But if rational thought is permitted, the homework dilemma can be brought under control.

Purpose

Rather than to determine *mastery*, it is suggested that homework be used to check students' *understanding*, provide additional *practice*, and help teachers determine what and with whom *reteaching* is needed. Properly constructed, homework is an extension of unit activities and is thus directly related to one or more standards. It can yield helpful information about a student's level of understanding—providing students have done their own work. In some instances, the homework may be deliberately structured as a group effort; in such cases, it is not intended to determine individual understanding. But teachers would do well to remember that with today's technology and the pervasiveness of the social networks, the likelihood of each student doing his and her very own work independently will be impossible to control.

Feedback

For homework to be truly helpful to the student, teachers must provide affirming feedback to reinforce accurate responses and corrective feedback where students "missed the boat." Suggestions should be offered or questions posed to help students rethink their group and/or individual responses. Where it would be productive—and not punishment or busywork—students and/or student groups could be asked to redo the missed items.

District Guidelines

To prevent the abuses and missteps listed in the earlier section—and to maintain quality control in the implementation of the course tools—districts should adopt a policy that reflects its philosophy about homework and operating guidelines that establish parameters for districtwide implementation. These parameters should include requirements such as the following:

- The homework must be directly related to unit standards.
- The homework must be extensions or applications of unit activities and not busywork.
- Homework should have no bearing on the letter grade.
- Affirming and corrective feedback must be provided to students in a timely manner.
- If group homework is assigned, each student must have a role in its completion.
- Homework may not be used as punishment.
- Homework may not be used for extra credit.
- The only class time that may be used for homework is a few minutes to make sure students realize what to do (e.g., the first item or so).

Research on Homework

Elementary Homework: Anne Swank (1999) examined the differences in test scores among fourth graders who either did or did not do homework. Her findings indicate no differences in math achievement scores between students in the two homework groups. Lyn Corno and Jianzhong Xu (2004) call homework the job of childhood. They examined taped sessions and interviews with parents and students, and they discovered that homework helped third graders learn responsibility and develop time-management and job-management skills. The students also learned to work on schoolwork when they did not want to and to adjust their attentiveness to the demands of a specific assignment.

Homework in Math vs. Reading: Harris Cooper, Jorgianne C. Robinson, and Erika A. Patall (2006), who have extensively studied the research on homework, report that, if anything, the correlational studies suggest a slightly more positive effect of homework for math than for reading. This phenomenon might occur because children are more likely to read after school regardless of whether it is assigned as homework, whereas math activities are less naturally embedded in students' afterschool environments.

How Much Homework Students Should Do: Cooper, Robinson, and Patall (2006) report that for Grades 1–6 (a) short practice assignments do improve performance on class tests and (b) teachers also use homework assignments to accomplish other learning-related objectives. In addition, for junior high school students, the positive association with achievement appears for even the most minimal amount of time spent on homework but disappears after about 90 minutes of homework a night. For high school students, the positive relationship between homework time and students' achievement levels peaks at about two hours and may even decline for hours beyond this. This suggests an optimal amount of homework for high school students of between 90 minutes and two and one-half hours a night.

Homework Connected to Grade: Jaan Mikk (2006) examined the association between homework and math achievement in 46 countries and found that student achievement was lower in countries where homework counted toward grades, where it was the basis of classroom discussion, and where students corrected homework in class. Patricia Scriffiny (2008), high school math teacher, reports changing how homework is used in her classroom as a result of moving to standards-based grading. She reports that originally she was sure students would not complete homework if they did not get points or a grade. However, what she found was that some students had been good at "playing school" and earning points without really learning. Other students had taken a hit on points for not doing homework, but they were passing the tests. However, her research supports our findings for what makes homework viable: (1) systematic and extensive feedback on assignments sends a message to students on what they need to practice in their homework. (2) Homework assignments consist of a small collection of problems, each of which is linked to a standard, where she makes connections for students that she wants them to eventually do on their own. (3) When assigning homework, she discusses how it applies to their assessments so students understand the bigger picture. (4) Even though a student may not do all of the homework assigned, her students know they are accountable for mastering the standards connected to that homework; it becomes a matter of student choice.

Practices That Make a Difference: One big question about the amount of homework has people stacking up on both sides of the issue. But there is one point of agreement—homework is largely ineffective and unproductive. A study reported in a recent *Economics of Education Review* (Ozkan & Henderson, 2011, pp. 950–961) contends that homework in science, social studies, and English language arts "has little or no impact" on student test performance. But a *New York Times* education writer feels the problem lay not in the <u>amount</u> of homework but in the <u>type</u> of homework assigned. Annie Murphy Paul (2011) reports three evidence-based learning techniques that have been documented as increasing student test scores. She suggests that the application of these techniques to homework could similarly advance student learning.

(1) "Spaced repetition" is the method of breaking up the assigned activity into smaller segments (e.g., not the entire Renaissance but single aspects of it such as art, politics, literature) and then repeating it across time. The idea is to focus on smaller amounts of information at once but with re-exposure for a cumulative effect. Paul reports two studies. In a collaboration between psychologists at Washington University in St. Louis and teachers at nearby Columbia Middle School using spaced repetition, the science and social studies test scores of students in Grades 7 and 8 improved by 13 to 25%. Another study from the University of Southern California-San Diego reports that Grade 8 history students who used a "spaced" approach to learning had nearly double the rate of retention of students who studied the same material in a consolidated unit.

(2) "Retrieval practice" is the method of using a practice test and/or practice test items for homework in place of additional practice of classroom activity. According to one experiment reported by Paul, language learners who employed the "retrieval practice" strategy to study vocabulary words remembered 80% of the words they studied, while learners who used conventional study methods remembered only about a third of them. In another study from Purdue University, students who used "retrieval practice" to learn science retained about 50% more of the material than students who studied in traditional ways.

(3) "Interleaving" is the technique of mixing up different kinds of situations or problems to be practiced instead of grouping them by type. Paul reports that when students do not know in advance the kinds of knowledge or problem-solving strategies needed to answer a question or solve a problem, "Their brains have to work harder to come up with the solution" (p. 2), and the result is that students "learn the material more thoroughly" (p. 2). **Paul** reports an "interleaving" study published last year in the journal *Applied Cognitive Psychology.* Grade 4 students were asked to work on solving four types of math problems. On the test to determine how well they had learned, the scores of the students whose practice problems were "interleaved," or mixed up, "were *more than double* the scores" (p. 2) of those students who had practiced one kind of problem at a time.

Perhaps one of the hottest controversies about monitoring student performance—and the one most misunderstood—is homework. It is not about assigning homework as a teacher's right, but all of the key decisions that go into making homework meaningful and informative for subsequent teaching. Philosophically, homework is a topic that engenders more debate than just about any other topic as far as how it is to be used, how it is to be "counted," and the teacher's responsibility in dealing with completed versus or incompleted homework.

GRADING RELATIVE TO MASTERY

Urgency. In schools across America, the traditional letter-grade, or 5-point grading scale, is so long-entrenched, it has and will continue to meet stiff resistance to any sort of adjustment. From the tiniest-tot preschools to the hallowed halls of higher education, parents, professors, and prospective employers have come to rely on some equivalent of the A, B, C, D, or F to get a fix on the level student performance. This is also the method used to disaggregate high-stakes test scores and to rate the schools in many states. Unfortunately, the public at large has been relatively unfazed by 90 years of evidence that failing grades do not improve achievement (Guskey, 2000). We honestly think there would be less resistance to taking a quarter out of football or moving the date of Christmas Day than changing the grading system in America's schools.

But with the advent of the more rigorous Common Core standards in Math and English Language Arts as well as newly adopted state content standards in Science and Social Studies, and in view of the push to integrate the 21st century skills into the curriculum of every district in the country, the tide may at last be turning. It has become apparent that the accumulation of points—which are then divided into percentages of 90%, 80%, 70%, etc.—will not be appropriate to reflect the mastery of such complex and higher-order performance expectations as are now being required.

But it is not our intent in this book to insist on the complete "reform" of the grading system. That will come eventually but not until the new standards have been in place for two or three years and American educators discover en masse that they need a better way. Grading will finally catch up to the transformation of the curriculum. Until that happens, we suggest that districts give serious thought to their grading systems and make a few sensible tweaks that will swap out some destructive habits in favor of some more appropriate ones. Oh, and one other thing; every teacher's grade book should include a large mirror that pops up with every entry—just to remind them of what the grade often *really* reflects.

Common Missteps. Below are some of the most common missteps in the current grading system that could be rectified with a dose of common sense and a commitment to quality control. Some of these practices have been referred to by Doug Reeves as "toxic" (2008), and he insists that to reduce the failure rate, schools don't need a new curriculum, new staff, or new technology—they need a new grading system. We have inserted our thoughts as well.

• Most districts are continuing with a **percentage system** for awarding grades that sets forth 90 or 93% for an A, 80 or 84% for a B, and so on. These systems equate "points" earned with the strength of mastery, irrespective of what actual performances the student has demonstrated. There is no indication of what students know or can do, only how many points they have earned. The use of points to reflect mastery flies in the face of what is expected in the new standards and in the 21st century skills—a series of performances that reflect mastery.

• Not only have most Boards of Education adopted a grading policy that sets forth 90 or 93% for an A, 80 or 84% for a B, and so on, but they then walked away! Under the cloak of "academic freedom," teachers in many districts have been permitted to decide independently **what *comprises* the grade** and in **what proportion.** In our experience, some count homework, and some do not; those who do may allow it to count 10% and the teacher next door 40%. Tests may count 60% or 20%, and final projects may or may NOT count at all. Thus there is often an untenable inconsistency within the same grade level and within the same building, resulting in a profound inequity for students. Doug Reeves (2008) claims that in hundreds of workshops nationwide, his simple activity of giving participants a series of scores and asking them to determine a final letter grade yields every conceivable grade from and A to an F.

• The determination of a student's mastery is too often an **average** of the scores across a grading period. This is a total contradiction to the concept of mastery learning. The idea behind mastery—and particularly of the new standards—is that every student is expected to attain mastery, eventually and to some degree. Thus, the determination of mastery should be based on a student's performance by the end of the grading period. Nothing new, this misstep has been condemned by Ken O'Connor (2007), Robert Marzano (2000 and 2007), and Doug Reeves (2008) and has been redisparaged by Tom Guskey (2011).

• Another of Reeves's (2004c, 2008) "toxic" grading practices (and Guskey before him, 2000) is the **use of zeroes** for missing work. They consider this not only a mathematical distortion but a silly way to punish students for not doing their work. We would add that in our experience, the net effect of zeros for work not completed is **more a disciplinary sanction** than an academic rating, since there is no academic work to judge.

• Another toxic grading practice according to Reeves (2004c and 2008) is the "semester killer"—the **single project, test, lab, paper,** or other **assignment** that will make or break students. This practice puts 18 weeks of other work at-risk based on one assessment. And safeguards such as the *quality control, equity,* and *consistency* are often nonexistent—thanks to academic freedom.

• Several more missteps have been more recently identified by Tom Guskey (2011), long-time school reform researcher and tireless advocate of improved grading practices.

  o The **"bell curve"** remains in many districts, predetermining that some students must fail, some do well, but most will be in the middle. Guskey explains that the bell curve originated as a method to sort scores or other numeric values without any intervention. Our opinion is that since the new standards require mastery of all students—more a J-curve than bell-shaped—and classrooms are the very heart of intervention, the "bell curve" is obviously invalid. Just think how ludicrous it would be if none or only a few of the students mastered a majority of the standards on a given test, and the teacher assigned the "best" of this nonmastery an A. The grade inflation would be astounding and the indication of "true mastery" impossible to determine. The bell curve must go!

o In too many cases, grading fosters unproductive **forms of competition** among students; i.e., "let's see who does the best job of ____" or "let's see who finishes first," and so on. It's as if there are winners and losers in the mastery of standards, a concept totally anathema to the new standards and the 21st century skills.

o Guskey agrees with Reeves that students should not be allowed to fail due to their lack of completing work. Instead, Guskey suggests these students **receive an "Incomplete"** and be required to complete the work at an inconvenient time (similar to Reeves). We have offered that solution to many districts, but the most frequent push-back is that this type of student will never complete the work—no matter what the arrangements or inducements.

o The notion of boiling down to **a single grade** a student's work during the entire quarter is problematic on at least two fronts: (1) it **ignores the specific standards** a student has mastered very well and those perhaps not as well and even those not mastered at all; and (2) it **obscures any growth or progress** experienced by a student as he or she develops along the quarter.

o An often ignored, dimension of this "single-grade" system is that it includes very **little substantive feedback** to students about the strengths and weaknesses of their work and how they might proceed to overcome mistakes. Every researcher decries this flaw, including Carolyn Tomlinson and Jay McTighe (2006); O'Connor (2007); Marzano (2000, 2007); Scriffiny (2008); Reeves (2008); and Guskey (2000, 2011).

Strategies for Improving the Grading Process. With the probable certainty that conventional letter-grading may indeed hang around for at least awhile longer, we contend that there are strategies and methods to improve poorly-conceived grading systems. With some thoughtful adjusting, districts can make substantive improvements that are consistent with the demands of the new content standards and the 21st century skills and—thought imperfect—will reduce many of the damaging effects mentioned above.

1. Set and enforce board grading policies and procedures. Boards of Education should adopt a grading policy and set of procedures that specify what *comprises* the grade and in what *proportion*. These policies and procedures should establish grading policies that prescribe allowable categories and a minimum-maximum range of weights for each; for example, tests, quizzes, projects, authentic products, and—if they *must*—homework. This would at least stop the inequities within the same grade levels and buildings and across entire districts. More importantly, building principals must be accountable for consistently and thoughtfully enforcing these policies and procedures throughout the district.

A note about **academic freedom:** Because we hear it so often, we must address the expression "academic freedom." It originated at the collegiate level, where students (who paid tuition to attend) could drop course—and thus the professor—if the instruction and/or requirements were not to his or her liking. Somehow, the concept migrated to public school, where many unions have wormed it into the labor contract. It's hard to imagine how any administrative teams could have missed that concession, but several did. In many cases, the results have been to lose managerial control of curriculum, instructional strategies, and grading practices.

In our opinion, there is no academic freedom in public schools for two major reasons: (1) the teachers are not independent providers—they sign a contract to follow the directives of the Board of Education and are paid by the Board; (2) although their salaries are subsidized by the taxpayer, the students (as the children of those taxpayers) do not have the right to drop a teacher's class (unless it is a high school elective); they are "stuck," irrespective of teacher quality. Hence, teachers are subject to their employers and must follow the board policies and procedures, and that should include how grading relates to standards mastery.

   2. Shift from points to performance and standards-based grading. With the Common Core standards, the new content standards, and the 21st century skills being all about *performance*, districts should seriously consider standards-based grading. This is certainly not a new suggestion (the details below are from Tomlinson and McTighe in 2006), but it bears repeating and reconsideration. While still keeping the venerable letter grade, it places the priority on performance, not points. Tomlinson and McTighe suggest that:

   o The *A* means a student has completed **proficient** work on **all** course standards and **advanced** work on some objectives.
   o The *B* means a student has completed **proficient** work on **all** course standards.
   o The *C* means a student has completed **proficient** work on the **most important standards**, although not on all. The student can continue to the next course.
   o [**NOTE:** In the NEW standards, there are no designations as to "most important" (a.k.a. "power" or "priority" standards).]
   o The *D* means a student has completed **proficient work** on **at least one-half** of the course standards but is **missing some important standards** and is at **significant risk of failing the next course** in the sequence. The student should repeat the course if it is a prerequisite for another course.
   o The *F* means a student has completed **proficient work** on **fewer than half** of the course standards and cannot successfully complete the next course in sequence.

Before we leave this topic, classroom teacher Pamela Scriffiny (2008) has adjusted the Tomlinson and McTighe system by replacing letter grades with the categories Advanced, Proficient, Partially Proficient, and Not-Yet Proficient. Every student's mastery of each standard receives one of the above designations, and a formula is applied to determine an Overall Mastery designation for the quarter. Unlike traditional grading—where once a grade or number of points is earned or lost, that's that—Scriffiny's approach allows students to keep working at a standard to raise the mastery designation throughout the quarter. In reality, however, colleges and universities still think they need a "grade," and categories such as Scriffiny's will doubtless get wedged into some letter so as to enable the determination of a grade point average.

3. Designate mastery at the end of the grading period, not an average. Mastery learning and performance-based learning—particularly in the new standards—intends that every student is given the opportunity to attain mastery. Further, it is the mission of every school that all students will achieve some degree of mastery, though perhaps at different rates and through different channels. It is anticipated that mastery is more *developmental* than *spontaneous* and takes more than one opportunity to occur. Thus, the determination of mastery should be based on student's **final performance by the end of the grading period.** This is in sharp contrast to the prevailing sentiment that a student's final grade be an average of all his or her performances throughout the grading period. Nothing new, this concept has been supported by Ken O'Connor (2007), Robert Marzano (2000, 2007), Pam Scriffiny (2008), and Doug Reeves (2008) and has been reasserted by Tom Guskey (2011).

4. Eliminate the "zero" and facilitate work completion. Instead of awarding students with zeroes for failing to complete their work, it is recommended that students be **required to *complete the work*** at a time that is *inconvenient* to them (to prevent their taking advantage of the delay tactic). The times may be before, during, or after school, during study periods, at quiet tables during lunch, or at other times not favorable to students. It's known as taking the unpleasant consequences for an earlier bad decision—but STILL having to do the work.

5. Avoid end-of-semester "killer" tests and projects. As detailed in the missteps above, Reeves (2008) feels that high-stakes end-of-semester tests and projects (he calls them grade-killers) should be disallowed. Although we agree with Reeves, semester exams have become as firmly entrenched as the faculty lounge and to drop them would be extremely unpopular. In a slight perversion of that practice, many districts have begun to offer students the reward of skipping the semester exam as a trade-off for successfully completing other assignments, including passing the high-stakes test—and it's been working!

6. Disallow competitive, comparative grading practices. To most educators, the use of grades to spur **competition** among students is more destructive than inspiring. It sets up a system of winners and losers, and being "first" or having the highest grade or greatest number of points becomes the end in itself, and the strengths and weaknesses of the performance is overshadowed. Unlike the Olympics, where not everyone can win, *everyone can learn,* and **all students can master the content standards**. How quickly that occurs and who does it ahead of whom is not the point. As a matter of fact, the 21st century skills are all about collaborative efforts among students and learning the value of cooperation to get a job done.

Several years ago, this notion was powerfully illustrated to one of us as a grad student, but it remains a vivid reminder of how destructive competition is to learning. A well-meaning but ill-advised workshop leader attempted to prove this by administering an achievement test to 25 teachers on day one of the two-week summer workshop. That evening, he scored the tests and posted the scores (with names) the next day, arranged from the highest to the lowest. To say that the chemistry within the group—and between the group and him—soured for the rest of the two weeks would be an understatement. And although most consultants certainly know better than to ever do such a thing, our guess is that none of those teachers EVER used grades to spur public competition among their students.

It is well understood that *state officials* may need to play the game of "my dog's bigger than yours" with other states—which takes the idea of "grading" to a whole different level of dysfunctionality. But vanity and bragging rights among politicians should be kept totally away from measuring mastery in the individual classroom.

7. Require teachers to provide substantive feedback on assessments. As encouraged by researchers for a decade (e.g., Tomlinson and McTighe, 2006; O'Connor, 2007; Marzano, 2000, 2007; Reeves, 2008; Scriffiny, 2008; Guskey, 2000, 2011), substantive feedback to students about their test and project performance is *crucial* to sustained mastery. The specific detail of this affirmation and correction provides students with direction for subsequent performance and how to overcome mistakes. The "right/wrong" of a single number or letter cannot inform students about *why* and *what* and *how*.

8. Expand the traditional "one grade" to three. One of Guskey's (2011) most powerful suggestions is to replace the one-grade system with three grades:

o **Product**, or the *quality of the work produced* by the student as a reflection of mastery;
o **Progress**, or the extent to which the student experienced *growth or gain* during the course of instruction; and
o **Process,** or how the student *conducted him and herself* while working toward mastery, including collaboration with others, the use of time and resources, sincerity of effort, and self-direction.

We would add that these three levels are also reflective of the requirements of the 21st century skills!

The reform of grading will probably not command the national interest until the national K–12 curriculum is driven by the Common Core standards in Math and English Language Arts, the new Science and Social Studies standards, and the 21st century skills. But in the meantime, this section of the chapter has attempted to suggest key points for discussion about grading and to offer doable adjustments that can be made in districts' current grading systems. Since the new standards are performance-based, the method of "marking" mastery or assigning a "grade" will need to adapt accordingly. But traditions in American education die hard, and the time-honored A, B, C, and so on will be no exception.

Implementation and Accountability 7

"Even if you are on the right track, you will get run over if you just sit there."

—Will Rogers

In the first six chapters, we hope to have shown what a major systemic undertaking it is to transform a district's curriculum to reflect the Common Core standards in Math and English Language Arts, state content standards in Science and Social Studies, and the 21st century skills. But we also hope to have made it equally clear that the task is an *unprecedented opportunity* to restore integrity and rigor to the instructional program. In fact, claims Common Core researcher Tim Shanahan (2012), to think the standards impossible to implement is "an urban myth." We see it as a chance to replace outmoded and ineffective practices with those proven to yield higher levels of student performance. In a way, it's like cleaning and reorganizing the cupboards and closets in the ones' entire house. Nobody likes the thought of it, and it's tempting to put it off since no one really sees what's inside. But once it's done, oh how great it feels and how much better and more efficiently the household operates! But the key, of course, is to approach it strategically and then to maintain it once it's been done. That same approach works when transforming the district's curriculum and instructional program.

Taking a quick look back, districts who have accomplished what has been addressed in the previous chapters would have achieved the following:

a. They have **established the districtwide infrastructure** (and allocated the human and financial resources) necessary to develop, enact, and support the new curriculum and instructional program; they have:

(1) chosen the subject areas and grade levels to work on in succession [Note: It is typical for these two phases of the work to take 10–12 release days, or 60–72 clock hours per work team.];

(2) appointed teacher work-teams to examine the standards and devise the course tools for classroom implementation;

(3) established work schedules and either (a) lined up substitutes for release days or (b) allocated stipend money;

(4) arranged with local university or regional service providers to facilitate the work;

(5) reworked principal job descriptions and performance evaluation criteria to include specific responsibilities in the transformational project (i.e., serving on work teams; being trained to support and monitor classroom implementation; learning to use student performance data to continuously monitor progress; and developing collaborative supervision skills to help teachers overcome difficulties); and

(6) established monthly grade-level meetings to review student performance and adjust the course tools as needed.

b. **developed valid course tools (curriculum maps and unit plans)** to implement the standards-based program; these have been adopted by the board of education as the official teaching documents of the district; and

c. put in place **procedures to continuously monitor** student and staff performance and to make adjustments in the course tools as needed.

While each of these is an integral step in the transformation process, none can be successful by itself. The fourth transformative feature—the one that binds them together to make the whole process work—is **a set of official structures or strategic practices for implementation and accountability**. Although these have been alluded to throughout the book (i.e., grade-level teams, on-site monitoring by central office staff, classroom visits by the principal, quality control of course tools and assessments, etc.), they are the direct focus of this chapter. To be precise, these structures for implementation and accountability are not a *separate* step; they actually *accompany the other three*, and many occur simultaneously.

GRADE-LEVEL OR COURSE TEAMS

This section addresses the hugely important role of the teacher work teams who review the standards and translate them into course tools for classroom implementation. Bear in mind that the board adopts these course tools as the official curriculum and instructional program of the district—for which all teaching and administrative staff are accountable and by which they will be evaluated. How could there possibly be a more legitimate and authentic voice for teachers than to actually develop the instructional program? For that reason, the teachers (and coaches, where applicable) for each work team must be carefully selected and their work fully supported. What follows are suggestions to secure the "implementation-accountability" for the work of these teams.

Selection of the Work Teams. The teachers selected for these teams must have the trust and respect of their colleagues. Because their work will set the course for entire grade levels in a subject, these teachers must be knowledgeable about their content areas and effective in the classroom. Their major concern is student learning. These work teams should also include at least one central office administrator and one building principal. Otherwise, the administrators remain detached from transforming the instructional program, unaware of the exchange of ideas and intense deliberations that accompany the process. Worse, they are excluded from the "best-practices" training and the careful thought that goes into developing unit plans and planning for differentiation. The truth is that unless the administrators work through the course tool development with teachers, they have very little credibility when it comes to monitoring their implementation. This participation in the work teams should be included in every administrator's job description.

The Role of Central Office in Preparing the Course Tools. As was described in Chapter 2, the analysis of the new content standards and the 21st century skills is an enormous job for the grade-level work teams in each subject. So is the development of the course tools to implement them in every classroom. The considerable time required for the standards and course tool work must be factored into the equation when the district makes its commitment. There are several other reasons to include a central office administrator on each work team. These include:

a. to help monitor the work team process as well as to participate in the deliberations;

b. to help maintain the developmental flow between grade levels and to provide continuity among the teams;

c. to answer questions about district-level matters (e.g., the availability of materials and technology; the district assessment schedule; professional development);

d. to coordinate the efforts among science, social studies, and English language arts teachers to address the Literacy standards—particularly in terms of the research papers.

Circulation of the Drafts for Consensus. In smaller districts, each work team may indeed be the entire grade-level or all of the teachers assigned to a course. But in larger districts, the work teams are typically representative. In these larger districts, the drafts of the course tools should be circulated among the other grade-level or course teachers to obtain their input and strengthen consensus. The important thing is to ensure that every teacher has a voice in these all-important course tools and *fully understands his or her accountability* for their use.

Regular Meetings and "Green Ink" Going Forward. Once the course tools are developed and then adopted by the Board of Education, they become the new curriculum and instructional program throughout the district. The teachers involved thus begin the implementation process. Among the strategic practices for implementation and accountability are **regular meetings** (at least monthly) of these grade-level and course teams to discuss student performance. In particular, how specific techniques "worked" with students—or did not; how easy or difficult the activities were to implement; and the results or level of success.

To provide the material for these grade-level team meetings, we have found it very helpful for every teacher to be given a **green** pen to make marginal notes and edits to the course tools as they go along, noting how students responded and any adjustments that had to be made. This is not to imply license to "do whatever they wish." The teachers are still accountable for using the course tools as written, and they bring their green ink to the grade-level or course team meetings for consideration. Collectively across the school year, this green ink—in conjunction with student performance—becomes the substance of the edits to the course tools for the next year.

Annual Course Tool Revisions. The task of the central office staff, principals, coaches, and other support staff is to oversee this transformation process via their respective job duties. Their role is to maintain quality control of the daily delivery and assessment of instruction while supporting candid but responsible discussions among practitioners about how the course tools are working—and what would make them stronger, but always keeping the standards as the primary consideration. Along with the green ink compiled by the teachers, these administrators will be analyzing student performance data on both the classroom and district levels. At the end of the year, the administrators are accountable for approving and submitting to the board valid adjustments to the course tools to be approved for the subsequent year. Their challenge is to balance teacher recommendations with student performance.

. . . And from those who REALLY know. . . .

*As I worked with a team of district math teachers to "unpack" the Core Math Standards and build curriculum maps and unit plans, we were not sure how things would go with our students in the classroom. "Green inking" as we taught the unit was a necessary step to plan for adjustments that need to be made going forward. The time for reflection on what we did instructionally after we saw how the students did on both traditional and authentic assessments also helped us know what adjustments we need to make for the units to be stronger. Using our student data, talking with students about the units, and discussing with other teachers what worked and what did not has made all of us stronger for the next time we teach the units.—**Melissa Rhode, Department Math Chair, Chaney High School, Youngstown City Schools***

DIRECT ASSISTANCE TO STAFF

Another key implementation-accountability practice is the direct assistance to staff and students by academic coaches, principals, supervisors, or other support staff. To help teachers in the delivery and assessment of instruction, some districts have the resources to hire academic supervisors and others have used categorical dollars to hire academic coaches. By design, these supervisors and coaches are themselves master teachers and are thus equipped with the necessary competencies and records of success to (a) train intervention specialists to provide the most effective intervention services possible and (b) model for and counsel teachers who are struggling. The following suggestions are offered to secure the implementation-accountability for the direct assistance to teachers.

Students. Districts who follow a response to intervention plan often assign their supervisors or academic coaches to provide training to the teachers who are assigned to provide intervention services to Tier II students. Proficient in the "best practices" themselves and having been involved with the work teams in the development of the course tools, these coaches and supervisors fully understand what is needed to maximize student performance. Coaches help intervention teachers understand that the standards must be mastered, and students who fall short must be taught the enabling skills to accomplish the standards. The curriculum cannot be "dumbed" down so that strugglers earn counterfeit points but show no lasting gains in their academic achievement. If needed, the coaches and supervisors should model appropriate intervention techniques for teachers to give them ideas about what to do. While some principals provide direct services to students, in the majority of districts, the role of the principals is facilitation of this assistance.

Teaching Staff. Academic coaches, supervisors, and principals may be asked to assist struggling teachers to overcome their weaknesses in planning, delivery, and/or assessment of instruction. One way is in a discrete, low-key capacity or as part of the teachers' "growth plan." Another way is through direct referral for an intervention. Either way, the effective coach, supervisor, or principal has the competency and perceptive skills needed to help a struggling teacher become successful. An integral part of the transformation process is to establish the infrastructure for—as well as the expectation of—direct assistance to teachers who are unable to use the course tools with fidelity. Informally, if teachers are willing to seek assistance, or formally, if principals are doing their job with classroom observations and walk-throughs, no teacher should be left to fail.

Administrative and Supervisory Staff. In some districts, there will be principals, supervisors, coaches, and central office curriculum-instructional staff who were unable to be members of a teacher work team to develop the course tools. These individuals must receive parallel training in the standards-review process, the development of course tools, and the best practices to deliver and assess classroom instruction. Otherwise, the district's transformational effort is fragmented, since some staff are aware and others not. This training also involves collaborative observation (to be explained later in this chapter) to make the implementation-accountability process more seamless and inclusive of every staff member.

. . . And from those who REALLY know. . . .

Thankfully, we no longer provide special needs students a separate curriculum and/or pull them away from the general ed students as a separate group. Except for students with extreme deficits (who are served in self-contained classes), we "include" our special needs students in the general education classrooms. These students are fully integrated into the class and are expected to do the same work with on-level standards as their general ed peers. In several "inclusion" classes, a special needs teacher works full-time with the general ed teacher, and in other classrooms, the special needs teacher provides part-time services.

This expectation that our "inclusion" students be academically part of the general ed classroom community cannot be accomplished simply by directive. To change what has been a prevailing culture of separation, we've had to change an entire mindset. We've provided encouragement, training, and facilitation. Early on, we made sure that the general ed and special needs teachers met to discuss how they would implement the unit plans. In particular, what role would each teacher play in presenting the material, and how would activities be differentiated to serve the special needs students? Throughout the year of developing unit plans, we included a special needs teacher as part of each grade-level work team in the four core content areas. Including the voice of special needs in each unit has yielded various adaptations and accommodations that can be used for all struggling students—low-functioning nonidentified as well as special needs. In addition, we've provided 1:1 consultation and in-class visitation services for teachers who have specific questions or particular needs.

*It hasn't been the easiest thing we've ever done, but it's certainly been one of the most beneficial for students!—**Lori A. Kopp, executive director of the Department of Special Education, Youngstown City Schools***

THE OBSERVATION AND ANALYSIS OF CLASSROOM INSTRUCTION BY THE PRINCIPAL

Probably the most important implementation and accountability practice is the direct supervision of instruction by the building principal. This is accomplished through frequent and structured classroom observations, followed by the collaborative development of follow-up plans for continued growth or corrective action. The observation technique most heavily supported in the research is to note the teacher behavior and its impact on students. This authentic teacher-student interaction is in sharp contrast to focusing on bulletin boards, introductions and conclusions, or looking for a checklist of static practices that may or may not be relevant to that lesson. With the right training and continued support from the central office, principals can become very skillful in observing and collecting authentic classroom data. Being thoroughly familiar with the course tools, principals know if teachers are teaching the curriculum as well as using appropriate teaching strategies. And through the objective analysis of classroom data and appropriate questioning, principals can collaborate with teachers to enhance or improve performance. Once it is understood what the standards expect of students and teachers, principals can use their awareness and authority in a positive way to help teachers improve the effectiveness of classroom instruction and help move students toward mastery.

The Principal's Schedule. There is absolutely no substitute for principals spending time each day in classrooms observing the teacher behaviors and the impact of those behaviors on students. To prevent being pre-empted by other duties, these visits must be planned as part of the principal's daily schedule. Paul Bambrick-Santoyo (2012), managing director of Uncommon Schools-North Star, insists that it is key to observe more frequently and for less time; therefore, by grouping several 15-minute observations into a block of time such as an hour or two hours, principals can reduce time lost trying to move between class visits and other activities. This represents a significant change for many principals, who have conducted classroom observations only if time in the day permitted. In our experience, far too many principals are either assigned to—or manage to find—all sorts of noninstructional ways to spend their time. They perform clerical or logistical tasks that should be handled by someone else, run interference on discipline, attend off-site meetings through the day, and/or deal with paperwork that could be completed after-hours.

We have discovered that this reluctance to observe the teaching-learning process and to perform the duties of an instructional leader is more about discomfort and lack of training than willful refusal (Peters & March, 1999, 2007). But to be fair, it is also about the expectations set and upheld by *district leaders.* With each state now mandating new practices and measures for teacher evaluation—tied significantly to student performance—this is one of the single most important aspects to changing what happens in classrooms. Our focus on classroom observation as the most crucial aspect of any teacher evaluation system is supported by the nation's foremost teacher appraisal researcher, Charlotte Danielson (2012).

Retooling and Changing the Focus. The current debate about teacher evaluation appears to be whether it is a tool to *measure* teachers or one to *develop* them (Marzano, 2012). States are mandating new teacher evaluation systems that include a multifaceted teacher evaluation and not the single classroom observation with an overall rating rubric (Stecher, Garet, Holtzman, & Hamilton, 2012). Among the facets that states are including is that of student test scores through value-added measures to reflect the competence of a teacher (DiCarlo, 2012). Indeed, the biggest names in the business are writing about teacher evaluation and outlining elements for a system that will create effective teaching (Darling-Hammond, 2012). But key to the whole undertaking is that districts upgrade the skill sets of principals to help them develop the proficiencies and confidence they require to actually function as instructional leaders.

The new curriculum, with its increased expectations for students and staff and the use of the course tools to deliver and assess it, provides a golden opportunity for principals to modify their practices in the supervision and evaluation of teachers. If principals sit in with the work teams as the course tools are developed, they will be perceived as partners in the transformation of the curriculum. Moreover, the principals' work with the best-practices techniques will have shown them how to recognize when such practices are and are not being used and how to analyze instruction and conference with teachers about these practices. Following authentic classroom observations, the principal and teacher collaborate on the development of a growth plan. Unlike traditional systems where only struggling teachers receive a follow-up plan, experts such as Danielson (2012) agree with us that everyone can be better at what they do and that growth plans are not reserved only for teachers who are struggling. For teachers doing well, the "plan" outlines continued growth, and for teachers who are falling short, the "plan" is corrective. Each action plan sets forth specific strategies, the criteria for success, and a time frame for completion.

The Approach With Teachers. The collaborative discussions between a principal and teacher assure that the action plan is something that is not dictated, but rather reflects a common understanding and agreement between the teacher and principal of what will happen for the teacher to demonstrate growth. This helps principals understand it is not about having all of the *answers* to "fix" every teacher, but rather it is about asking teachers the right questions (Danielson, 2012; Marzano, 2012). By focusing on teaching behaviors and how they impact students, the principals can help teachers reflect on their classroom practices through conversation and analysis that lead to how to make teaching stronger. Treating teachers with respect and empathy—but being clear in expectations for quality instruction—the principal is perfectly positioned to impact what happens in classrooms. Invested with the responsibility for evaluating teachers, the principal also has the impact with teachers to use the course tools with fidelity.

Some researchers are calling for elimination of the "announced" classroom observation and going with up to 10 shorter unannounced visits followed with timely, face-to-face feedback (Marshall, 2012). It is our belief that some of each type of observation is needed. To that end, the **walk-through** visits as well as the **longer class observation** are essential to capture what really is happening in the classrooms of a building. We propose that a principal use a list similar to that in Table 7.1 when doing walk-throughs to document what was happening while he or she was in the class. The key to the walk-through concept is that there be face-to-face dialogue following the classroom visit. In many places where we work, the emphasis for the walk-through is to have an "app" on an iPad, and the principal sends the teacher an electronic form of what was observed. In our opinion, this practice replaces the human interaction with an impersonal judgment about what was happening in the class. The feedback we have gotten from teachers about the electronic feedback is that they never had a chance to discuss what happened with anyone, and it seems to be a "gotcha" tool rather than a tool for professional growth.

The Unit as the Lesson Plan Tool. It is suggested that teachers submit the unit plan—highlighted as to where they are working each week—as their lesson plans. If they do so, the principal always has a sense of where the lesson for today fits into the bigger picture, what has come before and what is to follow, along with how students will be assessed to show mastery of the standards. Without this "big-picture" view, the principal is guessing, and the teacher can play a game of "but you don't understand what has happened, or where I am headed." It is incumbent on the principal to work with the unit plans and the accompanying assessments to improve the school's instructional program. Since the unit plan is electronic, the teachers can submit it electronically, or they can print the paper copy and highlight with color the work they are doing for a given week. It is critical that principals have a sense of how a teacher is proceeding through the units to understand student progress. Also, this allows the principal to discuss with a teacher the materials used, any additional materials that might be needed, and how specific students are progressing on the standards for that unit.

Table 7.1 Ideas for Best-Practices Walk-Throughs

Best Practice	Definition/Explanation
Higher-order thinking	Re: Bloom's *Taxonomy*
Goal-setting	Academic and personal
Recognition and reinforcement	Substantive and specific for good citizenship and self-management
Continuous monitoring with feedback	Substantive (to affirm and correct) and criterion referenced to the standards
Questioning and cueing	At various levels of thinking (literal, inferential, synthetic, evaluative, what-if, etc.)
Vocabulary and context	A series of steps to unlock word meaning; i.e., structure, syntax, context clues
Organizational patterns of text	For example, compare-contrast; cause-effect; chronological sequence; problem-solution; etc.
Note-taking	Re: organizational pattern
Graphic organizers	Re: organizational pattern
Summarizing nonfiction	Re: organizational pattern
Summarizing fiction	Re: who, what, when, where
Mathematical problem analysis and problem solving	Re: looking for *start, change,* or *result* (as per Appendix A of Math Core Content Standards)
Similarities and differences: Categorization	Labeling a group of people, objects, places, events, actions, conditions, and concepts according to the attributes they share or have in common
Comparison	Identifying how people, objects, places, etc. are alike and different using T-charts, Venn diagrams, or comparison matrices

(Continued)

Table 7.1 (Continued)

Best Practice	Definition/Explanation
Critical attributes	Looking for the attribute that makes a concept different from related concepts; accomplished through examples and nonexamples
Metaphor	A figurative device that uses the features of a familiar object to understand an unfamiliar one (e.g., his hands were steel mallets as they worked the metal)
Analogy	A double metaphor or two terms related to two other terms by function, synonyms, antonyms, symbols, etc. (e.g., wine : grape :: vinegar : apple)
Hypothesizing and testing to verify (a.k.a. inquiry)	Guiding students to ask questions or predict "whats" and "whys" and then checking out their hypotheses to discover the answer or another direction to pursue
Differentiation, using varied amounts of: **Time**	
Assistance	Unassisted—>—Peers—>—Aide—>—Teacher
Length of material or number of problems	
Level of difficulty	
Concreteness	Working with models and manipulatives versus dealing with the abstract
Practice	
Sophistication	Simple or basic through more elaborate (higher levels of thought)
Structure	Products ranging from a list of bullet points through written discourse

The Impact of Ongoing Student Performance Data. As was suggested earlier, one of the principal's most important responsibilities as an instructional leader is to spearhead the building's use of student performance results to inform instruction. This might be through common assessments, discussion at the teacher-based team meetings that focus on how a unit is going, what additional instruction is called for, and what supplemental materials would better meet student needs. If the data to be discussed are actual test scores by standard, with analysis of student error, the principal must make sure that the data are provided to teachers quickly and in a user-friendly format. These data are then analyzed by the teacher teams, and the strengths and weaknesses revealed are used to make adjustments in classroom instruction. While it is the teachers who are to use the data, they are far less likely to do so with any consistency or deliberate purpose unless they are provided the opportunity and the expectation to do so by the principal. We see it as key for the principal to set the tone for these meetings.

> **!** *Lesson Learned!* An important lesson from actual experience is not to focus so heavily on numbers that the skill deficits and strengths they represent are totally overlooked. In one district, the emphasis was so much about charts of numbers that when teachers tried to talk about something in the unit with which students struggled, the leader of the meeting shot it down and directed the teachers back to the numbers on the data sheet. There is more to being data driven than looking only at numbers. Teachers need time to discuss and analyze why students did well or not well on certain types of questions and concepts. Moreover, what distinguishes the students who mastered a standard from one who did not? Teachers need opportunity and encouragement to determine what they need to adjust going forward as well as what they can continue. Most important of all, what is working well for which students and what not so well for others?

The Collaborative Observation Process. The need for a collaborative process is perhaps now more important than when we first began work with the classroom observation for teacher growth many years ago (Peters & March, 1999, 2007). We believe that the use of a preobservation conference, followed by the in-class data collection through scripting, followed by a postobservation conference that yields an action plan for growth is critical to making the process meaningful and something done *with teachers, not to teachers.* Our work has been further reinforced by that of the country's leading school reformers (Bambric-Santoyo, 2012; Danielson, 2012; Darling-Hammond, 2012; Marshall, 2012; Marzano, 2012).

> *. . . And from those who REALLY know. . . .*
>
> *When we set out to reorganize our teacher evaluation system, we knew we had to focus more directly on the teaching and learning going on in our classrooms. We needed to make sure our principals could recognize methods of delivery and assessment and distinguish those that were effective from those that were not. We provided them training and practice in a collaborative observation process that helped them form their teachers into a professional learning community. And the key to the success of the process was to develop it around the course materials we had put in place. The preconference included questions about the teacher's planning—not just for this lesson but how this lesson fit into the context of the larger unit. The in-class observation focused on the teacher's behaviors and how students responded. The postconference consisted of a joint reflection on the learning response of students and posed alternate methods of delivery. The culmination of the observation process was a growth plan, collaboratively developed by each teacher and principal. It included jointly identified strategies for continued growth or improvement, criteria for success, any needed assistance, and a time frame. But again, the secret has been to make sure those strategies relate directly to classroom practices that will lead to improved performance among students.—**Susan Kahle, former assistant superintendent, Alliance City Schools**

The collaborative observation process components are outlined here. In addition, there is a template to guide each part of the process to ensure consistency in the work done. The forms are based on Ohio's teacher evaluation standards but are easily adaptable to any state's requirements.

The Preobservation Conference (a set of questions discussed that relate to the unit/lesson)

- ☑ Conducted as a face-to-face interview
- ☑ Designed to gather an overview of the daily lesson in the context of the unit plan
- ☑ Allows teacher to identify particular aspect(s) of the lesson he/she wants the observer to see

In-class data collection (scripting) and analysis

- ☑ Is the descriptive recording of classroom drawing; time frames; teacher behaviors; student responses; and teacher-student interactions
- ☑ Includes objective analysis—strengths and concerns or questions—expressed as teacher behavior and impact on students

The Postobservation Conference

- ☑ Is the "plan" for debriefing on the lesson with the teacher; the observer actually plans what points of emphasis he/she wants to use in the postconference
- ☑ Identifies those areas that both the teacher and the observer thought were strengths and concerns/questions
- ☑ Identifies *tentative* strategies for growth, expansion, or corrective action

The Collaborative Action Plan

- ☑ Culminates the postobservation conference to guide continued growth or corrective action
- ☑ Identifies **area(s) of focus** for growth or corrective action
- ☑ Specifies **strategies**, techniques, or activities to accomplish the plan
- ☑ Details the intended **impact on students**
- ☑ Specifies **time frames**
- ☑ Identifies helpful **resources** to accomplish the growth

---

The specific templates that accompany each of the components above are inserted here for clarity in how the process is to work. Note that the numbers behind each question or section relate to the teaching standards for Ohio. Most importantly, the templates can be customized for each client to reflect the client's unique priorities and circumstances. In addition, Appendix H: Collaborative Observation Samples shows a sample of the forms with data.

. . . And from those who REALLY know. . . .

*As a principal new to my present district, I am using the process outlined in the book for my classroom visits and analysis of instruction. I had previously worked with the process in another district and had great success with my teachers! The important key in classroom visitation and analysis is getting the opportunity to have a conversation with teachers about what is happening in the classrooms and getting them to reflect on their lessons. When meeting with the teachers in my building, I find that there is a lot of input from them through their reflection.—**Susan Koulianos, principal, Harding Elementary School, Youngstown City Schools***

The following pages have sample forms that we have used for the processes outlined. They are modified according to the district/state guidelines for teacher evaluation.

INDIVIDUAL LESSON PREOBSERVATION CONFERENCE

Teacher _____Building _____

Grade(s) _____ Subject(s)_____

Observer _____ Date of Conference _____ Date of Observation _____

[NOTE: The principal will have reviewed the unit plan from which this lesson is taken and will have a copy with him/her.]

1. How does this **unit** build on the previous one and lead to the next one?

2. I understand the lesson I'll see is taken from the **unit** on _____.
   Which **lesson** will I be seeing? [Teacher should be able to "point to" on the marked unit plan.]

   _____

   _____

3. Which **standards** will you be addressing in this lesson? [Teacher should be able to "point" to unit plan.]

   a. _____

   b. _____

   c. _____

   d. _____

4. Summarize for me what **strategies YOU'LL be using** and what you expect the **STUDENTS to do** to process the information and construct meaning for themselves. [Teacher should be able to "walk" through the proposed lesson; should be fairly decent match to Motivation, Teaching-Learning, Traditional Assessment, or Authentic Assessment sections of the unit plan.]

Time	Teaching Behaviors/ Strategies	Student Responses	Materials/Technology

5. What **learning "needs"** have you discovered among your students that have widened the "gap" between successful and unsuccessful performance?

6. How have you planned to **differentiate** your lesson for:

   a. the more accelerated students?

   b. students with disabilities?

   c. students at risk of failure?

7. What types of assessments are you using in the unit to:

   a. determine what students know at the start of the unit?

   b. determine understanding throughout the unit?

   c. determine mastery of the standards at the end of the unit?

8. Are there any students for whom you have a particular plan—academically or behaviorally? OR Are there any students you want me to note in particular?

IN-CLASS DATA COLLECTION

CLASSROOM DRAWING AND RECORD OF MOVEMENT AND RESPONSES	Observer _____ Teacher Observed _____
	Date: _____ Number of Students: _____
	Materials/Equipment for Differentiation:
	Notes:

RECORDING OF LESSON DESCRIPTION

TIME	TEACHER BEHAVIOR	STUDENT BEHAVIORS/RESPONSES

LESSON ANALYSIS

STRENGTHS	QUESTIONS/CONCERNS

Subsequent pages of the script template do not bear the classroom drawing and the other identifying information in the top right corner.

POSTOBSERVATION CONFERENCE PLANNING

1. **Positive points** from the preobservation conference and script that the observer wants to reinforce. These should be stated as Teacher Behavior/Impact on Students and should focus on 2–3 key items from the analysis.

2. **Questions/concerns** from the preobservation conference and script that the observer wants to address. These should be stated as Teacher Behavior/Impact on Students and should focus on 1–2 key items from your analysis.

3. **Area for growth** that the observer would like to see the teacher pursue at the end of the postconference.

4. **Alternatives**: What other activities, strategies, or techniques might also be effective for teaching a lesson such as this?

5. Other areas in planning from the **preconference** form for the teacher asked for you to observe and provide feedback.

POSTVISITATION CONFERENCE AND ACTION PLAN

Observer _____ Teacher Observed _____ Date of Postconference _____

Things that went the way the teacher had intended:
(what s/he felt *went well* and how the students responded)

Things that did not go the way the teacher had intended:
(what s/he felt *did not work* and how the students responded)

Target Area	Specific Strategies for Teacher to Try (Begin with a verb . . .)	Criteria for Success (So that . . .)	Time Frame for Plan	Role of Support Personnel (If any)

Without exception, principals tell us that when they did their training/ graduate work, the evaluation of classroom teaching and helping teachers grow was not part of their program. Indeed, for many, their first administrative job was as an assistant principal, and they spent their days doing little more than discipline. However, when one is to be the instructional leader of a building and required to evaluate teaching, the expectation shifts from "holding the lid on the place" to making the school strong instructionally through the analysis of teaching and learning. Therefore, one must learn how to be an instructional leader. As former college professors, who taught courses for the "to-be" principals, we required similar work to what is outlined in this book— working with standards, writing curriculum, conferencing with teachers, and collecting data, and analyzing instruction. Yes, the graduate students could be heard groaning for miles away! However, even today, we receive phone calls to consult in the schools where these people have become principals because they are using the practices that we outline here. They realize that what they learned about quality instruction truly does make a difference in student learning.

Why include collaborative observation as part of the curricular and instructional transformation process? In our many years of experience, it is not only a valid and important component to monitor the enacted reforms, but it is also the most seamless and job-embedded process available to help administrators work collaboratively with teachers for the benefit of students.

. . . And from those who REALLY know. . . .

As a high school principal, I often felt that not being an expert in all of the content areas was a detriment to me helping improve the teaching in my school. But, when I began working with the collaborative observation process and focused specifically on describing the teacher behaviors and the student responses/behaviors, I found that I had a tool that opened the door for discussing what was happening in each classroom. Working with the classroom teacher to analyze where we are and where we want to be, we collaboratively develop a plan of action for making the teaching stronger. We operate with the idea that all of us can be better at what we do, so everyone has a growth plan, and the process is not deficit oriented. With the walk-throughs, I am able to support and reinforce what teachers are trying to implement with their students as part of their plan. Subsequent to each walk-through, there are follow-up conversations with the teacher that focus on the specific teaching behaviors and how the students responded.

In addition to the collaborative observation process, my involvement in professional development around the core standards as well as our State Science and Social Studies standards helped me to understand the changes these new standards were bringing. Working with curriculum mapping and unit planning that our teachers have been doing, as well as engaging in "hands-on" best-practices professional development gave me the confidence to know I can work with our teachers on using these strategies to engage students in a more meaningful manner.—Holly Seimetz, principal, East High School, Youngstown City Schools

Summary and Sustainability 8

"Let us reform our schools, and we shall find little reform needed in our prisons."

—John Ruskin (1819–1900)

As we draw the book to a close, we thought this Ruskin quote especially apropos—just in case there's anyone on the planet who is convinced that the need to transform schools began with the Common Core and the 21st century skills. Improving schools has been one of humankind's missions since the first school bell rang and classes got underway. This book has been an attempt to set forth the fundamentals of incorporating the Common Core standards in Math and English Language Arts, the new state content standards in Science and Social Studies, and the 21st century skills into the district curriculum and instructional program. This final chapter offers the reader a process checklist of the "to-dos" from the first seven chapters. The checklist is structured to help a district maintain quality control in the process and yet allow sufficient flexibility to accommodate emerging local developments, state issues, or mandates from the U.S. Department of Education.

The process checklist will set forth the following:

✓ Each individual **task** or **procedure** necessary to complete and sustain the transformation

✓ A **status indicator** (i.e., to identify the extent to which each task or procedure is being implemented as planned):

[3] If it is going well, a set of action steps to maintain and sustain it.

[2] If it going fairly well but experiencing difficulties, a set of actions steps to shore it up.

[1] If it is going poorly, a set of action steps to redirect the effort and get it back on track.

✓ For each action step, at least one specific **task** (many will include options) for each, and for each task:

- the person(s) responsible
- sample procedures or logistics to accomplish
- criteria for success (i.e., "going well" in the status indicator)

PROCESS CHECKLIST FOR TRANSFORMATION OF DISTRICT CURRICULAR-INSTRUCTIONAL PROGRAM

Integrating the Common Core Standards in Math and English Language Arts, State Standards in Science and Social Studies, and the 21st Century Skills

	Chapter 1: No Longer Business as Usual	
Task or Procedure	**Status Indicator** 3 . . . 2 . . . 1	**Planning for Action Steps** Who will do What in what Time Frame, and how it will be Monitored
1.0 Preview the **transformation process** and the district plan with all staff (including tasks, timelines, and means for monitoring); preview a synthesized version with parents and interested community members.		
1.1 Review major differences between **current standards** and Common Core (also, new Science and Social Studies); focus on higher cognitive demand and constructing meaning (vs. rote memory).		
1.2 Review major differences between **classroom strategies** with previous standards and those needed for the new standards and the 21st century skills. (Table 1.2)		
1.3 Review the basic structure of the **21st century skills**, including (a) connections to the content standards; (b) global awareness; (c) the literacies; (d) thinking and reasoning for decision-making; (e) communication and collaboration; (f) information technology and media literacy; (g) initiative, flexibility, and collaborative skills.		
1.4 Review the **urgency for American students** to perform on competitive tests as well as students of competing countries—this as a rationale for the new content standards and the demand for increased academic rigor in the nation's schools.		
1.5 Review the **implications for leadership** of the transformation process; i.e., (a) the differences in the standards; (b) the use of course tools to implement the standards; (c) differentiation; (d) dealing with special needs students; (e) the review of unit assessments and the use of high-stakes and classroom data to adjust instruction; (f) the use of walk-throughs and collaborative observation to monitor classroom instruction; and (g) the facilitation of regularly scheduled grade-level meetings.		
Other/Special Notes		

(Continued)

Chapter 2: Developing Course Tools to Build the Instructional Program

Task or Procedure	Status Indicator 3 . . . 2 . . . 1	Planning for Action Steps Who will do What in what Time Frame, and how it will be Monitored
2.0 Develop the district **game plan** for the transformation, including the schedule for subjects and grade levels; the design for work teams—membership and logistics; the adjustments in infrastructure necessary to support the work and implement the adopted materials, arrangements for the training and facilitation; and the allocation of human and financial resources needed to accomplish and monitor the "plan."		
2.1 Secure the **commitment from the Board of Education** for human and material resources to devise, implement, and monitor a plan: (a) appoint *work teams* to devise course tools, consisting of teachers, principals, and support staff; (b) create a workable meeting schedule (release time or afterschool); (c) provide for sharing drafts to obtain consensus; and (d) develop parallel administrator training schedules to prepare for implementation and monitoring of the course tools.		
2.2 Unpack, cluster, and sequence the **content standards**. Help work teams (a) understand the structure and spirit of the standards; (b) establish topics or themes (units) around which to cluster standards to provide context to maximize learning and transfer; (c) analyze the literacy skills intended for Science, Social Studies, and technical subjects, including Math—and determine ways to collaboratively address them with English Language Arts; and (d) examine the 21st century skills to determine where each can be integrated into the content areas, K–12.		
2.3 Devise curriculum maps for each subject and grade level that (a) place the units into the most appropriate learning or developmental sequence; (b) repeat standards, as needed, in multiple units; (c) assign time frames to each unit; (d) devise a physical format that best meets the needs of teachers to organize the school year; and (e) circulate the first drafts among other teachers at each grade level and subject for feedback.		
2.4 Devise **unit plans** based on each curriculum map to guide the daily delivery of classroom instruction. Work teams are shown (a) the research base for the unit plan format to fully understand its alignment with the requirements of the new standards and (b) the unit plan components to lead students toward constructive mastery.		
Other/Special Notes for 2.0 (Course Tools)		

Chapter 3: Integrating Best Practices to Help Students Construct Meaning		
Task or Procedure	**Status Indicator** 3 . . . 2 . . . 1	**Planning for Action Steps** **Who** will do **What** in what **Time Frame,** and how it will be **Monitored**
3.0 Part 1—Insert the appropriate **best practices into the unit plans**—selected to correspond to the content and cognitive demand of the standards and the information requirements of each Unit.		
3.1 Include **multiple levels of thinking** (re: Bloom's *Taxonomy*) to ensure students process information at a balance of basic to higher levels.		
3.2 Include student **goal-setting**: teacher models with own goals and sample academic and personal goals until students can formulate their own. Include progress on goals in letter grade.		
3.3 Plan activities that show students how to examine nonfiction texts for the **organizational pattern** chosen to convey the author's message; include (a) chronological sequence; (b) cause-effect; (c) compare-contrast; (d) "how-to"; (e) persuasion; and (f) problem-solution.		
3.4 Include lessons that show students how to **process information** to coincide with organizational patterns; include (a) summarizing; (b) note-taking; and (c) using graphic organizers.		
3.5 Develop **multiple levels of questions** (Level I, II, and III) to help students process information at various levels of comprehension; at Grades 4–12, teach **students to develop** these Level I, II, and III questions to exchange with fellow students.		
3.6 Integrate activities that require students to use **similarities and differences** to master standards; include (a) categorization; (b) comparisons; (c) critical attributes; (d) metaphors; and (e) analogies.		
Other/Special Notes for 3.0 (Best Practices—Part 1)		

(Continued)

(Continued)

Chapter 4: Integrating Best Practices Into Unit Plans

Task or Procedure	Status Indicator 3 . . . 2 . . . 1			Planning for Action Steps Who will do What in what Time Frame, and how it will be Monitored
4.0 Part 2—Insert the appropriate **best practices into the** unit plans—selected to correspond to the content and cognitive demand of the standards and the information requirements of each unit.				
4.1 [Math] Plan lessons to review with students the core steps to math **problem analysis** and problem solving: finding (a) the *START*; (b) the *CHANGE*; and (c) the *RESULT*. In addition, provide opportunity for students to use the 8 **math practices** that are part of the Common Core: (1) make sense of the problem; (2) reason abstractly and quantitatively; (3) construct viable arguments and critique reasoning; (4) model with mathematics; (5) use appropriate tools strategically; (6) attend to precision; (7) look for/make use of structure; and (8) look for and express regularity in repeated reasoning.				
4.2 Identify **key vocabulary** words and **domain-specific language** that students will need to understand; prepare demonstrations and practice exercises for (a) context clues, including the five most frequently used types of clue; (b) multiple meanings, the correct one based on context; (c) connotative meanings, or feelings associated with language; and (d) word parts or structural clues like roots and affixes.				
4.3 Insert **delivery strategies** that are appropriate to individual unit plans.				
4.3.a. *Lecture or explanation*, specifying the role of the teacher as well as what students will do to process the information.				

Task or Procedure	Status Indicator 3 . . . 2 . . . 1	Planning for Action Steps: Who will do **What** in what **Time Frame**, and how it will be **Monitored**
4.3.b. *Demonstration*, specifying the role of the teacher as well as what students will do to process the information.		
4.3.c. *Guided discussion*, specifying the role of the teacher as well as what students will do to process the information.		
4.3.d. *Inquiry*, specifying the role of the teacher as well as what students will do to process the information.		
4.3.e. *Advance organizer*, specifying the role of the teacher as well as what students will do to process the information.		
4.4 Insert cues to provide **recognition and reinforcement** for student effort and accomplishment; plan specific ways to respond similarly to teachers, parents, and support staff.		
4.5 Plan for **continuous monitoring** of student performance, and include substantive feedback—both to affirm accurate responses and to specify corrections for responses that held errors.		
4.6 Observe each of the **basic assumptions** necessary for the successful implementation of the unit plans.		
4.6.a. Use district-level (high-stakes) classroom tests and student **performance data** to plan and adjust instruction.		
4.6.b. Plan alternate strategies to **differentiate instruction**—both to remediate and to enrich; include adjustments to any of the following as appropriate to the student: (1) **T**ime; (2) **A**ssistance; (3) **L**ength of text or number of problems assigned; (4) **L**evel of **D**ifficulty of the material or task; (5) the number of **C**oncrete examples; (6) the amount of **P**ractice needed; (7) the **S**tructure of the product; and (8) the **S**ophistication of the product.		

(Continued)

(Continued)

Task or Procedure	Status Indicator 3 . . . 2 . . . 1	Planning for Action Steps Who will do What in what Time Frame, and how it will be Monitored
4.6.c. Provide students with **options or choices** to complete tasks and to demonstrate mastery, and hold them accountable for following through on those choices with fidelity.		
4.6.d. Include activities and materials to address the **Literacy Standards,** and make collaborative arrangements with the English Language Arts department as needed to complete written projects.		
4.6.e. Establish efficient classroom **routines and procedures** to maximize student engagement and prevent wasting instructional time.		
4.6.f. Use a variety of strategies for the class to **read longer text passages,** including oral reading by the teacher, oral reading by student volunteers, students reading aloud to a partner, student silent reading, etc. Move students toward reading 600–900-word passages independently to build stamina for high-stakes tests.		
Other/Special Notes for 4.0 (Best Practices—Part 2)		

Chapter 5: Continuous Assessment to Monitor Results		
Task or Procedure	**Status Indicator** **3 . . . 2 . . . 1**	**Planning for Action Steps** **Who** will do **What** in what **Time Frame**, and how it will be **Monitored**
5.0 Develop a strategic plan to **continuously monitor student performance**, using the results of high-stakes tests, district benchmark tests, and teacher-made classroom tests to **plan for and adjust instruction**; include specific **roles and responsibilities** for teachers, principals, and central office staff.		
5.1 Prepare **high-stakes test results** in a format easily interpreted by staff in terms of specific *skill strengths* (green highlights) and *weaknesses* (red highlights) by grade level, classroom, and individual student.		
5.1.a. Train staff in the definitions and uses of **high-stakes tests** and their results; include both (1) *short-term* analyses (for immediate use) and (2) *longitudinal* scrutiny for patterns and trends.		
5.1.b. Avoid **common missteps** in the use of high-stakes data, including: (1) failure to consider trends and patterns; (2) focusing only on overall scores, missing individual results; (3) failing to use the data collected to impact instruction; (4) using the data to "track" students—especially Tier III and special needs.		
5.1.c. Compare **how standards are tested with how they are taught** to remove any discrepancies; rework the time frame and the method of teaching to coincide with the high-stakes tests—paying special attention to the errors made by struggling students.		
Other/Special Notes for 5.1 (High-Stakes Test Results)		
5.2 Prepare or purchase valid **standards-based benchmark assessments** that measure student performance on standards taught in the unit plans; distribute results by individual student to indicate mastery or the need for remediation.		
5.2.a. Develop the most viable **timetable for benchmark tests** (e.g., by unit, by month, quarterly) to maximize productive use—and not over- or under-test.		

(Continued)

(Continued)

Task or Procedure	Status Indicator 3 . . . 2 . . . 1		Planning for Action Steps Who will do **What** in what **Time Frame**, and how it will be **Monitored**
5.2.b. Avoid **common missteps** in the use of district benchmark assessment data, including (1) testing too frequently; i.e., spending more time testing than teaching; (2) using test items that do not match in content and/or the cognitive demand the standards being assessed; (3) including test items already used in the unit; (4) using items that are improperly constructed; and (5) including test formats other than multiple choice and constructed response (i.e., these are the two formats students will see on high-stakes tests; including true-false, matching, etc., is a waste of time).			
5.2.c. Develop benchmark tests that **reflect the standards** in both content and cognitive demand; in addition, ensure that there is alignment between the way the standard is assessed and how it is taught, but avoid using text, problems or scenarios, and test items already learned in classroom instruction. For maximum validity, include 3–5 test items per standard assessed.			
5.2.d. Organize an efficient and timely **compilation and analysis** of benchmark results and real-time **access** to staff; require staff to examine the data to discuss at team meetings, including specific implications for individual students and adjustments in unit plan activities.			
Other/Special Notes for 5.2 (District Benchmark Test Results)			
5.3 Devise a system of **classroom unit tests** to formatively and summatively monitor student performance; decide if there are to be common tests at a grade level and when the tests are to be given; arrange to train work teams to develop multiple-choice and constructed response items that reflect the content and cognitive demand of the standards.			
5.3.a. Develop **formative assessments for each unit plan** consisting of oral, written, and observational formats; ensure that they accommodate the lead-up skills as well as the standards and yield diagnostic results for subsequent instruction.			

Task or Procedure	Status Indicator 3 . . . 2 . . . 1		Planning for Action Steps Who will do What in what Time Frame, and how it will be Monitored
5.3.b. Avoid **common missteps** in the use of **formative assessments**, including (1) assigning a grade to formative assessments as if they represent mastery—they are to be diagnostic; (2) over-testing, or spending more time testing than teaching; (3) including on the test items already used in the unit; and (4) a lack of congruence between the way the standards are being taught and tested.			
5.3.c. Develop **summative assessments for each unit plan**—typically, the end-of-unit test, consisting of (1) traditional multiple-choice and constructed-response items in sync with high-stakes and district benchmark assessments and (2) authentic or performance testing items; ensure that all summative tests match the content and cognitive demand of the standards assessed.			
5.3.d. Avoid **common missteps** in the use of **summative assessments**, including (1) including test items already used in the unit; (2) including too few items to validly determine mastery—usually trying to include too many standards; (3) clustering all of the items for one standard together and/or placing all of the constructed response items at the end of the test; and (4) a lack of congruence between the way the standards are being taught and tested.			
5.3.e. Include in each unit plan **performance or authentic assessments** for a majority of the standards for the unit; devise scoring rubrics from the standards themselves; ensure that the teaching-learning activities in the unit prepare all students to successfully complete these performance tasks.			
Other/Special Notes for 5.3 (Formative and Summative Assessments)			

(Continued)

(Continued)

Chapter 6: Homework and Grading—Two Critical Issues for Success

Task or Procedure	Status Indicator 3 . . 2 . . 1	Planning for Action Steps Who will do What in what Time Frame, and how it will be Monitored
6.1 Adopt a districtwide **homework policy and procedures** to support the curricular-instructional transformation plan; include specific definitions and guidelines for what is "allowable" as homework, requirements for feedback, and how homework is to be used and evaluated.		
6.1.a. Consider the **recent research** on homework and its connection to the new content standards and the 21st century skills, including positive and negative impacts on students at various grade levels; promising variations such as spaced repetition, retrieval practice, group or partner homework, and interleaving.		
6.1.b. Avoid **common missteps** in the use of **homework**, including (1) additional practice on problems or tasks that students did not understand in class; (2) rote copying or fill-in from texts; (3) mindless busywork to fill time; (4) providing the "answers" the next day and similar disincentives; (5) the use of homework as punishment or extra credit; and (6) grading homework or otherwise using it to indicate individual student mastery.		
6.2 Adopt a districtwide **grading policy and procedures** to support the curricular-instructional transformation plan by focusing on the content standards; include a grading scale for each developmental level, specific guidelines for determining standards mastery and what student performance comprises each letter grade, and a districtwide system for communicating student progress to parents.		
6.2.a. Avoid **common missteps** in the **grading system**, including (1) the use of percentages (of points) for letter grades without guidelines for how points relate to standards mastery; (2) the misuse of academic freedom to create inconsistencies in determining grades; (3) the use of averages rather than level of mastery, thus obscuring growth; (4) the inclusion of extra credit toward a grade; and (5) the lack of feedback as to specific deficiencies and needs.		
Other/Special Notes (Homework and Grading)		

Chapter 7: Implementation and Accountability

Task or Procedure	Status Indicator 3 . . . 2 . . . 1			Planning for Action Steps Who will do **What** in what **Time Frame**, and how it will be **Monitored**
7.0 Establish an **infrastructure and operating procedures** to ensure and safeguard the process of developing and maintaining the highest quality course tools; a responsive and effective monitoring process, connecting student performance to classroom instruction; and continuous embedded professional development and the ongoing improvement of classroom instruction through collaborative supervision.				
7.1 Devise a process for appointing and training grade-level **work teams** for each subject to **devise the course tools** and make continuous **adjustments** as needed, based on student performance. Include on each team general and special needs teachers, principals, and central office staff to nurture collaborative ownership and maximize district resources. Clarify to all staff their respective responsibilities for implementing the course tools as the basis for their annual performance evaluations.				
7.1.a. **Minimize the negative impact** of work team members' involvement by determining with them meeting schedules that are least disruptive to their regularly assigned duties; check in with them regularly to address concerns.				
7.1.b. Assign key **central office staff to work teams** as an integral part of their job descriptions; their role includes overseeing quality control of the work, maintaining developmental flow between grade levels, and channeling district technology and print resources to each subject and grade level as needed.				
7.1.c. **Circulate drafts of course tools** as they are developed to all teachers working at the respective grade level and subject; obtain feedback from all staff to identify (1) hazards or concerns that may have been overlooked by work teams and/or (2) additional ideas or features that will strengthen the course tools. Ensure that teachers realize that the course tools will be adopted by the board as the district instructional program.				
7.1.d. Hold grade-level/course **team meetings** regularly to discuss student performance and what adjustments are needed in the course tools; clarify expectations to teachers that they are to bring data on student performance and "green ink" revisions to the course tools.				

(Continued)

(Continued)

Task or Procedure	Status Indicator 3 . . . 2 . . . 1			Planning for Action Steps Who will do What in what Time Frame, and how it will be Monitored
7.1.e. Subject all **course tools** to an **annual review** that involves the work teams; use student performance and any developments in state standards to make adjustments for the next school year; submit the revised course tools to the board for approval.				
Other/Special Notes for 7.1 (Work Teams and Course Tools)				
7.2 Establish a series of **professional development** activities for all staff to strengthen their competence in providing specific services to stakeholders in the curricular-instructional transformation plan. To avoid fragmentation and conflicting priorities, ensure that ALL professional development activities are **directly connected to the transformation plan.**				
7.2.a. Monitor the intervention **services provided to special needs** and/or struggling students (i.e., if using response to intervention, that would be Tier II and III students) to ensure they are being provided instruction using the **adopted course tools,** the appropriate modifications and adaptations are being made; and there is no tracking or pulling out except for students with severe issues, needing a self-contained environment.				
7.2.b. Provide **teachers, coaches, central office staff,** and **principals** who were not placed on work teams **parallel training** in the course tools (their structure and implementation), "best practices," and various monitoring techniques; establish roles and responsibilities for all staff in the implementation and maintenance of the transformation plan.				
7.2.c. Identify staff who are unable to fulfill their duties in the transformation plan and provide them the remediation or intervention they need to be successful.				
Other/Special Notes for 7.2 (Professional Development)				

Task or Procedure	Status Indicator 3 . . . 2 . . . 1		Planning for Action Steps Who will do **What** in what **Time Frame**, and how it will be **Monitored**
7.3 Establish a **districtwide plan** to **monitor classroom instruction**, including policies and procedures that set forth classroom implementation of the course tools as the basis of teacher evaluation.			
7.3.a. Reorganize the **principal schedules and job duties** to ensure they spend the majority (70%) of **each day in classrooms** in the form of walk-throughs and/or in-class observations; also include specific responsibilities for dealing with student data and working with teachers to use it in the adjustment of classroom instruction.			
7.3.b. Establish with teachers a **collaborative** rather than adversarial **relationship** in providing classroom supervision and teacher evaluation; share walk-through and classroom observation templates and jointly decide how to use student performance data in the evaluation process.			
7.3.c. Use the unit plans **as basis of daily lesson plans** to provide principals the larger context from which each day's lesson is derived; teachers highlight where they are each week rather than waste time copying codes and notes into square boxes.			
7.3.d. Formulate the **walk-through template** to coincide with the elements of the unit plans; include "best practices," routines and procedures, and differentiation strategies. Work collaboratively with teachers to devise the procedures for the walk-through, including how to provide affirmative and corrective feedback.			
7.3.e. Use the four-part system of collaborative observation to perform classroom visits and monitor instruction; include (1) the preobservation conference; (2) in-class data collection using scripting of teacher behavior and student response; (3) the postobservation conference; and (4) the collaborative action plan for continued growth or specific corrections.			
Other/Special Notes for 7.3 (Monitoring Classroom Instruction)			

Appendices

Appendix A
Goal-Setting Examples

ENERGY (GRADE 9 SCIENCE)

Academic/Content Goals

- explain the difference between energy and work and give examples
- distinguish between conductors and insulators

Personal Goals

- do an energy analysis of my home or some other building
- be able to propose ways to conserve energy in my home

CIVIC INVOLVEMENT (GRADE 11 AMERICAN GOVERNMENT)

Academic/Content Goals

- pick a civic issue that I support and say three things I could do
- summarize what the Democrats say about civic responsibility compared to what the Republicans say

Personal Goals

- take notes each day, and ask a peer to check
- avoid being tardy at least 95% of the time

THEOREMS ABOUT LINES AND ANGLES (HIGH SCHOOL GEOMETRY)

Academic/Content Goals

- prove theorems about lines
- prove theorems about angles

Personal Goals

- learn to use the TI-Nspire technology
- write vocabulary for the unit in my journal

Appendix B

Questioning

SOME STRATEGIES FOR BETTER QUESTIONING

1. **Plan ahead.** Although many of the best questions are spontaneous, it is silly to rely totally on spur-of-the moment inspirations to decide what to ask. The most effective questioners plan ahead, devising substantive prompts that tap into students' deep-level understanding and encouraging reflectivity. [Be sure to include an effective balance of Is, IIs, and IIIs.]

2. **Redirect.**

    a. Ask a second student the same question, then have a third student compare the two responses. This can be expanded to several students at once if the issue is a debatable one and it appears that students are taking sides.

    b. Ask the same student a related question, such as: "So, what would be an example of such a thing?" or "So then what would the opposite of your point be?" or "How might an opponent argue with you about that position?"

3. **Avoid multiple questions** without adequate think time. Students learn quickly whether you will forget about the earlier questions you asked. They soon know whether you'll tire of no hands going up and answer the questions yourself. Finally, they quickly discern whether you will only call on students whose hands are raised.

4. **Probe or delve.** Incorrect or incomplete answers should not be overlooked or simply passed over. The correct answer must be obtained from the students or provided by the teacher. But the students who gave the incorrect answers should not be embarrassed at having taken a risk. Give dignity to the response by "winding him or her back through" the line of reasoning. For example:

Q: Which President is considered the father of our country?
A: Ben Franklin

Q: What made you think of him?

A: I read somewhere he had a bunch of illegitimate children.

[Ride the laugh; join in; say you hadn't heard it put that way before]

Q: When he wasn't having children, what else does history say he did?

A: Flew kites 'n stuff—invented things.

Q: Tell us a couple things he did invent.

A: [silence-pause]

Q: Jonas is absolutely right; he did invent several things. Who can help us list some to those things? [Getting back to the "father of our country" will take a few more minutes, but it can be approached by Washington's affiliation with Ben Franklin, Franklin's support of Washington as the Commander-in-Chief of the Revolutionary forces, etc.]

5.   **Encourage an answer, even if student claims not to know.** If necessary, ask an easier question via redirect. The idea is that the student neither look like a failure (thereby reinforcing his or her reluctance to take a chance), nor "get by" with refusing to make an attempt. Giving dignity to reluctant responders should not be contrived or patronizing. Make it clear you've reserved the option to ask that student another question and have left the door open for him or her to offer an answer.

6.   **Ask the same student a follow-up question.** One of the things students often count on is that once they have answered, they're off the hook and can tune out. Develop the habit of doubling back—unexpectedly—so that students must remain engaged. Never, never fall into the 1950s trap of the "round-robin" approach.

7.   **Coupling or building-on**. Ask students to paraphrase each other's responses; then ask the *original student* if that's close to his or her intent. Ask students to redirect questions to each other, paraphrase, compare with intent, and so on. This can chain several topics together and engage several students at the same time.

Appendix C
Categorization Activity

Originally, all 105 of the words on the following chart could have been listed alphabetically—without the major categories of people, objects, places, events, and so on. But to be practical, words are rarely useful in such giant alpha lists (except to locate them, if needed), and so the natural human reaction is to *organize* them in some way—usually to **classify or sort them into large categories**, as we did.

(Continued)

(Continued)

SUBJECT	EXAMPLES			CATEGORIES
PEOPLE (e.g., surgeon; nurse)	actor congressman forward guitarist shortstop	goalie senator comedian president sprinter	mayor quarterback magician governor dancer	☑_____ ☑_____ ☑_____
OBJECTS (e.g., scalpel; masks; clamps)	wagon six-shooter snaps stroller spurs	Velcro motorcycle lariat staples roller skate	branding iron train buttons saddle paper clips	☑_____ ☑_____ ☑_____
PLACES (e.g., an army field hospital; an operating room)	temple restaurant rainforest tavern chapel	cathedral desert smorgasbord tabernacle tundra	church bistro steppe cafe savanna	☑_____ ☑_____ ☑_____
EVENTS (e.g., surgery)	floods computer weddings tsunamis manned flight	anniversaries hurricanes penicillin retirements electricity	earthquakes birthdays horseless carriage volcanoes graduations	☑_____ ☑_____ ☑_____
ACTIONS (e.g., removal of appendix)	remodel measure modify abandon estimate	detach compute amend gauge resign	improve impeach restructure calculate divorce	☑_____ ☑_____ ☑_____
CONDITIONS (STATE OF BEING) (e.g., inflamed or infected)	mistrust disarray mayhem prepared disbelief	eager pandemonium wariness bedlam trained	suspicion willing anarchy primed misgiving	☑_____ ☑_____ ☑_____
CONCEPTS (THEORIES, IDEAS, NOTIONS, ETC.) (e.g., if infected tissue is not removed, patient at risk of death)	guarantee manipulate negotiate promise compel	blackmail treaty assurance cooperation entrust	extort barter pledge filibuster interdependence	☑_____ ☑_____ ☑_____

Appendix D

Critical Attrbution for Similarities and Differences

We use *three approaches* to applying the critical attribute method as a learning construct with students:

Approach 1: The Concept is not Announced; Examples and Nonexamples Given Separately. The teacher does not announce the concept but provides clear <u>examples</u> and asks students to describe the attributes of each. This initial list is followed by additional examples, and the teacher asks students to be sure their attributes still hold. Any criteria that do not hold for the examples are dropped. The teacher then poses <u>nonexamples</u> to compare against the examples, describing how they are different. The following is an example from a Grade 5 class studying fruits and vegetables.

The teacher shows the *examples* of an apple cut in half and a sliced tomato.

    Students give the description as things we eat; *things that are alive; and things that grow on plants.*

The teacher shows *nonexamples* of a rock and a carrot sliced in half.

    Students re-examine the three ideas/criteria they previously said. Since a carrot meets the criteria of *things we eat, things that are alive, and things that grow on plants,* and we know that a carrot is **not** an example, we have to ask questions that will force students to think more deeply, as these three criteria no longer hold, the students attempt to refine their thinking to develop new criteria.

    Students may come up with: *parts of a plant that we eat that are above the ground.*

The teacher gives examples of avocado, peach, squash, and orange.

Students now come up with: *things we eat with seeds in them.*

The teacher gives more nonexamples: *celery, head of lettuce, artichoke, and potato.*

Students will finally get the attributes of the examples and discover the concept is:

Fruits are foods we eat with seeds in the edible part; some foods commonly thought of as vegetables are really fruits.

A variation of approach 1 is to provide students examples through pictures, illustrations, and so on—both as line drawings and as they appear in the environment—one at a time. For example, if teaching four types of angles (acute, obtuse, right, and straight), the teacher might show students one or more samples of an acute angle and ask them to identify the attributes. These are recorded on a piece of wall chart paper. Before going to the next drawing(s), the teacher would affix the first picture(s) to its attributes. This continues through the four types of angles. Once finished, students note the lists and attempt to identify similarities and differences, moving to the distinguishing attributes of each type of angle. Finally, students should be able to cite examples of how each type of angle appears in the environment.

A variation on the use of drawings or physical models is to use landforms on a map. By circling the Yucatan, Florida, Cape Cod, and so on, students get the idea that they are all land connected to a larger piece of land, jutting into an ocean or bay, surrounded on three sides by water. Putting the technical label on the concept is not as important as students showing they can identify others on the map and that they can distinguish them from other land-forms. The name "peninsula" is not as important as the concept.

A more challenging approach is to allow students to predict the concept from the examples. If students are given the following list of words:

bookcase   *carport*   *earplugs*   *fireplace*   *sunshine*

most will get to the notion of compound words. When asked to identify the attributes of compound words, they typically say two words joined to make one word. But when students are shown this next group:

angel   *carpet*   *format*   *father*   *carrot*

they are perplexed, because these words fit the definition, but they know that this group is different from the first group. Eventually, students get around to the core attribute of compound words: two words joined together to form a word that retains part or all of the meaning of the original words.

Approach 2: The Concept is not Announced; Examples and Nonexamples are Mixed. A second approach is to provide a list that contains <u>both</u> examples and nonexamples, and—without revealing the concept—ask students to separate the items. In so doing, they reflect on what distinguishes the two groups. An example of this approach to teach the concept of complete sentences is shown here.

Consider the following list:

1. *Hazel runs each morning*

2. *At 5:00 a.m. in the peace and quiet*

3. *Hazel finds morning a preferred time to run*

    4. As compared with running in the evening

    5. The danger of evening traffic

    6. Carlos enjoys running with Hazel

    7. One morning, the mist rolling, Hazel and Carlos

    8. Carlos was nowhere in sight

    9. What began as a feeling of puzzlement but became a pang of fear as she saw what lay ahead

Most students can see that the list contains complete and incomplete sentences. The next step is to ask students to distinguish between them; most eventually see that there must be an "actor" and an "action" for the sentence to be complete. They can deconstruct each of the items to discover that 1, 3, 6, and 8 are complete sentences, and the others are not. As a test of mastery, students should be asked to revise the incomplete sentences to make them complete and to provide complete sentences of their own.

A variation of the approach 2 is to present the items already labeled as Yes or No, asking the students to identify how the "Yeses" differ from the "Nos." This removes the need for students to do the initial sort, making it a bit easier to focus on the distinctions.

Approach 3: The Concept is Announced; Examples and Nonexamples Mixed. A third approach is to announce the concept at the outset (e.g., the relationship between fact and inference), and provide students a combined list of examples and nonexamples for <u>facts and inferences</u> that address a common topic. The students must separate the facts from the inferences, identifying the critical attributes that distinguish one from the other while identifying the linkage between them.

FACT OR INFERENCE???

F 1. The print-shop owner found a baby boy, carefully bundled in a small wicker basket, on his door stoop.

I 2. The boy appeared to be about 6 months old.

I 3. It must have been placed there by some neglectful mother who foolishly counted on the printer to find the child before it died.

_____ 4. Aleesha and Latricia Mills, the famous sailing twins who recently won the Challengers' Cup, arrived at San Diego two hours ahead of their projected schedule.

_____ 5. Their 36-foot cruiser—name *Gemini*—is appropriate, given the space exploration program of the same name.

(Continued)

(Continued)

_____ 6. "It's about time women are recognized for their sailing prowess," Commodore Steward said. "The Mills victory proves they are as capable as men on the high seas."

_____ 7. The United Nations' initiative to provide food and clothing for the southeast Asian countries devastated by the tsunami has been jeopardized by another storm that makes it impossible for the planes to land.

_____ 8. Without these supplies, the survivors are at further risk of disease and starvation.

_____ 9. The nations located nearby have agreed to come forward with aid, provided they are compensated by the United Nations.

Students typically realize even though facts and inferences are separate ideas, they are related. A valid inference is *built on* a verifiable fact. However—and this may be the tricky part for some students—facts do not necessarily "announce" their own inferences.

A variation in the approach where the concept is announced is to *show students separate lists* to illustrate the concept. For example, the *commutative property of addition and multiplication* might be shown as follows:

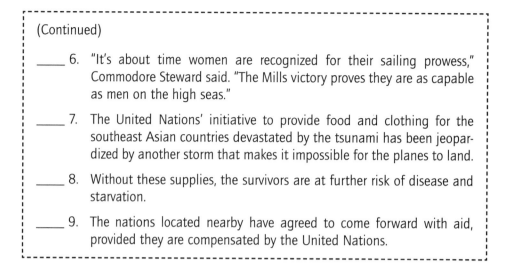

Examples:

$4 + 3 = 3 + 4$ $\qquad$ $45 \cdot 23 = 23 \cdot 45$

$1 \cdot 2 = 2 \cdot 1$ $\qquad$ $91 + 18 = 18 + 91$

$18 + 22 = 22 + 18$ $\qquad$ $71 + 16 = 16 + 71$

$12 \cdot 4 \cdot 3 = 3 \cdot 12 \cdot 4$ $\quad$ $3 + 2 + 6 = 2 + 6 + 3$

Students can see that the problems deal with addition and multiplication and that the answers are identical on both sides of the equal sign. No matter what the **order**, the answer is the same

Nonexamples:

$4 - 3 \neq 3 - 4$ $\qquad$ $45 - 23 \neq 23 - 45$

$2 \div 1 \neq 1 \div 2$ $\qquad$ $91 \div 18 \neq 18 \div 91$

$22 - 18 \neq 18 - 22$ $\qquad$ $71 - 16 \neq 16 - 71$

Students can see that these problems deal with subtraction and division. By contrast, the answers are NOT identical on both sides of the equal sign when the **order** is reversed.

When students have truly internalized this concept, they realize that the "order" property holds for addition and multiplication, but it does not hold for subtraction and division. Students can identify their own examples and nonexamples, even to the point of creating word problems to illustrate their mastery. As students get older, they use the property to simplify computation with more complex numbers.

The entire point of the critical attribute method is to give students prompts that exemplify a concept, and—with the help of some nonexamples—assist them to deduce the concept for themselves. It's almost as if the concept is actually clarified by what it is NOT.

Appendix E
Teaching the Metaphor for Similarities and Differences

WHEN TEACHING A CONCEPT USING METAPHORS

A. THE LIFE METAPHOR

The teacher should model for students how his or her life is like a _____ in that. . . . Examples include:

1. A carousel
2. A roller coaster
3. An amusement park
4. A dance (generational)
5. A puzzle
6. A party
7. A race (or a marathon)
8. A symphony
9. A shopping mall
10. A Wal-Mart
11. A building under construction
12. A circus (or carnival)
13. A voyage (or cruise)
14. A playground

B. CONCEPT TO METAPHOR

Step 1: Break the concept into its individual parts.

e.g., Manifest Destiny

✓ When:
   mid-1840s . . . lasted until after the Civil War

✓ What:
   belief that the U.S. was destined to expand across the continent—shore to shore and north to south

   manifest = apparent, was already underway without force

   destiny = inevitable, foreordained to be thus

(Continued)

(Continued)

- ✓ *Rationale:*

  superiority of the noble American experiment—i.e.,
  - – *representative democracy*
  - – *freedom from tyranny*
  - – *commitment to the ideals of human rights and privileges*
  - – *guided by a Higher Power; etc.*

- ✓ *Method:*
  - – *nonviolent*
  - – *occurred naturally from human enterprise and sense of adventure*
  - – *current occupants would be fortunate and appreciate the opportunity*
  - – *replaced savagery with civility and natural chaos with discipline and order—thought certainly the right thing to do!*

- ✓ *Pros (Democrats):*

  Expanding the country would strengthen it and guarantee longevity; hoped to acquire Texas, Oregon now, Canada, and Mexico later

- ✓ *Cons (Whigs):*

  Better to deepen prosperity by strengthening the economy and social structures of current territories and states

- ✓ *Fallout*

  Native Americans and other indigenous peoples whose customs varied from the "American" way; oppression of entire segments of the population

Step 2: Think of examples familiar to Ss to illustrate each part and the relationship among them.

e.g., The commons area [older students] or the playground [younger students]

- ✓ *When [where]:*

  21st century; the commons area is where all of the students hang out, but the largest and most influential group is the circle group. They are the ones who made the commons area possible and stood up to the principal to get the rights to use it. They have decided to work with the other grade levels to help them use the area effectively.

- ✓ *What:*

  belief that the circle group was destined to expand across the commons—shore to shore and north to south

  manifest = apparent, was already underway without force

  destiny = inevitable, foreordained to be thus

- ✓ *Rationale:*

  superiority of the circle group's noble experiment—i.e.,
  - – *representative democracy*
  - – *freedom from tyranny*
  - – *commitment to all things circular*
  - – *guided by a Higher Power; etc.*

- ✓ *Method:*
  - – *nonviolent*
  - – *occurred naturally from human enterprise and sense of adventure*

> – *current occupants would be fortunate and appreciate the opportunity*
> – *replaced squares, rectangles, and rectangles with all things circle—thought certainly the right thing to do!*

✓ *Pros (for the circles' dominance):*

Expanding the circles across the commons would strengthen the students' control over the area and guarantee longevity; hoped to acquire the sections now occupied by the other shape groups—the triangles, squares, and rectangles—but they can certainly continue to use the commons

✓ *Cons (against the circles' dominance):*

Better to deepen the effectiveness of the portion of the commons currently occupied by the circles and allow the other shape groups to do their own thing.

✓ *Fallout*

All of the triangles, squares, and rectangles have disappeared.

Step 3: If students lack the background information (the back story), provide it; otherwise, the concept will never take root and be remembered.

e.g., reminding students of previous patterns in math before attempting new ones
e.g., using students understanding of photosynthesis to attack respiration
e.g., spending some time playing chess to help students understand military strategy
e.g., using a bucket of water to illustrate centrifugal force to explain the concept of gravity

C. METAPHOR TO CONCEPT (adapted from Wormeli, 2009)

Step 1: Break the familiar object into its parts (structure, function, process, reminders of . . .).

Step 2: Think of extensions or "reminders of. . . ." that could become metaphors.

e.g., an apple

step 1 [break into familiar parts]

✓ Peel
✓ Stem
✓ Leaf
✓ Meat or insides
✓ Seeds
✓ Pies
✓ Cobblers, crisps, dumplings
✓ Vinegar

step 2 [think of reminders, extensions that could become metaphors]

☑ must break the surface to get to the juicy parts
☑ the outside doesn't reveal what lies inside
☑ the apple may look sweet but be bitter
☑ the meat gets mushy over time
☑ the best-tasting apples may not look the prettiest outside
☑ the apple can be tart or sweet, depending on its family background

(Continued)

(Continued)

☑ its parts are used to create all sorts of things

☑ the seed pattern in the middle is like a star—like the birthplace of energy for the planet

When thinking about specific content areas, the following might serve as possible ways to get students more engaged with the idea of how something unfamiliar is like something they already know.

SOCIAL STUDIES

1. [re: If the United States were an animal among other animals in the world, what would it be?] A big dog lying on the porch. It protects the house, while it stays dry and out of the elements—most of the time. If anyone approaches the house, it jumps to the defense, but otherwise, it rarely leaves the porch. The other dogs know how ferocious it COULD be, and that keeps them away.

2. Prussia was [like] a cornered mountain lion.

3. Historical figures coming down on both sides of the same fence

4. A politician's words adding salt to the wounds

5. A politician's platform

6. Draining the swamp

7. The earth's rotation-revolution relative to the sun is like the United States' relationship to the U.S. Constitution as it proceeds through time from 1789 through the 21st century.

8. The train became referred to as the iron horse.

9. The Civil War was a knife in the heart of the Union.

10. Racists of all cultures can hear nothing when their ears are filled with the cotton of prejudice and ignorance.

11. Just as weather forecasters predict changes in the wind, temperature, and precipitation—influencing the way we dress, economists predict changes in the production, distribution, and consumption of goods—influencing what we buy!

12. The industrial revolution was a train that transported an agricultural society to an industrial destination on the rails of invention and mass communication.

SCIENCE

1. One molecule flirting with another

2. The particle model of matter compared to a middle school dance; i.e.,

   a. all matter is made up of tiny particles = students at the dance

   b. the particles move and vibrate = what the students do when the music starts

   c. the particles in matter may be attracted to each other and bond = slow dance

   d. even bonded particles have spaces between them = teachers butting in to be sure there is space between the bodies

3. DNA as a genetic cookbook OR DNA is similar to a zipper

4. A Mercator projection is like a peeled orange.

5. The Krebs cycle is like an energy-processing factory for citric acid, consisting of six smaller interactions working together to create ATP (adenosine triphosphate).

6. Comparing how cars regulate their internal temperature to how mammals do so vs. reptiles

7. Photosynthesis is like an input-output machine.

8. A lunar eclipse is the moon being swallowed by the earth's shadow.

9. Gravity is the glue that holds us at home on the earth.

10. The water cycle is a Ferris wheel—up and down around the same point.

11. Mitosis is each cell making a Xerox copy of itself.

12. The molecules in the three states of matter are so many bumper cars; in solids, they are all clumped together and simply vibrate; in liquids, they glide past each other; in gases, they ricochet off each other.

MATH

1. How does *irrational behavior* in humans [vs. rational] relate to *irrational numbers?*

2. Students understand equations when they see either side of the equal sign as extended bars on a balance beam.

3. A thermometer turned on its side becomes a number line.

4. A line is a point that went for a walk.

5. Writing equations is balancing a set of scales with the equal sign as the fulcrum; both sides must be equal in value, even if they do not look alike.

6. Plotting points on a coordinate plane creates a partial picture, but it also allows us to predict the rest of the detail to complete it.

7. Finding the square root of a number is finding a pair of identical twins; finding cubed root is finding triplets!

LANGUAGE ARTS

1. Verbs as the workhorses of a sentence.

2. Parts of speech are like a house (verbs = foundation; nouns = frame; adjectives = decorative detail; adverbs = steps leading from foundation to the rest of the house; pronouns = roof; conjunctions = gutter connecting house to roof; pronouns = roof (they "cover" for the nouns); etc.

    The following page has a chart of familiar objects that are good to use when trying to get students to understand the concept of analogy.

(Continued)

(Continued)

FAMILIAR OBJECTS THAT MAKE GOOD METAPHORS OR ANALOGIES (A–Z)			
Anchor Ant Colony Apply	Ladder Laundry Landscape Light/Lamp	Radar Screen Railroad Train Recipe River Rock Russian Roulette	Umbrella Underdog
Baseball Basket Blind Date Bottleneck Boxing Match Bridge Brook	Kite	Sailing Savings Account Shadow Slogging Through Mud Snapshot Snow/Blizzard Song/Music Stage Play Stock Market Street (Avenue) Submarine Swamp	Vacuum Cleaner Violin
	Machine Map Marriage Menu Military Battle Mirror Mosaic Mountain Museum		Wal-Mart Watch Wheel Windmill Window Wrapping (For Gift Box)
Camping Card Game Circus Clock Closet Cloud Cupboard Curtains	Neighborhood		
	Oreo Cookie Orchestra Outer Space		
Dog	Parade Pencil Sharpener Photocopier Pine Cone Portrait	Teeth Theme Part Thermometer Traffic Traffic Signal Tree Tug of War	Yo-Yo
Engine			Zoo
Factory Family Farm Fence, Hedgerow			
Garden Gridlock Guitar	Quicksand Quilt		
Horse Race			

Appendix F

Math Problem Solving

PROBLEM TYPE: JOIN (ADD/MULTIPLY)

RESULT

Grade 3: David grew 12 pea plants; Karen grew 17 pea plants. Write a number sentence to show how to find the total number of plants they grew.

Grade 6: Evelyn rode her bike $3\frac{1}{2}$ miles on Monday, $2\frac{1}{4}$ miles on Wednesday. On Saturday, she rode $5\frac{1}{8}$ miles. How many miles did Evelyn ride in the 3 days?

CHANGE

Grade 3: What is the rule for this input-output table?

Input	Output
3	12
5	20
8	32

Grade 7: The following table shows the total balance in four people's savings accounts at the end of each month:

Name	Jan	Feb	Mar	Apr	May	Jun
Julie	50	65	80	105	120	135
Stuart	70	80	90	100	110	120
Sarah	100	120	140	160	180	220
Mike	90	100	110	130	150	180

In which person's account did the balance show a constant rate of increase over the six-month period?

(Continued)

(Continued)

START

Grade 3: In the Bean Bag Toss game, a player can score points by tossing a bean bag in a hole of 5 points, 6 points, 7 points, 8 points, and 10 points; Max tossed three bean bags in the same hole and two bean bags in a second hole. What is the highest score that Max could receive for these five tosses? Alissa also tossed five bean bags into the holes. She scored 45 points; show how Alissa could have gotten this score.

Grade 6: A coach paid a total of $175 for 14 baseball uniforms. What was the price of each uniform?

Grade 7: Jackson bought groceries that totaled $16.07; he received $4.00 in change. What amount did Jackson pay the cashier for the groceries in order to receive the $4.00 change?

PROBLEM TYPE: SEPARATE
(SUBTRACT/DIVIDE)

RESULT

Grade 8: Rob wants to buy a $20 CD that is on sale for 15% off. He estimates that he will save at least $4. Tell whether Rob's estimate is reasonable, and show how you determined your answer.

CHANGE

Grade 9: The pilot of a small aircraft was given permission to land, and she lowered the wheels at an altitude of 1,500 feet. Two and a half minutes after lowering the wheels, the aircraft landed. What was the plane's rate of descent, in feet per second, from the time the wheels were lowered to the time the plane landed?

START

Grade 7: The Acme Carpet Company received an order for 240 square feet of carpeting. The order form showed that the length of the rectangular room was 20 feet. What width should the company cut the carpeting to fit the room?

Grade 8: Mrs. Stanley has 32 pieces of ribbon, each ¾ yard long. How much ribbon did Mrs. Stanley have to cut her pieces of ribbon?

PROBLEM TYPE: PART—PART/PART-WHOLE

WHOLE UNKNOWN

Grade 7: The Amazon basin has received 23 inches of rain so far this year. This amount is 25% of the average yearly rainfall. What is the average yearly rainfall in the Amazon basin?

PART UNKNOWN

Grade 6: *Ms. Andrews allowed her students to print, write in cursive, or type their essays. 60% of the students printed; 10% of the students used cursive; and 30% of the students typed their essays. Ms. Andrews teaches 150 students; how many students typed their essays?*

Grade 7: *A book that sells for $13.50 is on sale for $10.80. What fraction represents the discount being offered on the book?*

PROBLEM TYPE: COMPARE

DIFFERENCE UNKNOWN

Grade 9: *Two years ago, Monique paid $5.50 for the rookie baseball card of her favorite New York Yankees player. The card is now worth $17.00. Sean, her brother, paid $12.00 for his favorite card, and it has a current value of $27.00. Sean says that his card has increased more in value than Monique's card. Monique says that her card has increased more in value than Sean's card. Show how both Monique and Sean can be correct. Support your answer by showing work or providing an explanation.*

COMPARE QUANTITY UNKNOWN

Grade 7: *Patty found the table below on the back of a pasta box. She needs 10 cups of cooked pasta. How many ounces of uncooked pasta does she need?*

Amount of Uncooked Pasta in Ounces	Amount of Cooked Pasta in Cups
4	2
8	4
16	8

Grade 9: *The population density of a state, in people per square mile, is found by dividing the population of the state by its area in square miles. Florida has an area of 53,936 square miles. In 1998, Florida had a population of 14,915,980 and a population density of 276.5 people per square mile. Describe the conditions under which a different state could have a smaller population than Florida but have a greater population density.*

REFERENCE UNKNOWN

Grade 7: *A water tower casts a shadow 70 meters long; at the same time, a fence post 1 meter tall casts a shadow 1.4 meters long. How tall is the water tower?*

Appendix G
Vocabulary

Syntax or the Function in a Sentence. Most adults learned the parts of speech as grammar and spent countless hours completing worksheets to label each word in a sentence—more like 10 sentences—according to its part of speech. In our work with teachers, we are helping them correct this misapplication by shifting the focus from the *label* to the *function* of the word in the sentence. For example, depending on the context, the word *base* can be a noun, a verb, an adjective, or an adverb. But that's not the important point; what counts is how the words are USED in the sentence, or the syntax.

We have had great success showing teachers how to introduce new vocabulary words in "nested" sentences that actually illustrate their meaning in a real-world context—this in sharp contrast to a list of isolated words. Here are a few examples, using words taken from the SAT lists.

1. Several flags were thrown after the play, and it took several minutes to sort out who committed the **blatant** penalties.

2. The Hindenburg **debacle** prevented the airship from becoming a major weapon in aerial warfare.

3. Although spiritual beliefs are based on faith, an important part of worship centers around religious **icons**.

4. The treasure was divided **proportionately** among the families who found it.

5. Judges often **sequester** the jury for high-profile cases that have created strong public feelings.

Many students can use a grammar template to replace the bolded words and thus decide how the word is used in the sentence. For example, students know that *car* is a noun, *fits* is a verb, *blue* is an adjective, and *perfectly* is an adverb. To be sure, they know the various "parts" of speech of *"The blue car fits perfectly"* and can add prepositional phrases such as "into the parking space" or "with the red truck," or "inside the garage." Once they become facile at this template sentence, they can make substitutions in the previous sentences.

1. Several flags were thrown after the play, and it took several minutes to sort out who committed the **blatant** penalties. [In testing each word,

the student quickly realizes that " . . . *blue*," the *adjective*, can be substituted.]

2. The Hindenburg **debacle** prevented the airship from becoming a major weapon in aerial warfare. [In testing each word, the student quickly realizes that " . . . *car*," the *noun*, can be substituted.]

3. The treasure was divided **proportionately** among the families who found it. [. . . *perfectly*, or the *adverb*, can be substituted]

4. Judges often **sequester** the jury for high-profile cases that have created strong public feelings. [. . . ."*fits*," or the *verb*, can be substituted]

5. Although spiritual beliefs are based on faith, an important part of worship centers around religious **icons**. [. . . the plural of *"car"* or *cars, the noun, can be substituted]* .

One foolproof way for students to remember syntax is to use their own names in the teaching sentences. As an example, each of the eight sentences below includes the name of an actual participant in one of our training sessions. Again, the bold words used are from the SAT lists.

1. When you see her positive intervention with autistic children, it's clear why Karen is known as an **advocate** of students with special needs.

2. It's a good thing Andrea is so **gregarious**; she didn't know anyone on her staff in September, but now you'd swear she's known them all for years.

3. In the dictionary under the word **camaraderie** are the pictures of Kathy, Amy, and Becky; no wonder they're called The James Gang.

4. Dismayed by the lack of dollars to take students on field trips, Cindy began calling several **philanthropic** organizations to support her "Medieval Feast" campaign.

5. Hearing about a colleague's struggle with small groups, Jennifer offered her services as a way to **ameliorate** the situation in that classroom and preserve the teacher's dignity.

6. As the **consummate** sports mom, Darcy makes all sorts of sacrifices to attend every event where her children participate.

7. Sensing that not everyone on the team agreed, Chris **sagaciously** walked them through the material and made adjustments that would meet everyone's need.

8. Being accustomed to conflicting directives about planning, Jennifer has a special **bent** for clarity and consistence.

9. With Emily's flair for insightful creativity, there's no excuse for **prosaic** writing among her students.

Appendix H

Collaborative Observation Samples

**INDIVIDUAL LESSON
PREOBSERVATION CONFERENCE**

Teacher #12
Grade(s) 7th
Observer: CW

Building John F. Kennedy School
Subject(s) Math
Date of Conference 10/8/2012
Date of Observation 10/10/2012

[NOTE: The principal will have reviewed the unit plan from which this lesson is taken and will have a copy with him or her.]

1. How does this unit build on the previous one and lead to the next one?

   This is the review of the first unit setting up for the second unit of the school year, and we started with rational numbers—adding/subtracting. Next, we will be working on multiplying and dividing. We are moving to ratio and proportion in the third unit.

2. I understand the lesson I'll see is taken from the unit on *adding and subtracting rational numbers*. Which **lesson** will I be seeing? [Teacher should be able to "point to" on the marked unit plan] Teaching-Learning #5 on working with fractions

3. Which **standards** will you be addressing in this lesson? [Teacher should be able to "point" to unit plan]

   7.NS.1 Apply and extend previous understandings of addition and subtraction to add and subtract rational numbers; represent addition and subtraction on a horizontal or vertical number line diagram.

   a. Describe situations in which opposite quantities combine to make 0. *(e.g., a hydrogen atom has 0 charge because its two constituents are oppositely charged.)* (7.NS.1a)

   b. Understand $p + q$ as the number located a distance $| \, q \, |$ from p, in the positive or negative direction depending on whether q is positive or negative. Show that a number and its opposite have a sum of 0 (are additive inverses). Interpret sums of rational numbers by describing real-world contexts. (7.NS.1b)

   c. Understand subtraction of rational numbers as adding the additive inverse, $p - q = p - (-q)$. Show that the distance between two rational numbers on the number line is the absolute value of their difference, and apply this principle in real-world contexts. (7.NS.1c)

(Continued)

245

(Continued)

d. Apply properties of operations as strategies to add and subtract rational numbers. (7.NS.1d)

7.NS.3 Solve real-world and mathematical problems involving the four operations with rational numbers. (Note: Computations with rational numbers extend the rules for manipulating fractions to complex fractions.)

4. Summarize for me what **strategies YOU'LL be using** and what you expect the **STUDENTS to do** to process the information and construct meaning for themselves. [Teacher should be able to "walk" through the proposed lesson; should be fairly decent match to motivation, teaching-learning, traditional assessment, or authentic assessment sections of the unit plan.]

Time	Teaching Behaviors/Strategies	Student Responses	Materials/ Technology
2 min	Greet students as they enter	Students take out Math Vocab books as they enter and be ready to start with these	Vocab Books SmartBoard
10 min	I review the least common denominator from yesterday, asking students to tell me what, why, and how	Take notes; some students may add to existing notes	SmartBoard notes
20 min	I intro the next phase—adding mixed numbers. First—I **demo** the entire thing and they copy; Second—I do partial, they tell me the rest; third—they do a few on their own and I walk around and check for understanding	They copy problems, work problems at seats, work with partners, and self-correct	
10 min	We debrief—talk about what is the big deal about fractions and mixed numbers in our lives	Students discuss what they have just learned and share ideas with the rest of the class	

5. What **learning "needs"** have you discovered among your students that have widened the "gap" between successful and unsuccessful performance? All students are very weak with fractions and decimals, especially with word problems and I am not even addressing the positive and negative aspect yet. They are very unsure of themselves.

6. How have you planned to **differentiate** your lesson for:

   a. the more accelerated students? Have students work on more sophisticated problems

   b. students with disabilities? I use numbers like half and fourth or decimals that are money related; try to give them something practical they will actually use.

   c. students at risk of failure? Same as students with disabilities.

7. What types of assessments are you using in the unit to:

    a. determine what students know at the start of the unit? Gave some problems to see what they knew about positive/negative numbers, decimals, fractions, etc.

    b. determine understanding throughout the unit? There are lots of practice problems with real-word examples in the unit.

    c. determine mastery of the standards at the end of the unit? Students take unit test, and they also do the authentic assessment where they analyze problems and create problems about what we have learned in the unit about adding and subtracting with rational numbers.

8. Are there any students for whom you have a particular plan—academically or behaviorally? I have students on individualized education plans (IEPs) and I have an inclusion teacher in the room with me; the kids on IEPs are struggling with these concepts.

Are there any students you want me to note in particular? (ELEMENTARY-MIDDLE SCHOOL) I would like you to notice the students who respond during the lesson and their level of understanding. Also, please chart which students make no effort to be engaged with what we are doing.

IN-CLASS DATA COLLECTION

Observer K Johnson	**Teacher Observed** # 15

Materials/Equipment for Differentiation: calculators; the overhead

Date: December 4, _____   **Number of Students:** 15 (Grade 7)

Notes:

This lesson is about adding fractions and mixed numbers. From an earlier lesson, the teacher begins by asking students to try creating improper fractions. The teacher then gives a step-by-step demo, followed by students working sample problems. All problems are straight computation; later, students will see samples in context.

CLASSROOM DRAWING AND RECORD OF MOVEMENT AND RESPONSES

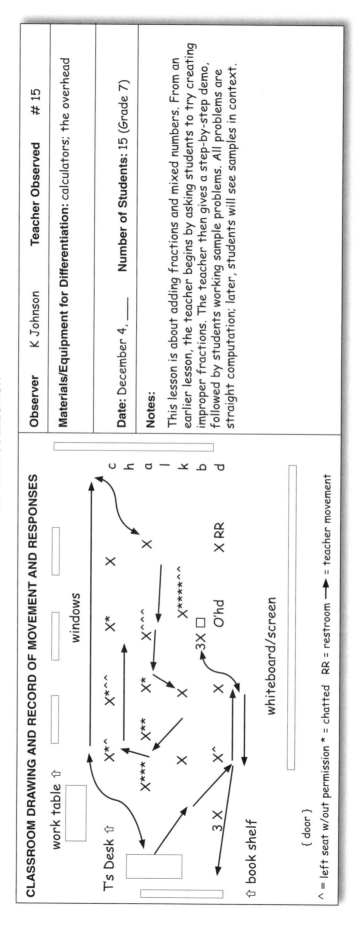

^ = left seat w/out permission   * = chatted   RR = restroom   ⟶ = teacher movement

248

	RECORDING OF LESSON DESCRIPTIONS		LESSON ANALYSIS	
TIME	TEACHER BEHAVIOR	STUDENT BEHAVIORS/ RESPONSES	STRENGTHS	QUESTIONS/ CONCERNS
10:45	T offers calculators to Ss as they come in		Helping Ss right away helps maintain focus, prevents off-task behavior . . . others know you're coming	Some Ss received calculators and not others did not; why? Why begin helping before all Ss are seated and working?
	T asks Ss to begin the day's work from the board	J begins work at desk		
	[converting mixed numbers to improper fractions]			
	[while helping J focus] "Let's all make $7\frac{2}{3}$ as an improper fraction."	Other Ss mosey to seats		What is the procedure for giving answers? Your behavior plan asks students to get permission before speaking out
10:50	T goes to closet, gets and hands out calculators to Ss with hands raised	3 Ss raise hands "we need calculators" Some Ss have multiplication tables in their notebooks		
	"Let me remind you . . ." [at board] "here's how we change improper fractions to mixed numbers and vice versa" . . . goes through the steps using $7\frac{2}{3}$			
	1. multiply denominator X whole number: $7 \times 3 = ??$	Ss call out 21	Asking Ss to provide answer as you go engages all Ss . . . several want to be involved	Saying 7 is wrong didn't help students realize WHY it is wrong
	2. add numerator: $21 + 2 = ??$ 23	Ss call out 23 . . . 23 over 7 !!		Is there a procedure for getting out of seats?
	"Nope; 23 over 3 !!"			
	"Suppose we have $\frac{33}{9}$ . . . how can we make that a mixed number?"	Ss call out $3\frac{6}{9}$		
	3. Divide the numerator by the denominator			How typical is this level of chatting while students work? How much of the chatting is work-related? Not everyone is focused.
	33 divided by 9 equals . . . ???	Several Ss chatting		

(Continued)

	RECORDING OF LESSON DESCRIPTIONS		LESSON ANALYSIS	
TIME	TEACHER BEHAVIOR	STUDENT BEHAVIORS/ RESPONSES	STRENGTHS	QUESTIONS/ CONCERNS
11:00	T puts $8\frac{3}{5}$ on the board . . . "Try this one on your own."	Several more Ss chatting; 2 get up to use pencil sharpener		
	T circulates . . . tells Ss to "look again at step 2" or "are you sure that's correct for step 3?" or "which is the whole number?" or "did you multiply only once?" . . . prompts Ss to examine own work	Ss continue to chat; several visit other Ss	Using prompts and indirect suggestions helps Ss discover their own mistakes rather than giving them the answer. This involves them in problem solving and requires them to examine their own work	
	T shushes . . . twice while circulating	Everyone BUT D____ immediately stopped chatting		
	"D____, shush"	Ss slowly start up chatting, walking around		
	T continues to circulate . . . helping	E____ asks for restroom pass		
	T gives E restroom pass	E____ leaves		
11:10	T puts 3 more problems on the board "Let's try these. Everyone is to be working at his or her own desk, please."	Ss chatting, and 2 or 3 at once mosey around the room, eventually returning to seats		
	T sharpens one S's pencil	2 Ss use pencil sharpener while T helps Ss		
	"W____, you're close. Check step 1." Goes to H____ "check the top number."	W____ and H____ fix their papers with T's prompt		
	"A, you were absent yesterday, right? Did you use Z____'s notes?" . . . T finds all 3 of A____'s problems are done correctly . . . "Good job!"			How are you checking for understanding for the remaining problems— those worked after you stopped at the desk?

	RECORDING OF LESSON DESCRIPTIONS		LESSON ANALYSIS	
TIME	TEACHER BEHAVIOR	STUDENT BEHAVIORS/ RESPONSES	STRENGTHS	QUESTIONS/ CONCERNS
11:20	"P___, where are your steps?" . . . walks her through	A___ said "yes"		
	"Let's switch gears now and open our Math Vocabulary Books!" Goes to board. "We need to add least common denominator to our books. What did we say it was? How does it work?	A___ said "Awesome!" E___ returns from restroom		Several students appear to not to be listening . . . .
	T uses another example on the board $\frac{1}{2}$ and $\frac{1}{5}$ "When we add fractions, we need a least common denominator."	J___ leaves room without permission (returns in 5 minutes with cough drop) 3 Ss in closet getting Math Vocabulary Books		still working on the 3 problems . . . not copying
	"Someone walk me through this. . . ." "Good, so the 2 and the 10 . . . what do I do?"	J___ returns to class with cough drop Ss chatting . . . none volunteer		How likely is it that only 1 student knew 10? How will you check the others? What if the denominators are 3 and 6?
11:30	T works the process. "Please copy this in your math vocabulary books." T writes definition of LCD on board . . . reads it aloud. Bell rings for class to end.	K___ finally says "10" Most Ss copy: some are looking for their books.		

POSTOBSERVATION CONFERENCE PLANNING

1. **Positive points** from the preobservation conference and script that the observer wants to reinforce. These should be stated as Teacher Behavior—Impact on Students.

   Interaction between NEARLY every student and the teacher

   Didn't just give students the correct answer; prompted them through the steps or specific processes to help them self-discover their mistakes

   Dignified even silly errors to encourage students

2. **Questions/concerns** from the preobservation conference and script that the observer wants to reinforce. These should be stated as Teacher Behavior—Impact on Students.

   Handing out calculators—and at different times—interrupted the flow of the lesson and created down time.

   It turned out that some students had multiplication charts (but some didn't??) and didn't need calculators; why the difference? How were students using the calculators?

   The lack of clear routines and procedures for the math vocab books, the calculators, pencil sharpening, leaving the room . . . created an atmosphere of confusion and disruptive chatter . . .

   all while you were trying to help individual students. Students lacked a sense to when to listen—even when you were presenting.

   Some students seemed not to realize when they were to copy and when to listen; how will you determine the level of understanding among less verbal students? How are the students being monitored once you leave their desks?

3. **Professional outcomes** that the observer would like to see the teacher pursue (e.g., focus on the district priorities, alternative strategies for teaching, etc.).

   You have an effective classroom behavior plan; stick to it (i.e., raising hands to be recognized before calling out; obtaining permission to leave seat; remaining seated during direct instruction).

   Establish a simple but efficient classroom routine for entering, getting to seats, getting and returning materials, focusing, and when and how to move about.

   Respond to each answer given by students during your direct instruction; it wasn't clear if you thought the answers right or wrong—and if wrong, what reasoning may have mis-led the student.

4. **Alternatives:** what other activities, strategies, or techniques might also be effective for teaching a lesson such as this?

   Use a shoe-holder that fastens over the door to store calculators and the math vocab books; or designate a student to pass out and collect each week or day

   Use title and inclusion special ed staff to help with guided practice; this will decrease the time students are left on their own.

5. Other areas in planning from the **preconference** to be considered:

   Observer's Note: Same methods for all students; no mention of differentiation or role of title and special ed staff

   Observer's Note: Various levels of questions: I—literal answer; II—why something happened; III—what if

   Observer's Note: Missing computation with decimals for all four operations

   Observer's Note: Are students actually determining the percent of savings and determining the "best buy"?

   Observer's Note: Add weather, economics, etc., from Science and Social Studies

POSTOBSERVATION CONFERENCE AND ACTION PLAN

Observer: KJ   Teacher Observed # 12   Date of Post-Conference: 12/5/08

Things that went the way the teacher had intended:
what s/he felt went well and how the students responded

Students discovered their own errors by going back through the steps

Things that did not go the way the teacher had intended:
what s/he felt did not work and how the students responded

He realized he didn't get a chance to ask many questions—and none at higher levels

He was upset about students wandering around, especially
- the student leaving without permission
- the 8-minute restroom jaunt

With so much noise and the distracting movements about the room, he had to repeat most of what he said—not to clarify but because they didn't hear it the first time

Target Area	Specific Strategies for Teacher to Try (Begin with a verb . . .)	Criteria for Success (So that . . .)	Time Frame for Plan	Role of Support Personnel (If any)
Behavior management	1. Enforce your discipline plan re: getting permission to leave seats; remain seated during direct instruction and raise hands/be recognized before calling out	There will be a businesslike yet encouraging atmosphere in the room; students will stay focused; and every student (not just the vocal ones) will feel he and she have opportunity to participate.	Begin the next day	Observe Mrs. N ____ to see the impact of not calling out
Routines and procedures	2. Establish and follow clear, simple, efficient routines and procedures that include coming into the room, getting required materials in hand and being ready on time; taking notes, completing board work, etc.	The level of noise will be reduced, the movement will be purposeful and deliberate, all students will have what they need at the time they need it, and everyone will be focused on the direct instruction.	Begin the next day	Meet with Dean of Students to discuss individual behavior plans for J and E Ask Mr. ____ about his routines to see if any might be appropriate
Best Practices	3. Teach students to find LCD by finding least common multiple as the strategy rather than multiplying the two denominators (e.g., with $\frac{2}{3}$ and $\frac{1}{6}$, your method will yield 18; the correct answer is 6).	Students will get the LCD and end up with answers in simpler form.	The next time LCD is taught	Principal will observe this in use, offer feedback

253

ACTION PLAN STRATEGIES FOR "STARS" (TEACHERS WHO ARE ALREADY HIGHLY SKILLED)

We operate under the premise that all of us can be better at what we do. Therefore, even the strongest teachers are encouraged to "grow" in some capacity. What we find, is that the strongest people usually have a list of things they want to work on to make themselves a better educator.

1. Attend a professional conference (local is fine!); share findings among peers.

2. Present at a professional conference; present a program/materials developed by you and/or peers, and invite feedback from attendees.

3. Work with building leadership team (BLT) to devise a strategy to solve a particular schoolwide or grade-level problem (e.g., a report card that reflects differentiation strategies; student-led parent-conferences; a "reading list" that reflects a balance across all genres and cultures, including classical as well as contemporary pieces; increasing levels of student engagement; incorporating levels of thinking—e.g., Bloom— into teaching, etc.).

4. Interview (via e-mail, telephone, etc.) an educational "hot shot" (e.g., the state Superintendent of Instruction, Larry Ainsworth, Mike Schmoker, Richard DuFour, Rick Stiggins, Robert Marzano, etc.); ask advice about specific classroom or building-level issues; disseminate the results of that exchange to members of the BLT.

5. Identify a particular topic of interest (e.g., gender issues for math; collaborative learning; differentiation among special needs students; ability grouping; student motivation; etc.); read three research articles, at least one of which includes the results of an actual study in a school with a population similar to ours, and formulate a viable recommendation for the building.

6. Find articles *written by teachers* about successful classroom strategies that would be helpful in this building; disseminate among staff. [NOTE: Sources might include *ASCD SmartBriefs, EdWeek, Ed Leadership, Phi Delta Kappan* magazine, etc.]

7. Conduct an "action research" project in your own classroom, trying out a specific technique to meet a specific need for your students; keep track of the impact, and determine if it would have implications building-wide.

8. "Exchange places" with a teacher at another grade level (and/or subject area) to experience working with students at another developmental level or to see one's own students in another setting; meet with exchange teacher in advance to discuss lessons and swap plans.

9. Initiate a mini-project with other teachers in the building (department, grade level) to improve grade-to-grade articulation re: curriculum, assessment, differentiation, literacy, etc.

10. Take a professional day to observe in (and then meet with teachers) a school that is rated as Excellent. See what they are doing with their students that would be meaningful for your students; share with teacher-based team or BLT, and set a course of action for your department or school.

References

Ainsworth, L. (2006). *Common formative assessments: How to connect standards-based instruction and assessment.* Thousand Oaks, CA: Corwin.

Ainsworth, L (2010). *Rigorous curriculum design: How to create units of study that align standards, instruction, and assessment.* Englewood, CO: Lead and Learn Press.

Ausubel, D. (1962). A subsumption theory of meaningful verbal learning and retention. *The Journal of General Psychology, 66*(2), 213–224.

Bambrick-Santoyo. P. (2012). *Educational Leadership, 70*(3), 26–30.

Bernauer, J. (2002). Five keys to unlock continuous school improvement. *Kappa Delta Pi Record, 38*(2), 89–92.

Bernhardt, V. (2002). *The school portfolio toolkit: A planning, implementation, and evaluation guide for continuous school improvement.* Larchmont, NY: Eye on Education.

Carpenter, T., Fennema, E., Franke, M. L., Levi, L., & Empson, S. B. (1999). *Children's mathematics: Cognitively guided instruction.* Portsmouth, NH: Heinemann.

Chappuis, J. (2005). Helping students understand assessment. *Educational Leadership, 63*(3), 39–43.

Chappuis, S., R. J. Stiggins, et al. (2004). *Assessment for learning: An action guide for school leaders.* Portland, OR: Assessment Training Institute.

Collins, J. (2001). *Good to great.* New York, NY: HarperCollins.

Common Core State Standards Initiative. (2012a). *Common Core State Standards for English language arts & literacy in history/social studies, science, and technical subjects.* Retrieved from http://www.corestandards.org/ELA-Literacy.

Common Core State Standards Initiative. (2012b). *Common Core State Standards for mathematics.* Retrieved from http://www.corestandards.org/Math.

Cooper, H., Robinson, J. C., & Patall, E. A. (2006). Does homework improve academic achievement? A synthesis of research, 1987–2003. *Review of Educational Research, 76,* 1–62.

Corno, L., & Xu, J. (2004). Homework as the job of childhood. *Theory Into Practice, 43,* 227–233.

Costa, A., & Kallick, B. (2010). It takes some getting used to: Rethinking curriculum for the 21st Century. In H. H. Jacobs (Ed.), *Curriculum 21: Essential education for changing the world.* Alexandria, VA: Association for Supervision and Curriculum Development.

Costa, A., & Kallick, B. (2012). *16 habits of mind.* Retrieved from http://www.apaceofchange.com.

Daniels, H., & Bizar, M. (2005). *Teaching the best practice way: Methods that matter.* Portland, ME: Stenhouse Publishers.

Danielson, C. (2008). *The handbook for enhancing professional practice: Using the framework for teaching in your school.* Alexandria, VA: Association for Supervision and Curriculum Development.

Danielson. (2012). Observing classroom practice. *Educational Leadership, 70*(3), 32–37.

Darling-Hammond, L. (2000). *Teaching quality and student achievement: A review of state policy evidence.* Seattle: Center for the Study of Teaching and Policy, University of Washington.

Darling-Hammond, L. (2011). From a blog to the *Washington Post,* cited by C. Perrius in the *National Equity Project Newsletter* March 24, 2011.

Darling-Hammond, L. (2012). The right start: Creating a strong foundation for the teaching career. *Phi Delta Kappan, 94*(3), 8–13.

Darling-Hammond, L., Ancess, J., & Falk, B. (1995). *Authentic assessment in action: Studies of schools and students at work.* New York, NY: Teachers College Press.

DiCarlo, M. (2012). How to use value-added measures right. *Educational Leadership, 70*(3), 38–42.

Edwards, J. (2012 November 1). Focusing on effective teaching strategies can change the conversation about professional development [Web log post]. Retrieved from http://www.marzanocenter.com/blog/article/effective-teaching-strategies-can-change-the-conversation-about-pd/.

Fleming, M., & B. Chambers (1983). Teacher-made tests: Windows on the classroom. In W. E. Hathaway (Ed.), *Testing in the schools: New directions for testing and measurement, No. 19* (pp. 29–38). San Francisco, CA: Jossey-Bass.

Fullan, M. (2002a). The change leader. *Educational Leadership, 59*(8), 16–20.

Fullan, M. (2002b). Leadership and sustainability. *Principal Leadership, 3*(4), 14–17.

Fullan, M. (2011b). *Choosing the wrong drivers for whole system reform.* East Melbourne, Australia: Centre for Strategic Education.

Fullan, M. (2012). *Change leaders: Learning to do what matters most.* New York, NY: Wiley.

Fullan, M., A. Bertani, & Quinn, J. (2004). New lessons for districtwide reform. *Educational Leadership, 61*(7), 42–46.

Guskey, T. R. (2000). Grading policies that work against standards . . . and how to fix them. *NASSP Bulletin, 84*(620), 20–29.

Guskey, T. R. (2011). Five obstacles to grading reform. *Educational Leadership, 69*(3), 17–21.

Hanushek, E. A., & Peterson, P. E. (2011, August 28). Why can't American students compete? *Newsweek Magazine.*

Hattie, J. (2012). *Visible learning for teachers: Maximizing impact on learning.* New York, NY: Routledge.

Hayes Jacobs, H. (Ed.). (2010). *Curriculum 21: Essential education for changing world.* Alexandria, VA: Association for Curriculum and Supervision Development.

Herman, J. L., & E. L. Baker (2005). Making benchmark testing work. *Educational Leadership, 63*(3), 48–55.

Hirsh, S. (2012). Common-core work must include teacher development: The standards movement must embrace teacher professional learning. *Education Week, 31*(19), 22–24.

Hunter, M. (1994). *Mastery teaching: Increasing instructional effectiveness in elementary and secondary schools, colleges, and universities.* Thousand Oaks, CA: Corwin.

Joyce, B., & B. Showers (2002). *Student achievement through staff development.* Alexandria, VA: Association for Supervision and Curriculum Development.

Leahy, S., C. Lyon, et al. (2005). Classroom assessment: Minute by minute, day by day. *Educational Leadership, 63*(3), 19–24.

Levin, B. (2008). *How to change 5000 schools.* Cambridge, MA: Harvard Education Press.

March, J. K., & Peters, K. H. (2007). *Instructional design: Making best practices work in standards-based classrooms.* Thousand Oaks, CA: Corwin.

Marshall, K. (2012). Let's cancel the dog-and-pony show. *Phi Delta Kappan, 94*(3), 19–23.

Marzano, R. J. (2000). *Transforming classroom grading.* Alexandria, VA: Association for Supervision and Curriculum Development.

Marzano, R. J. (2002). Standardized curriculum. *Principal, 81*(3), 6–9.

Marzano, R. J. (2003a). *What works in schools: Translating research into action.* Alexandria, VA: Association for Supervision and Curriculum Development.

Marzano, R. J. (2003b). Using data: Two wrongs and a right. *Educational Leadership, 60*(5), 56–60.

Marzano, R. J. (2007). *The art and science of teaching: A comprehensive framework for effective instruction.* Alexandria, VA: Association for Supervision and Curriculum Development.

Marzano, R. J. (2011). *Effective supervision: Supporting the art and science of teaching.* Alexandria, VA: Association for Supervision and Curriculum Development.

Marzano, R. J. (2012). The two purposes of teacher evaluation. *Educational Leadership, 70*(3), 14–19.

Marzano, R. J., Frontier, T., & Livingston, D. (2011). *Effective supervision: Supporting the art and science of teaching.* Alexandria VA: Association for Supervision and Curriculum Development.

McCarthy, B. (1990). Using the 4MAT system to bring learning styles to schools. *Educational Leadership, 48*(2), 31–37.

McTighe, J., & K. O'Connor (2005). Seven practices for effective learning. *Educational Leadership, 63*(3), 10–17.

Mikk, J. (2006, May) *Students homework and TIMSS 2003 mathematics results.* Paper presented at the International Conference Teaching Mathematics: Retrospective and Perspectives, Tartu, Estonia.

Mills, M. (2001). *Ensuring the viability of curriculum mapping in a school improvement plan.* Retrieved from ERIC database. (ED460141)

Mizell, M. H. (2003). Facilitator: 10, refreshments: 8, evaluation: 0. *Journal of Staff Development, 24*(4), 10–13.

Mizell, M. H. (2004). From muck to mountaintop. *Journal of Law in Education, 33*(2), 261–273.

Moon, T., C. Brighton, et al. (2005). Development of authentic assessments for the middle school. *Journal of Secondary Gifted Education, 16*(2/3), 119–133.

Moon, J., & L. Schulman (1995). *Finding the connections: Linking assessment, instruction, and curriculum in elementary mathematics.* Portsmouth, NH: Heinemann.

Niguidula, D. (2005). Documenting learning with digital portfolios. *Educational Leadership, 63*(3), 44–47.

O'Connor, K. (2007). *A repair kit for grading: 15 fixes for broken grades.* Portland, OR: Educational Testing Service.

Ohio Department of Education. (July, 2011). *The Ohio revised science education standards and model curriculum, introduction.* Columbus: Author.

Ohio Department of Education Social Studies Standards. (2012). *Introduction.* Retrieved from http://education.ohio.gov/Topics/Academic-Content-Standards/Social-Studies.

Olson, L. (October 19, 2005). Purpose of testing needs to shift experts say. *Education Week, 25*(8), 7.

Ozkan, E., & D. J. Henderson (2011, July). Are we wasting children's time by giving them homework? *Economics of Education Review, 30*(5), 950–961.

Paul, A. M. (2011 September, 10). The trouble with homework. *New York Times.* Retrieved from http://www.nytimes.com/2011/09/11/opinion/sunday/quality-homework-a-smart-idea.html?pagewanted=all&_r=0.

Peters, K. H., & J. K. March (1999). *Collaborative observation: Putting classroom instruction at the center of school reform.* Thousand Oaks, CA: Corwin.

Piaget, J. (1952). *The origins of intelligence in children.* New York, NY: International University Press.

Pink, D. (2005). *A whole new mind: Moving from the information age to the conceptual age.* New York, NY: Riverhead Books.

Popham, W. J. (2005, March 23). Standardized testing fails the exam. *Edutopia,* 1–3.

Quinn, T. (2002). Redefining leadership in the standards era. *Principal, 82*(1), 16–20.

Reeves, D. B. (2001). If you hate standards, learn to love the bell curve. *Education Week.*

Reeves, D. B. (2004a). *Accountability for learning: How teachers and school leaders can take charge.* Alexandria, VA: Association for Supervision and Curriculum Development.

Reeves, D. B. (2004b). *Assessing educational leaders.* Thousand Oaks, CA: Corwin, National Academy of Secondary School Principals.

Reeves, D. B. (2004c). The case against zero. *Phi Delta Kappan, 86*(4), 324–325.

Reeves, D. B. (2005). Constructive alternative in a destructive debate. *Principal Leadership, 5*(7), 38–43.

Reeves, D. B. (2008). Effective grading practices, *Educational Leadership, 65*(5), 85–97.

Rotherham, A., & Willingham, D. (2009). *21st century skills: Learning for life in our times.* San Francisco, CA: Jossey-Bass.

Schmoker, M. (2004). Tipping point: From feckless reform to substantive instructional improvement. *Phi Delta Kappan, 85*(6), 424–432.

Schmoker, M. (2011). *Focus: Elevating the essentials to radically improve student learning.* Alexandria, VA: Association for Curriculum and Supervision Development.

Scriffiny, P. (2008). Seven reasons for standards-based grading. *Educational Leadership 66*(2), 70–74.

Shanahan, T. (2012). The common core ate my baby and other urban legends. *Educational Leadership, 70*(4), 12–17.

Sharkey, N., & R. Murnane (2003). Learning from student assessment results. *Educational Leadership, 61*(13), 77–81.

Shepard, L. (2005). Linking formative assessment to scaffolding. *Educational Leadership, 63*(3), 66–71.

Stanford, P., & S. Reeves (2005). Assessment that drives instruction. *Teaching Exceptional Children, 37*(4), 18–22.

Stecher, B., Garet, M., Holtzman, D., & Hamilton, L. (2012). Implementing measures of teacher effectiveness. *Phi Delta Kappan, 94*(3), 39–43.

Stiggins, R., J. Arter, et al. (2004). *Classroom assessment for student learning: Doing it right, using it well.* Portland, OR: Assessment Training Institute.

Strong, R., H. Silver, et al. (2001). *Teaching what matters most: Standards and strategies for raising student achievement.* Alexandria, VA: Association for Supervision and Curriculum Development.

Stronge, J. H., Ward, T. J., Tucker, P., & Hindman, J. (2008). What is the relationship between teacher quality and student achievement? An exploratory study. *Journal of Personnel Evaluation in Education, 20,* 165–184.

Swank, A. L. G. (1999, July). *The effect of weekly math homework on fourth grade student math performance.* Johnson Bible College. (ERIC Document Reproduction Service No. ED433234.)

Taba, H. (1962). *Curriculum development: Theory and practice.* New York, NY: Harcourt Brace and World.

Taba, H. (1966). *Teaching strategies and cognitive functioning in elementary school children.* San Francisco, CA: San Francisco State University.

Taub, D. A. (2012, May 22). The Common Core Standards: How will they change teaching and assessment? *Special Education Advisor.*

Tomlinson, C. A. (2005). Quality curriculum and instruction for highly able students. *Theory Into Practice, 44*(2), 160–166.

Tomlinson, C. A. (2012, February 9). *Teaching today's students: A case for differentiated instruction.* Presentation to Knox College, Galesburg, IL.

Tomlinson, C. A., & McTighe, J. (2006). *Integrating differentiated instruction and understanding by design.* Alexandria, VA: Association for Curriculum and Supervision Development.

Trilling, B., & Fadel, C. (2009). 21st century skills: The challenges ahead. *Educational Leadership, 67*(1), 16–21.

Tucker, M. S. (2012, February 27). The Education Experts Blog; sponsored by the National Journal; Published in Print.

Tucker, M. S. (2012, February 22). How the Brown Center Report got it wrong: No relationship between academic standards and student performance? [Web log post]. Retrieved from http://blogs.edweek.org/edweek/top_performers/2012/02/how_the_brown_center_report_got_it_wrong_no_relationship_between_academic_standards_and_student_perf.html.

Tyler, R. (1950). *Basic principles of curriculum and instruction.* Chicago, IL: University of Chicago Press.

Wiggins, G., & McTighe, J. (2008). Put understanding first. *Educational Leadership, 65*(8), 36–41.

Wormeli, R. (2009) *Metaphors and analogies: Power tools for teaching any subject.* Portland, ME: Stenhouse.

Yaple, M. (2012). You don't know Charlotte. *School Leader.* Retrieved from http://www.njsba.org/school-leader/janfeb12.html#danielson.

Other Resources That Informed the Work

Adler, M., E. Rougle, et al. (2004). Closing the gap between concept and practice: Toward a more dialogic discussion in the language arts classroom. *Journal of Adolescent & Adult Literacy, 47*(4), 312–322.

Ainsworth, L. (2004). *Unwrapping the standards: A simple process to make standards manageable.* Englewood, NJ: Advanced Learning Press.

Ainsworth, L. (2011). *Rigorous curriculum design: How to create curricular units of study that align standards, instruction, and assessment.* Englewood, NJ: Advanced Learning Press.

Airasian, P. (2000). *Assessment in the classroom: A concise approach* (2nd ed.). Boston, MA: McGraw-Hill Higher Education.

Ancess, J. (2004). Snapshots of meaning-making classroom. *Educational Leadership, 62*(1), 36–40.

Ausubel, D. P. (1960). The use of advance organizers in the learning and retention of meaningful verbal material. *Journal of Educational Psychology, 51*, 267–272.

Ausubel, D. P. (1968). *Educational psychology: A cognitive view.* New York, NY: Holt, Rinehart & Winston.

Applebee, A., J. Langer, et al. (2003). Discussion-based approaches to developing and understanding: Classroom instruction and student performance in middle and high school English. *American Educational Research Journal, 40*(3), 685–730.

Barber, M., & M. Fullan (2005). Tri-level development: Putting systems thinking into action. *Education Week, 24*(25), 32–34.

Baxendell, B. (2003). Consistent, coherent, creative: The 3 C's of graphic organizers. *Teaching Exceptional Children, 35*(3), 32–34.

Bell, L. I. (2003). Strategies that close the gap. *Educational Leadership, 60*(4), 32–34.

Bell, R., L. Smetana, et al. (2005). Simplifying inquiry instruction. *The Science Teacher, 72*(7), 30–33.

Berry, B., D. Johnson, et al. (2005). The power of teacher leadership. *Educational Leadership, 62*(5), 56–60.

Berliner, D. C. (1989). The place of process-product research in developing the agenda for research on teacher thinking. *Educational Psychologist, 24*(4), 325–344.

Bernhardt, V. (2008). *Data, data everywhere!* Larchmont, NY: Eye on Education.

Blachowicz, C., & P. Fisher. (2002). *Teaching vocabulary in all classrooms* (2nd ed.). Upper Saddle River, NJ: Merrill Prentice Hall.

Bloom, B. S. (1956). *Taxonomy of educational objectives: The classification of educational goals: Handbook 1: Cognitive domain.* New York, NY: David Company.

Bloom, B., J. T. Hartings, et al. (1971). *Handbook on formative and summative evaluation of student learning.* New York, NY: McGraw-Hill.

Boardman-Moen, C. (May, 2005). Literature circles revisited: Learning from experience. *Book Links,* 52–53.

Brooks, J. G. (2002). *Schooling for life: Reclaiming the essence of learning.* Alexandria, VA: Association for Supervision and Curriculum Development.

Brooks, J. G. (2004). To see beyond the lesson: Why we must make meaning making the core of teaching. *Educational Leadership, 62*(1), 8–13.

Brophy, J., & Good, T. (1986). Teacher behavior and student achievement. In Merlin Wittrock (Ed.), *Handbook of research on teaching* (3rd ed., pp. 328–375). New York, NY: Macmillan.

Brophy, J. (1990). Teaching social studies for understanding and higher-order applications. *The Elementary School Journal, 90,* 351–417.

Brophy, J. (1998). Research on teacher effects: Uses and abuses. *The Elementary School Journal, 89*(1), 3–21.

Bruner, J. (1996). *Toward a theory of instruction.* Cambridge, MA: Harvard University Press.

Bruner, J. (1973). *Going beyond the information given.* New York, NY: Norton.

Buckley, G., N. Bain, et al. (2004). Adding an 'active learning' component to a large lecture course. *Journal of Geography, 103*(6), 231–237.

Chen, P., & D. McGrath (2004/2005). Visualize, visualize, visualize: Designing projects for higher-order thinking. *Learning & Leading With Technology, 32*(4), 54–57.

Chrisman, V. (2005). How schools sustain success. *Educational Leadership, 62*(5), 16–20.

Cooper, S. (2003). Some lecturing dos and don'ts. *Journal of Continuing Education in Nursing, 34*(3), 99–100.

Cooper, H. (2007). *The battle over homework: Common ground for administrators, teachers, and parents.* Thousand Oaks, CA: Corwin.

Culbertson, J. (2012). Putting the value in teacher evaluation. *Phi Delta Kappan, 94*(3), 14–18.

Danesi, M. (2004). *Poetic logic: The role of language in thought, language, and culture.* Madison, WI: Atwood Press.

Daniels, H., & Steineke, N. (2011). *Texts and lessons for content-area reading.* Portsmouth, NH: Heinemann.

Danielson, C. (1996). *Enhancing professional practice: A framework for teaching.* Alexandria, VA: Association for Supervision and Curriculum Development.

Danielson, C. (2002). *Enhancing student achievement: A framework for school improvement.* Alexandria, VA: Association for Supervision and Curriculum Development.

Darling-Hammond, L. (1995). Changing conceptions of teaching and teaching development. *Teacher Education Quarterly, 22*(4), 9–26.

Darling-Hammond, L. (1996). What matters most: A competent teacher for every child. *Phi Delta Kappan, 78*(3), 193–200.

Darling-Hammond, L., & Falk, B. (1997). Using standards and assessments to support student learning. *Phi Delta Kappan, 79*(3), 190–199.

Darling-Hammond, L. (1998). Teacher learning that supports student learning. *Educational Leadership, 55*(5), 6–11.

Dewey, J. (1933). *How we think: A restatement of the relation of reflective thinking to the educative process.* Boston, MA: Henry Holt.

Downey, C. J., Betty E. Steffey, & Williman K. Poston. (2009). *50 Ways to close the achievement gap. Curriculum management systems.* Thousand Oaks, CA: Corwin.

DuFour, R. (2003). Central office support for learning communities. *School Administrator, 60*(5), 16–17.

DuFour, R. (2004). What is a professional learning community? *Educational Leadership, 61*(8), 6–11.

DuFour, R. (2011). *Leaders of learning: How district, school, and classroom leaders improve student achievement.* Bloomington, IN: Solution Tree.

Eisner, E. (1997). Cognition and representation: A way to pursue the American dream. *Phi Delta Kappan, 78*(5), 348–353.

Eisner, E. (2004). Preparing for today and tomorrow. *Educational Leadership, 61*(4), 6–10.

Foote, C., P. Vermette, et al. (2001). *Constructivist strategies: Meeting standards and engaging adolescent minds.* Larchmont, NY: Eye on Education.

Fulton, K. P. (2003). Redesigning schools to meet 21st century learning needs. *T.H.E. Journal, 30*(9), 30–32, 34, 36.

Fullan, M. (2011a). *Change leader: Learning to do what matters.* San Francisco, CA: Jossey-Bass.

Fullan, M. (2011c). *The six secrets of change: What the best leaders do to help their organizations survive and thrive.* San Francisco, CA: Jossey-Bass.

Gabriel, R., & Allington, R. (2012). The Met Project: The wrong $45 million question. *Educational Leadership, 70*(3), 44–49.

Gardner, H. (1983). *Frames of mind: The theory of multiple intelligences.* New York, NY: HarperCollins.

Goodlad, J., Soder, R., & Sirotnik, K. A. (Eds.) (1990). *The moral dimensions of teaching.* San Francisco, CA: Jossey-Bass.

Gregorc, A. (1984). *Gregorc style delineator: Developmental technical and administration manual.* Columbia, CT: Gregorc Associates.

Grove, K. (2002). The invisible role of the central office. *Educational Leadership, 59*(8), 45–47.

Harvey, S., & Goudvis, A. (2002). *Strategies that work: Teaching comprehension to enhance understanding.* New York, NY: Stenhouse.

Hayes Jacobs, H. (1989). *Interdisciplinary curriculum: Design and implementation.* Alexandria, VA: Association for Supervision and Curriculum Development.

Hayes Jacobs, H. (2000). Upgrading the K–12 journey through curriculum mapping. *Knowledge Quest, 29*(2), 25–29.

Hayes Jacobs, H. (2001). New trends in curriculum: An interview with Heidi Hayes Jacobs. *NAIS independent School Magazine: Curriculum Conundrum,* 18–22.

Hayes Jacobs, H. (2004). *Getting results with curriculum mapping.* Alexandria, VA: Association of Supervision and Curriculum Development.

Hurley, V., R. Greenblatt, & Cooper, B. (2003). Learning conversations: Transforming supervision. *Principal Leadership (middle-school ed.), 3*(9), 31–36.

Jacobson, L. (2005). Book spells out 'core curriculum' for teaching training. *Education Week, 24*(25), 10.

Jenkins, J., M. Stein, et al. (1984). Learning vocabulary through reading. *American Educational Research Journal, 21, 787–787.*

Jennings, J. (2003, August 17). Keeping score: Tests are vital but will not fix education alone. *Chattanooga Times.*

Johnson, S. M., & Fiarman, S. E. (2012). The potential of peer review. *Educational Leadership, 70*(3), 20–25.

Kim, A.-H., S. Vaughn, et al. (2004). Graphic organizers and their effects on the reading comprehension of students with LD: A synthesis of research. *Journal of Learning Disabilities, 37*(2), 105–118.

Kolb, D. A., & R. Fry (1975). Toward an applied theory of experiential learning. In C. Cooper (Ed.), *Theories of group process.* London: Wiley.

Koppang, A. (2004). Curriculum mapping: Building collaboration and communication. *Intervention in School and Clinic, 39*(3), 154–161.

Kovecses, Z. (2002). *Metaphor: A practical introduction.* New York, NY: Oxford University Press.

LaBeau, B., & P. Morehead (2004). Successful curriculum mapping: Fostering smooth technology integration. *Learning & Leading With Technology, 32*(4), 12–17.

Lezotte, L. (1994). The nexus of instructional leadership and effective schools. *School Administrator, 51,* 20–22.

Liben, D., & M. Liben (2005). Learning to read in order to learn. *Phi Delta Kappan, 86*(5), 401–406.

Lin, C.-H. (2004). Literature circles. *Teacher Librarian, 31*(3), 23–25.

Love, N. (2002). *Using data to get results: A practical guide for school improvement in math and science.* Norwood, MA: Christopher-Gordon.

March, J. K., & Peters, K. H. (2002). Curriculum development and instructional design in the effective schools process. *Phi Delta Kappan, 83*(5), 379–381.

March, J. K., & Peters, K. H. (2003). A collaborative approach for small districts to use the Effective Schools Process for comprehensive school reform. *Journal for Effective Schools, 1*(2).

Manoucherhri, A., & D. Lapp (2003). Unveiling student understanding: The role of questioning in instruction. *Mathematics Teachers, 96*(8), 562–566.

Marshall. K. (2012). Fine-tuning teacher evaluation. *Educational Leadership, 70*(3), 50–53.

Marzano, R. (2004). *Classroom instruction that works: Research-based strategies for increasing student achievement.* Upper Saddle River, NJ: Prentice Hall.

Marzano, R. (2004, September 13). Why is there a need for these standards? from *Windows* on ASCD Website.

Marzano, R. J., Pickering, D., & Pollock, J. (2001). *Classroom instruction that works.* Alexandria, VA: Association of Supervision and Curriculum Development.

McNameed, G., & J.-Q. Chen (2005). Dissolving the line between assessment and teaching. *Educational Leadership, 63*(3), 72–77.

McTighe, J., E. Seif, & G. Wiggins (2004). You can teach for meaning. *Educational Leadership, 62*(1), 26–30.

McTighe, J., & R. S. Thomas (2003). Backward design for forward action. *Educational Leadership, 60*(5), 52–55.

Mielke, P., & Frontier, T. (2012). Keeping improvement in mind. *Educational Leadership, 70*(3), 10–13.

Memory, D., C. Yoder, et al. (2004). Creating thinking and inquiry tasks that reflect the concerns and interests of adolescents. *The Social Studies, 95*(4), 147–154.

Mizell, M. H. (2003, April 25). *NCLB: Conspiracy, compliance, or creativity?* Lecture to the Maryland Council of Staff Developers, Columbia, MD.

Morgan, R., J. Whorton, et al. (2000). A comparison of short-term and long-term retention: Lecture combined with discussion versus cooperative learning. *Journal of Instructional Psychology, 30*(1), 53–58.

O'Connell, S. (2000). *Introduction to problem solving: Strategies for the elementary math classroom.* Portsmouth, NH: Heinemann.

Olson, L. (2005). Benchmark assessments offer regular checkups on student achievement. *Education Week, 25*(13), 13–14.

Patterson, D., & C. Rolheiser (2004). Creating a culture of change. *Journal of Staff Development, 25*(2), 1–4.

Pollock, J. E., & Ford, S. M. (2009). *Improving student learning one principal at a time.* Alexandria, VA: Association of Supervision and Curriculum Development.

Reeves, D. (2006). *The learning leader: How to focus school improvement for results.* Alexandria, VA: Association for Curriculum and Supervision Development.

Reeves, D. (2009). *Leading change in your school: How to conquer myths, build commitment, and get results.* Alexandria, VA: Association for Curriculum and Supervision Development.

Reeves, D. (2010). *Elements of grading: A guide to effective practice.* Bloomington, IN: Solution Tree.

Richland, L., K. Holyoak, et al. (2004). Analogy use in eighth-grade mathematics classrooms. *Cognition and Instruction, 22*(1), 37–60.

Ritchhart, R. (2011). *Making thinking visible: How to promote engagement, understanding and independence for all learners.* San Francisco, CA: Jossey-Bass.

Ritter, G.W., & Shuls, J. V. (2012). If a tree falls in a forest, but no one hears. *Phi Delta Kappan, 94*(3), 34–38.

Rock, T., & C. Wilson (2005). Improving teaching through lesson study. *Teacher Education Quarterly, 32*(1), 77–92.

Rosenshine, B., & Stevens, R. (1986). Teaching functions. In M. Wittrock (Ed.), *Handbook of research on teaching* (3rd ed.). New York, NY: Macmillan.

Roth-McDuffie, A., & T. Youngs (2003). Promoting mathematical discourse through children's literature. *Teaching Children Mathematics, 9*(7), 385–389.

Ruebling, C., S. Stow, et al. (2004). Instructional leadership: An essential ingredient for improving student learning. *The Educational Forum, 68*(3), 243–253.

Sagor, R., & J. Cox (2004). *At-risk students: Reading and teaching them.* Larchmont, NY: Eye on Education.

Shepard, L. (1995). Using assessment to improve learning. *Educational Leadership, 52*(5), 38–43.

Simon, M. (2012). A tale of two districts. *Educational Leadership, 70*(3), 58–63.

Sousa, C., & C. Tomlinson. (2010). *Differentiation and brain: How neuroscience supports learner-friendly classrooms.* Bloomington, IN: Solution Tree.

Sronge, J., Tucker, P., & Hindman, J. (2004). *Handbook for qualities of effective teachers.* Alexandria, VA: Association for Curriculum and Supervision Development.

Starko, A. (2000). *Creativity in the classroom: Schools of curious delight* (2nd ed.). Mahwah, NJ: Lawrence Erlbaum.

Stien, D., & P. Beed (2004). Bridging the gap between fiction and nonfiction in the literature circle setting. *The Reading Teacher, 57*(6), 510–518.

Stiggins, R., & Chappuis, J. (2008). Enhancing student learning. *District Administration.*

Stiggins, R. (2011). *Introduction to student-involved assessment FOR learning* (6th ed.). Boston, MA: Addison-Wesley.

Strong, R., H. Silver, et al. (2003). Boredom and its opposite. *Educational Leadership, 61*(1), 24–29.

Strunk, K. O., Weinstein, T., Makkonen, R., & Furedi, D. (2012). Lessons learned. *Phi Delta Kappan, 94*(3), 47–51.

Tomlinson, C. A. (1999a). *The differentiated classroom: Responding to the needs of all learners.* Alexandria, VA: Association for Supervision and Curriculum Development.

Tomlinson, C. A. (1999b). Mapping a route toward differentiated instruction. *Educational Leadership, 57*(1), 12–16.

Tomlinson, C. A. (2000). Reconcilable differences: Standards-based teaching and differentiation. *Educational Leadership, 58*(1), 6–11.

Tomlinson, C. A. (2001). *How to differentiate instruction in mixed-ability classrooms.* Alexandria, VA: Association for Supervision and Curriculum Development.

Tomlinson, C. A. (2004). Sharing responsibility for differentiating instruction. *Roeper Review, 26*(4), 188.

Tomlinson, C. A. (2007). Learning to love assessment. *Educational Leadership, 65*(6), 8–13.

Tomlinson, C. A. (2008). *The differentiated school: Making revolutionary changes in teaching and learning.* Alexandria, VA: Association for Curriculum and Supervision Development.

Tomlinson, C. A., & M. Imbeau. (2010). *Leading and managing a differentiated classroom.* Alexandria, VA: Association for Curriculum and Supervision Development.

Trautwein, U., & Koller, O. (2003). The relationship between homework and achievement—still much of a mystery. *Educational Psychology Review, 15,* 115–145.

Udelhofen, S. (2005). *Keys to curriculum mapping: Strategies and tools to make it work.* Thousand Oaks, CA: Corwin.

Vacca, R., & J. Vacca (2004). *Content area reading* (8th ed.). Boston, MA: Allyn & Bacon.

Vansciver, J. H. (2004). Challenging students to achieve. *Principal Leadership, 88*(638), 39–42.

Van Voorhis, F. L. (2003). Interactive homework in middle school: Effects on family involvements and science achievement. *Journal of Educational Research, 96*(6), 323–338.

Waters, J. T., R. Marzano, et al. (2004). Leadership that sparks learning. *Educational Leadership, 61*(7), 48–51.

Weiss, I., & J. Pasley (2004). What is high-quality instruction? *Educational Leadership, 61*(5), 24–28.

Wenglinsky, H. (2004). Facts or critical thinking skills? What NAEP results say. *Educational Leadership, 62*(1), 32–35.

Wies Long, T., & M. Gove (2003). How engagement strategies and literature circles promote critical response in a fourth-grade, urban classroom. *The Reading Teacher, 57*(4), 350–361.

Wormeli, R. (2005). Busting myths about differentiated instruction. *Principal Leadership, 5*(7), 28–33.

Zemelman, S., H. Daniels, & A. Hyde (2005). *Best practice: Today's standards for teaching and learning in America's schools* (3rd ed.). Portsmouth, NH: Heinemann.

Index